Creative writing is one of the most
worldwide, but what does creative wr

In *Research Methods in Creative Writing,*
offer a diverse account of conceptions of research in the discipline
that involve not only critical analysis but also creative practice. They
examine a variety of approaches and consider the synergy that occurs
between undertaking creative writing and understanding creative
writing.

Ideal for student writers at all levels, and relevant to writers inside
or outside the academy, *Research Methods in Creative Writing* offers
a lively selection of research modes and methods that readers can
explore and on which they can build.

GRAEME HARPER directs The Honors College at Oakland University,
Michigan, USA, and is a Professor of Creative Writing. He previously
taught in the United Kingdom and Australia, and he is Editor of *New
Writing: The International Journal for the Practice and Theory of Creative
Writing.*

JERI KROLL is Dean of Graduate Research and Professor of Creative
Writing at Flinders University, Australia. She previously taught in the
United Kingdom and the U.S. A Past President of the Australasian
Association of Writing Programs, she co-edited *Creative Writing
Studies: Practice, Research and Pedagogy* with Graeme Harper.

Research Methods in Creative Writing

Edited by

Jeri Kroll and Graeme Harper

palgrave
macmillan

First published 2013 by
PALGRAVE MACMILLAN

Palgrave Macmillan in the UK is an imprint of Macmillan Publishers
Limited, registered in England, company number 785998, of Houndmills,
Basingstoke, Hampshire RG21 6XS.

Palgrave Macmillan in the US is a division of St Martin's Press LLC,
175 Fifth Avenue, New York, NY 10010.

Palgrave Macmillan is the global academic imprint of the above companies
and has companies and representatives throughout the world.

Palgrave® and Macmillan® are registered trademarks in the United
States, the United Kingdom, Europe and other countries.

ISBN 978–0–230–24266–1   hardback
ISBN 978–0–230–24267–8   paperback

This book is printed on paper suitable for recycling and made from fully
managed and sustained forest sources. Logging, pulping and manufacturing
processes are expected to conform to the environmental regulations of the
country of origin.

A catalogue record for this book is available from the British Library.

A catalog record for this book is available from the Library of Congress.

10   9   8   7   6   5   4   3   2   1
22   21   20   19   18   17   16   15   14   13

Printed in China

Contents

Contents

List of Figures

Acknowledgements

Jeri Kroll:
Thanks to my co-editor, Professor Graeme Harper, for being fearlessly energetic, for the support of a Flinders University Faculty Research Grant, and to my research assistant and doctoral student, Katrina Finlayson, of the eagle editorial eye. I also must acknowledge the ongoing support, stimulation and critical acumen of my colleagues in the Australasian Association of Writing Programs. Finally, thanks to my husband Jeff for helping me live through the process.

Graeme Harper:
Sincere thanks to the contributors, who have been engaged, enthusiastic, and fabulous. Warm thanks to my fine co-editor, Jeri Kroll. We've worked on a couple of books together; this time we've swapped our alphabetical order, or Jeri would never get to go first on the cover. That is simply not fair. A big thank you to you Jeri! Thanks to Katrina for her expert checking and assistance with indexing. Finally, to my wife Louise and our sons, Myles and Tyler, it's been a big year: much love.

We both want thank to Kate Haines for initiating this project at Palgrave Macmillan, and to Jenna Steventon for developing and supporting it so wonderfully, through to completion. Sincere thanks also to Felicity Noble.

Notes on Contributors

Donna Lee Brien, BEd (Deakin), MA (UTS), PhD (QUT), GradCert HighEd (UNE), is Professor of Creative Industries and Assistant Dean of Research, in the School of Creative and Performing Arts at Central Queensland University, Australia. Widely published in the areas of writing praxis and pedogogy, creative non-fiction and collaborative practice, her biography *John Power 1881–1943* (Sydney: 1991) is the standard work on this expatriate artist/benefactor. Donna is co-author with Tess Brady of *The Girl's Guide to Real Estate: How to Enjoy Investing in Property*, 2002, and *The Girl's Guide to Work* and *Life: How to Create the Life you Want*, 2004 (both Allen & Unwin, Sydney). Founding Editor of *dotlit: Online Journal of Creative Writing* (2000–2004), Donna is currently Special Issues Editor of *TEXT: Journal of Writers and Writing Courses* and Past President of the Australasian Association of Writing Programs.

Katharine Coles' fifth and sixth collections of poems, *The Earth Is Not Flat* and *Flight*, are forthcoming in 2013 and 2015 from Red Hen Press. She has also published two novels. Her poems, essays, and stories have appeared in such journals as *The Paris Review, The Gettysburg Review, Poetry, Image, Seneca Review, North American Review, Southwest Review*, DIAGRAM, and *Ascent* and have been translated into Italian, Dutch, and Chinese. In 2009–10, she served as the inaugural director of the Harriet Monroe Poetry Institute for the Poetry Foundation. She is a professor at the University of Utah, where she founded and co-directs the Utah Symposium in Science and Literature. In 2010, she traveled to Antarctica to write poems under the auspices of the National Science Foundation's Antarctic Artists and Writers Program. She is a 2012 Guggenheim Foundation Fellow.

Graeme Harper is Professor of Creative Writing and Director of The Honors College at Oakland University, Michigan, USA. An Honorary Professor in the United Kingdom, he was inaugural Chair of the

Higher Education Committee at the UK's National Association of Writers in Education (NAWE) and, from 2003, a research panelist at the Arts and Humanities Research Council. Writing as Brooke Biaz, his most recent novel is *The Invention of Dying* (2012), while other works include *Moon Dance* and *Small Maps of the World*. Recent critical works are *Inside Creative Writing* (2012) and *On Creative Writing* (2010). He holds doctorates from the University of East Anglia and University of Technology, Sydney. A National Book Council awardee, in 2012 he received a grant from the College of Physicians of Philadelphia for work on creative writing. He is Editor of *New Writing: the International Journal for the Practice and Theory of Creative Writing*.

Dr Dominique Hecq is Associate Professor at Swinburne University of Technology where she is Research and Discipline Leader in Writing. She has a PhD in literature and a background in French and Germanic languages, with qualifications in translating. She has published in the areas of literary studies, translation, creative writing, psychoanalysis, and pedagogy. She is the author of eleven major works of creative writing. *Out of Bounds* (Re.press) is her most recent collection and *Stretchmarks of Sun* is due out later this year. *The Creativity Market: Creative Writing in the 21st Century* has recently been released by Multilingual Matters.

Professor Jeri Kroll is Dean of Graduate Research at Flinders University in Adelaide, South Australia, and its founding Program Coordinator of Creative Writing. She has published over twenty titles for adults and young people, including poetry, picture books and novels, some of which were Children's Book Council of Australia Notables. On the Boards of *New Writing*, *Write4Children* and *TEXT*, she has won numerous awards for poetry and gained two Varuna Residencies and an International Exchange at the Tyrone Guthrie Centre in Ireland. *New and Selected Poems* and *Swamp Soup* came out in 2012. She is a Past President of the Australasian Association of Writing Programs. Her most recent critical book is the co-edited *Creative Writing Studies: Practice, Research and Pedagogy*. In 2011 a staged reading of a script based on her verse novel took place at the Kennedy Centre's 10th 'Page to Stage' Festival in Washington DC.

Kim Lasky has a doctorate from the University of Sussex, where her research explored the relationship between creative and critical writing. She has taught creative writing at undergraduate and postgraduate levels as well as in various community settings, and her interest in innovative approaches to teaching saw her lead an interdisciplinary project at Sussex using poetry to help Engineering and Design students learn a complex set of equations. Her poems have appeared in journals in the UK and US and the pamphlet *What it Means to Fall* was published by Tall Lighthouse. She is currently completing a science-inspired collection with support from the Arts Council. Find out more about Kim's work at http://www. kimlasky.com/

Marguerite MacRobert is a South African writer and creative writing researcher. As a lecturer in the Faculty of Education at Stellenbosch University, she teaches English pedagogy, creative writing and children's literature, as well as academic literacy. She has published a variety of poems, short stories and academic research articles in peer reviewed journals, in South Africa and internationally, as well as preparing primary school literacy textbook material and the occasional magazine article. Her research focus is on all facets of the creative writing process, using qualitative methodologies ranging from extensive interviews with authors to autoethnographic performance-as-research. Currently, she is working on a youth novel and an anthology of poems, and is involved in a school teacher development partnership project modeling creative writing workshop skills in striving schools. Marguerite wrestles for the computer with her husband and children and tries not to be too distracted by the mountains, vineyards and seaside surrounding their home town of Somerset West.

Graham Mort is Professor of Creative Writing and Transcultural Literature at Lancaster University where he directs the Centre for Transcultural Writing and Research. He has worked extensively in sub-Saharan Africa for the British Council, designing literature development projects and radio productions. *Visibility: New & Selected Poems* appeared from Seren in 2007, when he was also winner of the

Bridport Competition short story prize. His book of short fiction, *Touch*, was published by Seren in 2010 and won the Edge Hill Prize for the best book of short fiction in 2011. A new book of poems, *Cusp*, appeared from Seren in 2011.

Kerry Spencer, PhD, has never, personally, been arrested. But she does enjoy crossing higher order mathematics with bits of YA fiction and seeing what happens. Dr. Spencer received her BA and MA from Brigham Young University. She studied English, Chemistry and Music as well as worked in the Math lab, tutoring all levels of math up through partial differential equations. She received her PhD from the University of Wales in 2011; her dissertation utilized a statistical epistemology to glean new insights into the US YA fiction market and the books within it. She is currently faculty at Brigham Young University where she continues to horrify colleagues and English majors alike by pulling up graphs with numbers on them and saying words like, "Nonparametric Multiplicative Regression."

Introduction

Jeri Kroll and Graeme Harper

I Exploring creative writing research methods

The development of creative writing as a research discipline in universities and colleges has not yet been well documented, even though many teachers and students pursue it and many degree programmes incorporate forms of creative writing research. *Research Methods in Creative Writing* aims to address this lack by offering a diverse account of conceptions of research in the discipline as well as a selection of models that readers can explore and on which they can build.

Contributors to this collection hail from around the globe – the United Kingdom, Australia, the United States and South Africa. These contributors demonstrate how creative writing research encourages and supports creative and critical work and can lead to 'conventional' as well as 'experimental'[1] explorations. In addition, they each explore research definitions in an effort not only to provide insights into writing practice but also to illuminate how creative writing can provide new knowledge.

Here in the twenty-first century, creative writing is one of the most vibrant and alert of university disciplines, creating and critiquing itself as it moves the field forward. Indeed, the vitality of creative writing as a research field is never more obvious than when we observe the great numbers of teachers and learners engaged in the subject, and consider the ways in which their creative writing research draws concepts and inspiration from so many sources. While focused on practice, on producing that individual work that distills their vision, these researchers situate themselves within a cultural context and articulate what they contribute to their aesthetic domain.

These efforts demonstrate the synergy between the creative, the practical and the critical. Richard Sennett calls attention to the false divides between the artist, the craftsperson, the critic and the audience in this way: 'History has drawn fault lines dividing practice and theory, technique and expression, craftsman and artist, maker and user; modern society suffers from this historical inheritance.'[2] Creative writing research can be said, in many ways, to be occupied with healing these rifts.

Creative writing research is, therefore, concerned with actions as well as outcomes, with the individual as well as the culture and, furthermore, with concepts and theories that illuminate these complex interrelationships. Other disciplines engaged in expanding research possibilities share similar objectives and creative writing research often adapts or responds to these. For example, advocates of action research,[3] educational research,[4] and arts-based research in education and the social sciences[5] have championed new methodologies that can uncover knowledge inaccessible to quantitative methods alone, often by a flexible working method that combines research processes. Those who practise these variations of arts-based and action research and who train others in their methods form networks that enrich discipline-specific vocabularies, map appropriate epistemological frameworks and hence make possible collaboration with other disciplines as well as the mixed genre or hybrid projects that might result.

In the Arts, Humanities, Social Sciences and Natural Sciences, methods related to creative writing research can be found, therefore, and in many cases in this collection you will notice how contributors draw on a range of resources that can be found in these other disciplines. Creative writing research, however, is distinct in being primarily focused on the production of new works, and in the understanding of the processes as well as the ideas and actions that inform a project. In this respect, creative writing research is fundamentally 'practice-led'; or, to put it another way, it always has practice at its conceptual core, even when it is dealing with issues of critical understanding or with theoretical speculation. As craftspeople, therefore, writers attend to technique, but not in isolation, each establishing their own version of the practice-led research loop that drives any creative project forward. It is one of the essential premises demonstrated in this book that any creative writing involves imagination, practice and critical engagement, working together, questioning and supporting each other. Creative writing research simply builds upon this important premise.

Other arts – drama, music, dance, film-making, painting, design, for example – are also actively engaged in practice-led research, informed by a variety of critical and theoretical positions, and these fields have similarly seen considerable growth in and around universities and colleges in recent years. For example, Smith and Dean[6] consider research approaches in a range of art forms while Balkema and Slager[7] survey research developments in European visual arts in particular. Balkema and Slager's introduction suggests the bold sweep of current creative research of all types: 'One could claim that the artistic field comprises the hermeneutic question of the humanities, the experimental method of the sciences, and the societal commitment of the social sciences.'[8] This scope indicates why creative writing research readily draws concepts and inspiration from so many intellectual as well as artistic sources. As several contributors argue, writers from past centuries, whether inside or outside academia, have been doing just that – whether we call their research approaches 'poetics,' 'narratology' or, indeed, creative writing research.

Being one of the arts, creative writing of course has a connection with these other artistic fields as well as with literary ancestors who have interrogated how and why they practice and, in effect, how and why they research in order to develop. In comparison with other art forms, however, creative writing chooses words as the principal tools and words are the primary outcome. Other art forms may use words, but they are creative writing's substance, its essence.

As an art using words and producing artefacts made up primarily of words, the methods of creative writing research sometimes draw directly, and quite naturally, on notions surrounding written expression or text; for example, considerations of how certain imaginative arrangements of words can be used to unlock emotions or establish a relationship between the writer and a potential reader. At other times, research methods in creative writing refer to concepts that could be encountered in any form of human communication, written or otherwise – so, for example, investigations of meaning, inference or attitude. In that regard, a creative writer might explore the inference of a particular viewpoint or voice or the situating of a particular cultural or political attitude. Still further, research methods in creative writing can be located in systems of personal or cultural exchange. In this instance, the researcher might consider context or the relationship between their individual understanding and societal understanding, or they might locate a personal history in the realm of local, national or international histories.

What the examples above primarily point towards is research relating to *expression* or *approach*. Creative writing research can be located in a number of sub-sets of these broadly defined interests, and the research questions posed and explored can be situated according to definitions of type or end result. So, to take one instance, a creative writer seeking to explore a result that related to the form of art defined as 'expressionist', or to a mode of expression defined as 'postmodern', would be working within the realm of aesthetic or cultural definition and would most likely either be confirming or challenging notions associated with those established definitions of type or result.

A creative writing researcher, however, might equally be undertaking their investigations with their individual project as the initiator and definer of their progression and success. Such individualism will involve synthesising aspects of knowledge; however, ideas and terms already in place, and related mostly to the *end results* of creative practice, might be felt to serve the creative writer in undertaking and perceiving their work only partially. It might help your perception of the evolving structure of your novel to read another, already published novel, but your perception might also be helped by engaging with other creative arts or conventional disciplines. For example, you might watch a dancer perform or a chemist conduct an experiment or mix a solution. Viewing these actions might stimulate a sense of form in motion, a relationship with evolutionary human activity. That is not to say that a creative writer can work entirely without textual context. Far from it, given the textual nature of much of our practice. But we suggest here that a focus on individualism and the idea of creating something new are frequently reasons why someone undertakes creative writing. This individualism manifests itself in current, individual human action as well as in texts. We see this situation in the many human fields that create new things. The creative writer can therefore also be aiming to establish as well as respond to elements; they are evolving from their own creative engagements notions that might or might not have well-established definitions, even though they will have imaginative origins. In many ways, creative writing research continues to define itself as well as to respond to modes, methods and philosophies of knowledge that are already available.

What follows is a collection of approaches to researching in and through creative writing. In no sense would we suggest these are the only approaches that might be taken. In fact, if anything, these approaches suggest rather than define, they explore rather than discover, and they point towards rather than stand atop of our destination. Faculty and students continue to develop their research, and we certainly aim here in *Research Methods in Creative Writing* to provide further support and encouragement for what is, we believe, an enormously dynamic field. All the authors in this book provide potential pathways of investigation – pathways that can be followed by advanced creative writing undergraduates at university, as well as postgraduates and faculty. Using the book as a collection of signposts pointing to such exciting pathways is the suggested method of engaging with individual chapters. In fact, with this ideal in mind, the book has the potential to be of use to all writers who show an interest in what they create. Finally our joint, personal objective is to encourage the readers of this book to engage on a deeper level with their creative writing practice; to explore it in order to further understand it for the benefit of their own work and for the discipline generally.

2 The writers

Kim Lasky

This opening chapter nicely situates the present condition of research. Lasky speaks about ancient 'principles and forms of literary composition' in order to explicate some challenges to contemporary writers. That general sense of how we might construct a bridge from what has gone before to what might appear in the future could be the theme for *Research Methods in Creative Writing* overall. That is, research is always in essence about finding out 'what has been' and 'what is' in order to move forward. Here, the writer considers the history and background of poetics, but also its contemporary applications to creative writing research. She looks at some examples of creative writers speaking about being at practice – Henry James, John Fowles and Doris Lessing – and explores practice-led research in relation to what is indeed a considerable 'range of inputs'. Lasky's chapter concludes with a discussion of some innovative creative-critical work and, as with all the chapters you will find in this book, she offers some exploratory exercises.

Donna Lee Brien

In 'Non-Fiction Writing Research,' Donna Lee Brien investigates a complex field comprising a range of subgenres, such as life writing, journalism, and essays that can themselves be broken down into smaller units with their associated methodologies and 'procedural and ethical challenges'. Given the scandals in recent years about the degree of falsification in some high-profile non-fiction titles, this timely chapter considers how and why non-fiction writing needs to be clear about its purpose and techniques, since it depends on trust between author and audience. Brien offers a brief history of the contemporary non-fiction genre in order to ground her analysis of the types of research it entails (including process, archival and experiential research), explaining step by step how a 'research enquiry cycle' proceeds by tracking a project based around a birthday lunch. Significantly for those in higher education, Brien demonstrates how certain types of non-fiction writing can make original contributions to knowledge.

Marguerite MacRobert

What methods might we use for exploring creative writing as a process as well as a product? In each chapter in this book the author asks this question. In Marguerite MacRobert's chapter we find a timely reminder that no matter what answers we might have, we cannot forget that creative writing involves people and people can offer direct insights into the actions they undertake. Based in South Africa, MacRobert employs a qualitative research method, using interviews to investigate creative writing process among some South African writers. Questions of a writer's 'goal-setting' in the initiating and then re-visiting of a work-in-progress suggest to her additional investigations concerning how drafting of a work takes place, and what motivations lie behind a writer editing their work-in-progress. Indeed, we could ask what lies behind deciding a work is complete? Considering the research of Linda Flower and John Hayes, and that of Mihaly Csikszentmihalyi, this chapter ventures into discussions of creativity and theories of creativity, looking at aspects of the writers' 'world-making'. The context-bound elements of both the writing process and the eventual publishing of work also feature, providing a backdrop. So does the writers' sense of enjoyment.

Kerry Spencer

The wryly observant might say that it takes a very brave writer to approach a creative writing project through statistical analysis. Whether inclined to believe mathematics and creative writing exist in alternative worlds, or simply a little sceptical about the role of the numerical in approaching creative communication, on first glance readers might feel hesitant about the contents of Kerry Spencer's chapter. But what if, as a creative writer, you are working in a genre that is extremely market conscious? What if those companies who publish books in this genre take sales figures, readership figures, book shop records, very seriously? And what if, in developing your novel, you want to know if there is any firm relationship between what is statistically declared to be successful and the style, subject and approach of those 'successful' books? Then, some numbers might be just what you are looking for. Kerry Spencer's chapter draws directly from her PhD in Creative and Critical Writing, in which she produced both a young adult novel and a statistically informed consideration of the young adult fiction market. She makes a case for this kind of approach, and also for the possibilities inherent in what she calls inter-disciplinary methods.

Jeri Kroll

The metaphor of the laboratory underpins this chapter, focussing on creative writing researchers within an institutional community whose goal is the production of new knowledge. This chapter analyses the *where*, *what*, *why* and *how* of creative writing research and how it might be shared with a variety of publics. In particular, it draws parallels between scientific and artistic research to explore the way in which conventional definitions of research can apply to creative knowledge generation. The terms 'local' and 'global' research are coined to distinguish between what enriches a project and what engenders transferable knowledge. Addressing the most innovative types of research – in particular rhizomatic research – the chapter explores the dynamic relationship between practice, methodology, theory and artefact. A discussion of W. H. Auden's poem, 'Musée des Beaux Arts,' demonstrates how each artwork can have multiple entry points to aid teachers and students not only to 'read like writers' but to 'research like writers.' Especially at higher degree level, moreover, the twenty-first century writing workshop can function as an experimental site where members generate material, test hypotheses and contribute to the stock of knowledge and culture.

Graeme Harper

In the chapter 'The Generations of Creative Writing Research', it is suggested that when approaching research in and through creative writing we make a choice related to what might clumsily be called 'knowledge acquisition'. That is, we consciously go in search of new knowledge. It could be said that all creative writing does this; and, certainly, one of the greatest contributions to the world of finished works is that contribution associated with the exchange of understanding, between writer and reader, between the individual and others. It is argued here that in undertaking creative writing research we do it with the intention of discovering things about the action of creative writing itself. That is, we do it by concentrating on the actual process and work-in-progress, not only on the completed results. It is suggested that new knowledge found in creative writing research might not only be useful to ourselves, as individual writers, it might also be useful to others. If this is the case then creative writing research highlights the importance of writing as a widely undertaken human practice and it contributes to the sustainability of that practice by improving our knowledge about how it occurs. In that sense, research in and through creative writing contributes to 'generativity', the passing on of knowledge from one generation to another. Four avenues of creative writing research are discussed:

1 Creative Writing Habitats
2 Creative Domains
3 Activities
4 Artefacts of Creative Writing

Kate Coles

All the chapters in *Research Methods in Creative Writing* relate in some way to university and college teaching. Each chapter can be read as a 'case study' of creative writing research methods that, even if not directly adopted, might suggest other approaches, informing project work at undergraduate as well as graduate level. As a vibrant research discipline, methods of examining, developing and contributing new knowledge are not in any sense limited, and the excitement of defining new approaches is one of the joys we all experience. In Kate Coles' chapter the idea of developing original thinking rings clear, as does the idea of reading and readerly exchange between writers. What are the texts that are out there, where might we best find them and how might we best use them? Questions worth asking, Coles suggests, because creative writing is an activity that involves effort, 'discipline and sustained attention', and reading is one of the key elements of that attentiveness. Likewise, creative writing contributes to 'human and even to

9

academic knowledge', she says, in which case there is every reason to support the funding of such research – and she thus offers some advice for creative writers approaching research grant proposals, particularly in the United States.

Dominique Hecq

Dominique Hecq grapples with one of the most contentious and yet potentially fruitful aspects of creative writing research – the role of theory. She poses the critical question – What is theory? – in light of its 'apparent demise' in the past decade. A brief history of theory's influence in academia in the second half of the twentieth century grounds Hecq's discussion of creative writing research now. She argues that writers adopt a variety of theoretical postures, but what they have in common is a dual focus on 'process' as well as 'processor'. Using psychoanalysis as a case study, she recommends a 'theory without credentials', which embraces uncertainties as it focuses on new modes of understanding a subject that is 'constantly *in the making*'. Innovative teaching methods arise from engaging with this theory driven by what Hecq calls 'interactive narrative pedagogy', a new conceptualization of the teacher–student relationship.

Graham Mort

Graham Mort's chapter, 'Transcultural Writing and Research', looks at the role of creative practice-led research in 'an increasingly inter-nationalised academy' where inflections of cultural identity colour the creative and critical work of staff and students. His institution, Lancaster University, offers a case study for the way in which twenty-first century technologies that facilitate distance education not only attract new student populations but also themselves change the academic and writing culture of those in the home country. In particular, Lancaster has established a Virtual Research Environment that provides research-training modules for on-campus and remote (including off-campus UK as well as overseas) students, blending modalities. In doing so, Lancaster has formed a virtual research community that incorporates diverse cultures that span 'geographical and political borders.' At the online workshop and higher degree research level, English as the language of instruction and production highlights how significant not only reader–writer interaction is, but also culture in 'understand[ing] and locat[ing] literary works as manifestations of new knowledge'.

3 What follows

As a vibrant field that continues to evolve, and that attracts a growing number of faculty and students, creative writing in universities and colleges takes a variety of forms and resounds with many voices. This collection, thus, aims to encourage the members of that polyphonic audience to articulate not only how and why they write, but also to expand their awareness of the possibilities of creating new knowledge. We believe that the following chapters will stimulate and provoke. But we also believe that how readers individually choose to approach, and to use, this book will equally be part of the evolving field of creative writing, where ideas around research methods and research topics are as interesting and as complex as creativity itself and informed critical understanding. Creative writing is a field that will continue to develop because it is not only related to human creativity and to the significance of words as tools of human communication, but because it celebrates individuals as well as cultures. What follows in *Research Methods in Creative Writing* are indeed case studies, a selection of creative writing research approaches and associated research methods. The chapters reveal, therefore, the voices of practitioners who themselves have undertaken this new species of research and who want to share the insights that they have gained. What follows is not meant to be an encyclopaedic gathering or an authoritative road map, therefore, instructing you how to proceed on your own individual research journey. Filling in the details of your progress and destination is up to you. It is hoped that in reading this book you are encouraged to make your own lively contributions to the field of creative writing.

Notes

1 The term 'non-traditional' outcomes is used by the Australian Government in their research auditing system (*ERA 2010 Submission Guidelines: Excellence in Research for Australia, December 2009*). It has, therefore, influenced the way in which writers in the academy speak about their creative research in funding or promotion applications, for example. Below are the Australian government's definitions of 'traditional' and 'non-traditional' research.

5.4.2. List of eligible research output types
    There are four kinds of research outputs common to all disciplines, as detailed in section 5.4.9. These are referred to as 'traditional' types of research output:

Books—Authored Research;
Book—Chapters in Research Book;
Journal Articles—Refereed, Scholarly Journal; and
Conference Publications—Full Paper Refereed.

For some disciplines the following 'non-traditional' types of research output are also eligible, as detailed in section 5.4.10:

Original Creative Works;
Live Performance of Creative Works;
Recorded/Rendered Creative Works; and
Curated or Produced Substantial Public Exhibitions and Events.

2 Richard Sennett, *The Craftsman*, New Haven & London: Yale University Press, 2008, 11.

3 B. Dick 'Qualitative action research: improving the rigour and economy,' 1999. Online. http://www.scu.edu.au/schools/gcm/ar/arp/rigour2.html [Accessed July 2008]. David Tripp 'Action Inquiry, Action Research e-Reports', 017. 2008. Online. www.fhs.usyd.edu.au/arow/arer/017.htm. [Accessed 2008].

4 David Cormier, 'Rhizomatic Education: Community as Curriculum. *Innovate* Vol 4, No 5. http://www.innovateonline.info/index.php?view=article&id=550

5 Richard Sigesmund and Melisa Cahnmann-Taylor, 'The Tensions of Arts-Based Research in Education Reconsidered: The Promise for Practice', in Melisa Cahnmann-Taylor and Richard Sigesmund (eds) *Arts-Based Research in Education: Foundations for Practice*. New York and London: Routledge, 2008, 211–246. Also Patricia Leavy, *Method Meets Art: Arts-Based Research*, New York, London: The Guildford Press, 2009.

6 Hazel Smith and Roger T. Dean (eds) *Practice-Led Research, Research-Led Practice in the Creative Arts*, Edinburgh: Edinburgh University Press, 2009.

7 Henk Slager and Annette W. Balkema (eds) *Artistic Research*, trans. Global Vernunft, Amsterdam/New York: Lier en Boog, Editions Rodopi B. V, 2004.

8 Ibid., 9.

Works cited

Cormier, D. 'Rhizomatic Education: Community as Curriculum', *Innovate* Vol. 4, No. 5, 2008. Online. http://www.innovateonline.info/index.php?view=article&id=550.

Dick, B. 'Qualitative Action Research: Improving the Rigour and Economy', 1999. Online. http://www.scu.edu.au/schools/gcm/ar/arp/rigour2.html [Accessed July 2008].

ERA 2010 Submission Guidelines: Excellence in Research for Australia, December 2009. Canberra: Australian Government/Australian Research Council, 2009.

Leavy, P. *Method Meets Art: Arts-Based Research Practice*, New York, London: The Guildford Press, 2009.

Sennett, R. *The Craftsman*, New Haven & London: Yale University Press, 2008.

Sigesmund, R. and Melisa Cahnmann-Taylor 'The Tensions of Arts-Based Research in Education Reconsidered: The promise for practice' in Melisa Cahnmann-Taylor and Richard Sigesmund (eds) *Arts-Based Research in Education: Foundations for Practice*, New York and London: Routledge, 2008.

Slager, H. and Annette W. Balkema (eds) *Artistic Research*, trans. Global Vernunft, Amsterdam/New York: Lier en Boog, Editions Rodopi B. V., 2004.

Smith, H. and Roger T. Dean (eds) *Practice-Led Research, Research-Led Practice in the Creative Arts*, Edinburgh: Edinburgh University Press, 2009.

Tripp, D. 'Action Inquiry, Action Research e-Reports', 017. 2008. Online. www.fhs.usyd.edu.au/arow/arer/017.htm [Accessed 2008].

1   Poetics and Creative Writing Research

Kim Lasky

Chapter summary

One of the key challenges of creative writing research lies in successfully articulating the relationship between the creative work and the critical context, thinking, and outcomes associated with its production. The prospect of providing an introduction, commentary, or some other critical discourse related to their work often leaves students struggling to know how to address this relation.

This chapter suggests the concept of poetics as a useful way of tackling this issue. While the term 'poetics' has referred to the study of principles and forms of literary composition since Aristotle wrote his treatise in 330BC, coming later to refer specifically to the study of poetry, here, 'poetics' refers to the means by which writers across a range of genres formulate and discuss a critical attitude to their own work. This formulation recognises a range of influences: the traditions they write within and against, relevant literary, social, and political contexts, and the processes of composition and revision undertaken. Such a concept of poetics offers a means by which writers in the academy can develop an ethos towards their work in order to gain perspective on the interrelated aspects of practice and theory, and the critical and creative activities involved in the act of writing, helping them to express the knowledge gained through practice-led research.

Drawing upon the image of the triptych, whose three interconnected panels allow the two outer panels to hinge, folding over the central one in a dynamic movement involving close touching, I suggest that poetics might usefully become the anchoring panel at the centre of research practice that sets out to produce creative work in knowing close connection with critical and theoretical influences.

1   A kind of disconnection – the challenge of creative writing research

It is the start of summer term and my MA students are gathered in a sunlit room discussing the material they have written so far for their final dissertation submissions. They are animated, enthused, and full of well-developed ideas for their portfolios of creative work. We run through the submission format, and turn to the critical element. Noticeably, the room quietens. 'Oh', one of them offers, 'this part really freaks me out'. Two weeks later I meet up with a DPhil writing group where two of the members are writing critical prefaces, having worked over a number of years part-time while juggling jobs and families to write a collection of poems. They have developed into mature writers, and our meetings are always inspiring, our discussions full of wise insight. Yet talk about the critical accompaniment to their collection is punctuated by groans, a vocabulary of doubt and struggle. It strikes me that what is happening here is not simply a lack of critical confidence. These are all students who regularly interrogate essays on writing, the work of other writers, and literary theory. They have demonstrated insight into their own writing process and ability to revisit and edit work in progress. They discuss their work in terms of ideas drawn from all kinds of places, from philosophy, psychoanalysis, and art. They are passionate observers of the world around them. Yet there is something about the prevailing stance towards the critical accompaniment to creative work that causes this shift in thinking. It is a kind of disconnection. Somehow, conceptually, the creative and critical processes have become falsely separated. Faced with the task of producing a preface, introduction, commentary, or some other critical discourse related to their work, writers often forget that they have, actually, been engaged in a wealth of critical activity during the process of composition.

For me, this is one of the key challenges to the discipline of creative writing as it continues to consolidate its position in the academy. The relationship between creative practice and the critical understanding drawn from it is central to creative writing produced in an academic environment as practice-led research. The Creative Writing Research Benchmark Statement[1] reminds us that Higher Education defines research as an 'original contribution to knowledge', and suggests 'practice-led research in Creative Writing uses creative practice to explore, articulate, and investigate'.[2] I have witnessed my MA students and the DPhil group exploring and investigating through their writing practice, what they seem to be struggling with is the means to articulate the knowledge involved in, and engendered by, the process.

So how do we articulate this strange symbiotic relation between practice and theory, between process and outcome? How do we usefully speak of influences and inputs that might be intellectual and emotional, public and personal, and that necessarily involve failed attempts and the mysteriously instinctual in their happening dynamics?

The fact is writers have been doing this for some time, and calling it poetics.

2 Concepts of poetics

What exactly do we mean when we speak of poetics?

Let's glance back to 330BC. In *Poetics*, the oldest surviving work on the theory of literary and dramatic composition, Aristotle says he sets out to discuss 'the art in general' as well as characteristics of its individual forms, and to describe how basic elements might be assembled to produce a successful composition, the number and nature of the work's constituent parts, and 'all other relevant matters'.[3] Not a bad starting place for reflection upon the knowledge integral to the composition of a piece of creative writing. Of course, Aristotle was not writing about his own work. Since then, poetics has become the means by which writers formulate and discuss an attitude to their work that recognises influences, the traditions they write within and develop, the literary, social, and political context in which they write, and the processes of composition and revision they undertake. The word *poetics* shares *poet*'s etymological roots in the Greek *poiesis*, which means to create, to make (Oxford English Dictionary). So, the concept of poetics offers a useful means to articulate those processes involved in the making of a work. This etymology, however, fools us into thinking poetics might only be relevant to poets, the context in which the term is most widely used. However, many texts by fiction writers constitute statements of poetics. Let me direct you to three of these to begin to illustrate how the concept of poetics allows for the articulation of the various kinds of insight encountered during the writing process.

2.1 Henry James and the house of fiction

'The house of fiction has in short not one window but a million.'[4] This often-quoted statement from Henry James' preface to *A Portrait of a Lady* memorably captures James' philosophy on the layering of perspectives that enlivens fiction. Written in 1908, this preface looks back on his experience of writing the novel, which first appeared as a serial in *Atlantic Monthly* during 1880–1, before being published in October 1881. The setting of Venice – 'the bristling curve of the wide Riva, the large colour-spots of the balconied houses and the repeated undulation of the little hunchbacked bridges, marked by the rise and drop again, with the wave, of foreshortened clicking pedestrians'[5] – is depicted as one of those beautiful places that prove more distracting than inspiring to the writer, being 'too rich in their own life and too charged with their own meanings merely to help him out with a lame phrase'.[6] The piece considers the influence of other writers from Shakespeare to George Eliot, the development of the inner lives and values of James' characters in relation to those in his other novels, and suggests that in the house of fiction those windows 'either broad or balconied or slit-like and low-browed' constitute the 'literary form' yet are 'singly or together, as nothing without the posted presence of the watcher – without, in other words, the consciousness of the artist'.[7] Written in the same ornate style as his fiction, the preface constitutes a poetics in its articulation, at once theoretical and intensely personal, of his philosophy as a writer, addressing the context in which he writes, influenced by a specific cultural and historical moment, informed by tradition but looking beyond to original thinking.

2.2 John Fowles' 'Notes on an Unfinished Novel'

John Fowles' 'Notes on an Unfinished Novel' reflects upon the writing of *The French Lieutenant's Woman*.[8] Written concurrently with the novel, it describes how the idea for the book begins with a recurring vision of a woman who 'stands at the end of a deserted quay and stares out to sea'.[9] Unable to shake off this image, Fowles comes to understand the character as representing 'a reproach on the Victorian age. An outcast'.[10] The piece follows the process of composition through journal entries and 'memoranda to self' that formulate key critical intents. 'Remember the etymology of the word. A novel is something new. It must have relevance to the writer's now – so don't ever pretend you live in 1867; or make sure the reader knows it's a pretence'.[11] Issues with dialogue are thought through, the form of the novel considered in relation to theoretical essays as well as personal practice, and the purpose of fiction as a genre questioned. Again, the influence of other writers including Flaubert, Thackeray, and Hardy is acknowledged in this piece that depicts the emotional and intellectual, like the theoretical and practical, as closely interwoven.

2.3 Doris Lessing's *The Golden Notebook*

Doris Lessing's Preface to the 1971 edition of *The Golden Notebook*,[12] written as an impassioned response to debates inspired by the novel, reflects upon her intentions in structuring the book as an exploration of personal and social fragmentation, and the potentially healing effect of breakdown where it challenges false dichotomies and divisions. Looking back at the composition of the novel, which itself comments upon the many interconnected influences on the writing process, Lessing addresses feminism and Marxism, historical examples of the novel as social commentary, and the vexed relationship between writer and critic. Her position reflecting upon the writing process as it spans the movement from initial imaginative and intellectual impetus, through composition and editing, towards awareness of potential audience responses, in light of reader interpretations that were not necessarily what she expected, gives this example of poetics a particularly outward-looking perspective. Here, Lessing goes further than either James or Fowles in addressing the part the reader plays in the making of a work, highlighting the gaps always at play between intention and reception.

I draw attention to these as examples of places where writers articulate the strange symbiotic process involved in writing, where critical thinking feeds intimately into creative practice. This is not about explaining or interpreting the work but reflecting and commenting upon process. Contemporary poets offer further examples. Seamus Heaney's essay 'Feeling into Words'[13] speaks of a range of personal and literary influences on his development as a writer, including the Ulster dialect of his childhood and the poetry of Gerard Manley Hopkins. The piece looks at the work of other poets including Wordsworth and Robert Graves and includes a reading of his own poem 'Digging' in considering aspects of the writing process that Heaney distinguishes as 'technique' as opposed to 'craft'. Technique, Heaney suggests, involves not only 'a poet's way with words, his management of metre, rhythm and verbal texture; it involves also a definition of his stance towards life, a definition of his own reality'.[14] It is this 'definition of a stance' that lies at the heart of poetics.

Joan Retallack uses the term 'poethics' to capture this sense of responsibility within a process that draws its energies from forces of chance and unpredictability. In her introduction to *The Poethical Wager* she says, 'This is a question of po*ethics* – what we make of events as we use language in the present, how we continuously create an ethos of the way in which events are understood'.[15] Informed by scientific theories of the dynamic systems at work in our universe,

Retallack's work actively explores unpredictable forms of change, the nature of agency, and the collaborative making of meaning. Similarly, Marlene Nourbese Philip's award-winning collection *She Tries Her Tongue; Her Silence Softly Breaks* contains an afterword that reflects on her developing poetics. In the essay 'The Absence of Writing or How I Almost Became a Spy', Nourbese Philip recalls growing up in Trinidad and Tobago 'no stranger to books' but never thinking of becoming a writer.[16] The essay goes on to explore how she came slowly to 'accept the blessing and yoke that is writing',[17] and the implications for her, as an African Caribbean woman, of a personal and cultural history that excluded her 'from the fullness and wholeness of language'.[18] Looking to the linguistic theories of Noam Chomsky as well as journal excerpts reflecting on the composition of poems in the collection, this afterword speaks of how *She Tries Her Tongue* shows Nourbese Philip working towards her 'goal of decentering the language',[19] in order that she and other black female writers might 'begin to recreate our histories and our myths, as well as integrate that most painful of experiences – loss of our history and our word'.[20] The essays in Rachel Blau Du Plessis' *Blue Studios* tell of the personal, cultural, political, and literary influences upon her writing, and her stance towards 'the cultural work that poetry does and could do'.[21] At once autobiographical, critical, and poetic, these essays address a wide range of concerns, including feminism, Du Plessis' position writing within the sphere of influence of modernists including H. D., George Oppen, and Ezra Pound, and the thinking behind the composition of her ongoing long-poem project *Drafts*.

These examples illustrate the various elements feeding into the writing process, which span false divides often posited between public/personal, emotional/intellectual, and creative/critical. Developing a poetics, then, means drawing reflexively on a range of inputs:

- Writing practice – including exercises, first drafts, rewrites
- Experiences, observations, and thinking recorded in notebooks and journals
- The influence of other writers, contemporary and historical, working in the genre and beyond
- Essays by other writers and interviews with them

- Critical essays on the work of other writers
- Literary theory
- Entering into dialogue with other works, literary essays, and criticism through essays, creative interventions, unsent letters, arguments, and agreements
- Influences drawn from other disciplines, such as scientific theories or philosophical thinking
- Encounters, experiences, instincts, visions, dreams
- Consideration of alternative methodologies and their effects and implications
- Technical aspects such as dialogue, characterisation, plot structure, scenes, stage directions, prosody, metre, poetic form
- Understanding the history of the genre
- Challenging conventions
- Observing the world, its history and politics
- Seeing the contemporary by recognising the current cultural environment
- Pushing at boundaries, experimenting, testing, and reviewing
- Encountering desires and disappointments
- Rethinking and rewriting
- Developing ethics and testing beliefs.

All these activities converge to constitute process and product, and the active movement between. Encouraged to think of the critical discourse in relation to their creative work in these terms, far from feeling lost for words, students are more likely to echo Henry James' view that 'There really is too much to say.'[22]

3 The triptych of practice-led research

In thinking of the practice of writing as a process in which these elements meet and coalesce, the concept of poetics can help writers involved in practice-led research articulate the relationship between the creative work and its critical inputs and outcomes, so developing a mature perspective on their practice. This process might be figured as a triptych whose outer panels – the critical and theoretical inputs and

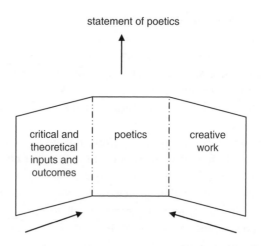

statement of poetics

critical and
theoretical
inputs and
outcomes

poetics

creative
work

Figure 1.1   The triptych of practice-led research

outcomes on one side, the creative work on the other – might hinge
to fold over and into the central poetics panel as in Figure 1.1.

Crucial to this image is the hinge between the panels that allows
for the movement between – a flexible, active, connection. Out of
this connected process, writers can formulate a statement of poetics
that might underpin the discourse that accompanies a piece of
creative work.

4   Towards reconnection

How, then, can this model be applied to creative writing teaching to
facilitate students in successfully developing their own poetics?

4.1   The challenge of creative writing research

Students cite three main challenges that seem to reinforce the
tendency towards disconnection between the activities of writing
and critical reflection:

1 Too much focus on product and outcomes leads to excessive
   self-consciousness, inhibiting the writing process and paralysing

the ability to write freely, risk, to take chances. *Being critical means I just keep second guessing myself, ending up unable to write anything.*

2   Taking a critical perspective means becoming a literary critic of your own work, applying theory to your work as if you had not written it. *Won't I just be pointing out its flaws? This is painful, and doesn't help me as a writer.*

3   Writing a critical piece in addition to the creative work is an academic exercise (in the pejorative sense of the term). It is jumping through academic hoops for little practical gain, simply to meet assessment criteria. *It's a waste of valuable time that I could better use writing creatively.*

Encouraging students to develop a concept of their own poetics positively addresses these key concerns.

Too much thought of reader expectations can indeed paralyse the writing process, as even the most accomplished of writers have found. Having waited years for recognition, when it finally came Gertrude Stein found herself unable to write under the burden of audience awareness she suddenly encountered. As she said, 'all your inside gets to be outside'.[23] Carole Satyamurti has a nice term for the interruption to the creative flow caused by the inner critic muscling in on the composition process – 'premature evaluation'.[24] The word *premature* is key here: this is all about time. Yes, there are times when a writer needs to sidestep judgement in order to free-write, or generate connections and associations that might not make logical sense, sound poetic, or gel well structurally. They also need time to stand back, read, reflect, edit, revise, and rewrite. The skill lies in allowing the two processes their own time. In a sense this is about permission – learning to demarcate activities opens up the space to do what is needed at a certain point in the writing process. Of course, in practice judgemental impulses feed into even free-writing; what we can do as writers is allow one mode to be in ascendancy when we need it most. This is akin to shaping and moulding clay by passing it from one hand to another – there is something in the energy of the movement between that is part of the dynamic of creating.

Encouraging students to develop a poetics helps with the confusion and paralysis caused by being too critical too soon by moving them away from simplistic value judgements about whether something 'is working or not'. Allowing them to understand the varied aspects of their practice and to consciously enter into dialogue with a wide range of influencing material shifts the emphasis to '*how* is it working?' This moves the notion of 'critical' away from negative connotations of disapproval towards a more productive concept of informed thoughtfulness. For example, creatively rewriting a favourite poem by an influential poet allows for intimate engagement and deeper understanding about the effects of line length and rhythm that will underpin a writer's own approach to these technical aspects. This is the kind of knowledge practice-led research develops, knowledge that grows in the shift between writing and reflecting modes. Such a perspective also supports the creative writing workshop format suggested by Katharine Coles,[25] whereby close attention is paid to formal characteristics of a piece in order to facilitate mature discussion of *how* it is working, rather than placing the focus on 'fixing' work in progress by committee.

The concept of poetics helps address the difficulty of assuming an uncomfortably artificial critical stance by encouraging students to see themselves not as a critic of their own work but as an informed practitioner articulating knowledge and beliefs. The challenge here is often one of form, the difficulty arising in the choice of discourse used to frame the discussion. First thoughts seem to suggest a critical discourse must be written from either an intensely personal perspective or a falsely distanced one. The directly autobiographical 'this is what I did and how' can feel too naked. Everyone knows how painful it is to attempt to describe a plot idea or the bones of a poem, as paraphrasing a creative work strips it of its life and energy; writers can feel as if they are being forced to say something differently that they have already said in the best way they know. It also feels like an invitation to highlight flaws – not a comfortable position at any time, least of all when submitting work for judgement and grading. Conversely, attempting to approach your work as a literary critic, reading it according to the tenets of critical theory as if it has been written by another writer is falsely distanced, and equally painful.

Once you have been so deeply immersed in a piece, it is impossible not to know what you know, intimately, about its composition.

Poetics helps address this dilemma. Not only does it help the student to develop a reflective critical perspective on their work continuously throughout the composition of a piece, it encourages them to gather together a storehouse of material that will inform a critical discourse about their creative work, including journal entries charting the challenges of composition, interviews with influencing writers, notebook entries recording responses to other work in the genre, drafts of work in progress where structural difficulties have been addressed, and so on. This storehouse then suggests other approaches to the critical discourse. For example, a writer influenced by Toni Morrison might structure a critical discourse on her own novella around a key theme in Morrison's work that is also central to her own, combining literary criticism on Morrison informed by critical theory with insight gained from her own writing practice and ethos. This opens up possibilities for active demonstration of, for example, how genre conventions and race/gender implications are being tested and subverted. This allows the student to speak from an informed critical perspective to demonstrate understanding of the context and tradition into which she writes, and to articulate how her own practice might further contemporary knowledge within the field.

Crucially, the concept of poetics is instigated during the compositional process as an integral part of that process, which makes for a critical perspective that is ongoing, rather than something to be addressed after the event, an afterthought. Again, the movement away from asking 'is it working?' to '*how* is it working?' enacts a crucial shift in perspective that allows for an informed consideration of aspects of the piece that may not have worked as intended. This allows for failed experimentation to be critically evaluated and the important knowledge gained to be shared, rather than denied. Rather than pointing out flaws to be negatively judged, this allows the writer to demonstrate the value of taking risks that advance knowledge even if they might not achieve initial aims – a crucial aspect of practice-led research, in which understanding emerges during the act of writing and reflection, and in which it should be recognised that as much, if not more, is often learnt when things do not work as expected.

It is true that academic and creative demands on the writer can feel antithetical. In her introduction to *Everybody's Autonomy*, Juliana Spahr speaks of those times when she felt pulled to look in opposite directions to satisfy the needs of poetic and academic communities as 'bifocal moments'.[26] However, the joy of poetics is that, as well as offering a means to address the academic need to demonstrate original knowledge and contribution to the field, it provides the writer with an invaluable perspective on their practice. Far from being an 'academic' exercise to simply meet assessment criteria, the benefits of formulating a poetics are ongoing, facilitating future change and growth for the writer, who will have developed an attitude towards their work that will go on enlivening their practice. In *The Necessity of Poetics*, informed in part by a UK English Subject Centre research project into forms of supplementary discourse, Robert Sheppard suggests an involvement with poetics might allow students to integrate skills and techniques 'into an ongoing practice that is involved with change'.[27] He says, 'I believe all students of creative writing should be inaugurated into the activity of poetics, since it is, of necessity, a self-sustaining part of all writerly process, born of the critical need to change practice'.[28]

4.2 Teaching strategies

Encouraging students to formulate a concept of their own poetics can be instigated at undergraduate level, and applied at postgraduate levels of study. As teachers we can do this in a number of ways:

- Suggest students seek out examples of poetics both historical and contemporary, including statements of beliefs from influential writers in essays as well as in conversations, interviews, blogs, and the like. Discuss how they might draw upon these examples to develop a philosophy towards their own practice. Collected works containing interesting discussions by poets include *Poetry in Theory*,[29] a collection of writings on poetry by poets from 1900 to 2000, and *American Women Poets in the 21st Century*,[30] which prints poems by contemporary innovative writers alongside their statements of poetics. *The Novel Today*,[31] edited by Malcolm Bradbury, contains examples of poetics by fiction writers, including those already mentioned by Doris Lessing and John Fowles, as well as an essay on 'The Novel as Research' by Michel Butor. Reading creative works in conjunction with essays written by the poet or author can be actively modelled in taught seminars. Particularly enlightening are those that directly address a specific work, such as Rachel Blau Du Plessis' essays in Section IV of *Blue Studios*[32] on the writing of *Drafts*, and Denise Riley's discussion of 'Affections of the Ear' in *The Words of Selves*.[33] Inspire students to seek out different forms of discourse by writers they admire, or writers they do not (which can sometimes be even more enlightening). As we all know, following that trail of strange connection that leads to an unexpectedly exciting text is part of the joy of discovery – many an inspiring work has been found just to the left of the one sought on the library shelf.

- Introduce creative methods of engagement, including different kinds of textual interventions. Charles Bernstein suggests innovative poetic approaches in 'Experiments' (http://writing.upenn.edu/bernstein/experiments.html), and Hazel Smith's *The Writing Experiment: Strategies for Innovative Creative Writing*[34] contains plenty of exercises working across poetry and fiction genres. Encourage the breaking down of perceived barriers between theory and practice by getting students to write a scene where a character from their work in progress is engaged in discussion with a critical theorist, or a scene in which an influential playwright wanders into the action of a drama to comment upon it. None of this writing need necessarily be submitted. It can, however, provide entertaining, sometimes startling, and usually enlightening insights into the creative process simply by allowing the writer to shift perspective by placing themselves, or their characters, or both, in an unexpected position. Similarly, students might practice expressing their poetics by answering general questions from interviews with other writers in terms of their own work.

- Encourage students to reflect upon their writing process on an ongoing basis by keeping a journal. Here they can record observations on the experience of drafting and editing, as well as noting responses to essays, interviews, critical theory, and other influencing material. Some students find it inspiring to split the page, noting thoughts on reading material on one side and poetic or fictional responses on the other, allowing the two to fold into ongoing conversation. Michelene Wandor warns against such journal material becoming 'a substitute for the conventional academic practice of study – reading and note-taking, while not giving adequate attention to the ways in which such accumulation of material might form resources for imaginative writing'.[35] Wandor points out the importance of directing students how to use these reflective resources to underpin critical thinking about their practice. Once again, the concept of a developing poetics helps to facilitate this, encouraging students to articulate a critical stance informed by this material, rather than simply submitting it, unprocessed, alongside creative work.

4.3 Assessment

As assessment criteria in creative writing increasingly move away from the often unquantifiable 'publishable standard', prey as that judgement is to the vagaries of markets and literary taste, towards the ability to demonstrate knowledge gained through practice, helping students develop a concept of poetics offers a number of benefits in terms of assessment:

- Providing a context for work to be assessed on its own terms, articulating *how* it is working and allowing for failed experiment where this is considered reflexively in light of knowledge gained.
- Providing the means for students to demonstrate awareness of the context and traditions within which they write, and how these are being drawn upon, developed, and challenged in order to progress knowledge in the field.
- Actively demonstrating engagement with critical and theoretical material to show how this body of knowledge is being tested and developed through practice.

4.4 Innovations

Increasingly there is active recognition of the performative aspect of the relation between creative and critical elements in works that inscribe a writer's poetics in their form. These can offer inspiration for more experimental, hybrid, forms of discourse, which actively comment upon the interconnected nature of these elements in inventive ways in order to better represent this relationship.

Juliana Spahr's *Spiderwasp or Literary Criticism* is an excellent example of this. Pages on one side of the book tell a poetic narrative that uses the metaphor of a pepsis wasp laying eggs on the body of a tarantula to explore the close touching involved in various relations, personal and social. On the other side is a critical essay discussing works 'that have themes and forms and aesthetics that join',[36] including Lisa Jarnot's *Sea Lyrics*, Jena Osman's 'The Periodic Table as Assembled by Doctor Zhivago, Oculist', and Joan Retallack's 'THE BLUE STARES'. Reflecting the thematic content, both pieces touch across the hinge of the page in active, joint, conversation, and in doing so they comment on the interconnectedness of the practice of writing poetry and literary criticism.

Some writers carrying out practice-led research have found innovative ways to address the relationship between critical and creative elements in order to demonstrate how the two are working in close connection within this research. In her 2009 Sussex University DPhil thesis, 'The Textual Skin: Towards a Tactile Poetics', Sarah Jackson says she attempts to forge a new poetics using different textures of writing as a means of inquiry. Exploring the textual skin of H. D.'s work through critical essays that draw on Derrida's conceptualisation of touch and Kristeva's notion of the semiotic, Jackson goes on to explore the skin between lucidity and dreaming, memory and imagination, inside and outside, and the self and others in *Pelt*, a collection of poems. The preface to the collection, situated in the space between the two modes of writing, playfully articulates the sensitive touching it is involved in through a consideration of tickling, which might cause laughter, but also create unease. Jackson notes, 'Thus, while the critical chapters in this thesis are not explicitly "about" my own poetry – they do not touch on it directly – my reading of HD rethinks the manner in which textual skins rub against each other, performing contact with the material, theoretical and creative history of my writing. It is critical, it is precarious, and yet it carries its own "primitive pleasure."'[37]

Abi Curtis' 2007 Sussex University DPhil thesis 'The Freud Effect: At the Limits of Psychoanalysis and Literature' combines three critical essays exploring Freud's marginalia and its effects upon his writing process with *The Hypnotist*, a novella underpinned by the same theoretical concerns. The movement between these modes of enquiry is bridged by an epistolary piece entitled 'Passing Hands', four letters concerned with hypnosis, automatic writing, detection, and telepathy, which both fuse and question academic and creative conventions.

These examples demonstrate the potential when critical and creative aspects of creative writing research are recognised as working in dynamic close connection, illustrating how this relationship might be expressed in engaging, informative, and progressive ways. Encouraging students to develop a concept of their own poetics as part of their writing practice provides them with an anchoring central panel linking their creative work and its critical influences. From this informed perspective students can gain valuable insight into the act of writing and, in place of a vocabulary of doubt and struggle, discover the means to successfully articulate the knowledge gained through practice-led research.

Exercises

1 Write a dialogue that is an imagined conversation between yourself and a writer whose work you admire, in which you discuss how you view your work in relation to theirs. Be as creative with this as possible – it can take the form of a short story, poem, or a scene from a play or radio drama.

2 Answer the following questions as though you were being interviewed by a literary journal:

   a Which other writer has been the biggest influence on you and why?

   b What is the key theme of your current work? How are you exploring this theme and why do you feel it is so important?

   c If you could write a manifesto for the genre you work in, based on three key ideas, what would those ideas be?

Notes

1 *Creative Writing Research Benchmark Statement*. Available at http://www.NAWE.co.uk

2 *Creative Writing Research Benchmark Statement* (11).

3 Aristotle, *Poetics*. Kenneth McLeish trans. London: Nick Hern Books, 1999, p. 3.

4 Henry James, *The Novels and Tales of Henry James, Vol. III, The Portrait of a Lady, Vol. I*. London: Macmillan, 1908, p. x.

5 James, p. vi.

6 James, p. v.

7 James, p. xi.

8 John Fowles, 'Notes on an Unfinished Novel', 1969.

9 John Fowles in Malcolm Bradbury (ed.), *The Novel Today*. Manchester: Manchester University Press, 1977, p. 136.

10 Fowles, p. 136.

11 Fowles, p. 139.

12 Doris Lessing, *The Golden Notebook*. Michael Joseph, 1962.

13 Seamus Heaney, *Preoccupations*. London: Faber, 1984, pp. 41–60.

14 Heaney, p. 47.

15 Joan Retallack, *The Poethical Wager*. Berkeley: University of California Press, 2003, p. 9.

16 Marlene Nourbese Philip, *She Tries Her Tongue; Her Silence Softly Breaks*. London: The Women's Press Ltd., 1993, p. 77.

17 Nourbese Philip, p. 77.

18 Nourbese Philip, p. 87.

19 Nourbese Philip, p. 88.

20 Nourbese Philip, p. 91.

21 Rachel Blau DuPlessis, *Blue Studios*. Tuscaloosa: University of Alabama Press, 2006, p. 1.

22 James, p. xxi.

23 Gertrude Stein, *Everybody's Autobiography*. New York: Vintage, 1973, p. 47.

24 Carole Satyamurti and Hamish Canham (eds), *Acquainted with the Night: Psychoanalysis and the Poetic Imagination*. London: Karnac, 2003, p. 42.

25 Graeme Harper (ed.), *Teaching Creative Writing*. London: Continuum, 2006, pp. 8–20.

26 Juliana Spahr, *Everybody's Autonomy: Connective Reading and Collective Identity*. Tuscaloosa: University of Alabama Press, 2001, p. xi.

27 Robert Sheppard, *The Necessity of Poetics*. Liverpool: Ship of Fools, 2002, p. 15.

28 Sheppard, p. 15.

29 Jon Cook (ed.), *Poetry in Theory, An Anthology 1900–2000*. Malden, MA: Blackwell, 2004.

30 Juliana Spahr and Claudia Rankine (eds), *American Women Poets in the 21st Century: Where Lyric Meets Language*. Middletown, CT: Wesleyan University Press, 2002.

31 Bradbury, ed., pp. 169–85, 136–50, 48–53.

32 Du Plessis, pp. 209–51.

33 Denise Riley, *The Words of Selves: Identification, Solidarity, Irony*. Stanford: Stanford University Press, 2000.

34 Hazel Smith, *The Writing Experiment: Strategies for Innovative Creative Writing*. Crows Nest, NSW: Allen & Unwin, 2005.

35 Michelene Wandor, *The Author is not Dead, Merely Somewhere Else*. Palgrave Macmillan, 2008, p. 221.

36 Juliana Spahr, *Spiderwasp or Literary Criticism*. New York: Spectacular Books, 1998, p. 7.

37 Sarah Jackson, 'The Textual Skin: Towards a Tactile Poetics'. Sussex University, DPhil thesis, 2009, p. 153.

Works cited

Aristotle, *Poetics*. Kenneth McLeish trans. London: Nick Hern Books, 1999.

Bradbury, Malcolm (ed.), *The Novel Today*. Manchester: Manchester University Press, 1977.

Cook, Jon (ed.), *Poetry in Theory, An Anthology 1900–2000*. Malden, MA: Blackwell, 2004.

Curtis, Abi, 'The Freud Effect: At the Limits of Psychoanalysis'. Sussex University, DPhil thesis, 2007.

DuPlessis, Rachel Blau, *Blue Studios*. Tuscaloosa: University of Alabama Press, 2006.

Harper, Graeme (ed.), *Teaching Creative Writing*. London: Continuum, 2006.

Heaney, Seamus, *Preoccupations*. London: Faber, 1984.

Jackson, Sarah, 'The Textual Skin: Towards a Tactile Poetics'. Sussex University, DPhil thesis, 2009.

James, Henry, *The Novels and Tales of Henry James, Vol. III, The Portrait of a Lady, Vol. I*. London: Macmillan, 1908.

Lessing, Doris, *The Golden Notebook*. London: Michael Joseph, 1962.

Nourbese Philip, Marlene, *She Tries Her Tongue; Her Silence Softly Breaks*. London: The Women's Press Ltd., 1993.

Retallack, Joan, *The Poethical Wager*. Berkeley: University of California Press, 2003.

Riley, Denise, *The Words of Selves: Identification, Solidarity, Irony*. Stanford: Stanford University Press, 2000.

Satyamurti, Carole and Canham, Hamish (eds), *Acquainted with the Night: Psychoanalysis and the Poetic Imagination*. London: Karnac, 2003.

Sheppard, Robert, *The Necessity of Poetics*. Liverpool: Ship of Fools, 2002.

Smith, Hazel, *The Writing Experiment: Strategies for Innovative Creative Writing*. Crows Nest, NSW: Allen & Unwin, 2005.

Spahr, Juliana, *Everybody's Autonomy: Connective Reading and Collective Identity*. Tuscaloosa: University of Alabama Press, 2001.

——, *Spiderwasp or Literary Criticism*. New York: Spectacular Books, 1998.

—— and Rankine, Claudia (eds), *American Women Poets in the 21st Century: Where Lyric Meets Language*. Middletown, CT: Wesleyan University Press, 2002.

Stein, Gertrude, *Everybody's Autobiography*. New York: Vintage, 1973.

Wandor, Michelene, *The Author is not Dead, Merely Somewhere Else*. Basingstoke: Palgrave Macmillan, 2008.

2   Non-Fiction Writing Research

Donna Lee Brien

Chapter summary

Although non-fiction writing has been a core part of such disciplines as history, journalism and literature (in the form of writing articles, essays and books), creative writers often find the instructions given regarding researching and writing non-fiction in these disciplines inadequate to serve the increasingly complex procedural and ethical challenges they face. In response, as more writers, undergraduate students, higher degree candidates and teachers of writing publish or study non-fiction, how to conduct research in, and about, this genre has become a prominent area of interest in creative writing studies. In the wake of a number of recent 'scandals' around non-fiction publications, moreover, the ethical issues involved in producing non-fiction texts have also come to the forefront as a concern for writers. At the same time, the recognition of such work as valid research in the university context, and the justification for this classification, is also important. This chapter defines research in the context of the discipline of writing generally and non-fiction writing more specifically. It focuses on the different ways non-fiction creative writing is researched and how this research can be validated. It also highlights the ethical issues involved in researching and writing non-fiction texts, and how the writer of non-fiction can approach and deal with these challenges.

History is always changing behind us, and the past changes a little every time we retell it.

(Mantel 2009)

1   Introduction – focus of chapter

With more and more writers, as well as students, teachers and higher degree candidates, seeking to publish or study non-fiction, how to research and write this genre has become a prominent area in creative writing studies. Although non-fiction has been a core part of such disciplines as history, journalism and literature (in the form of writing articles, essays and books), creative writers often find the instructions given regarding researching and writing non-fiction in these disciplines inadequate to serve the increasingly complex procedural and ethical challenges they face. In the wake of a number of recent scandals around non-fiction publications, moreover, the ethical issues involved in producing non-fiction texts have also come to the forefront as a concern for writers. A number of these scandals are discussed below, including when James Frey's *A Million Little Pieces*,[1] Margaret B. Jones's *Love and Consequences: A Memoir of Hope and Survival*[2] and Misha Defonseca's *Misha: A Mémoire of the Holocaust Years*[3] were found to be exaggerated or even wholly fabricated. At the same time as these challenges, the recognition of such work as valid research in the university context, and the justification for this classification, has also become an issue.

This chapter defines research in the context of the discipline of writing generally and non-fiction writing more specifically. It focuses on the different ways non-fiction creative writing is researched and in which circumstances this work can be validated as practice-led research that moves beyond authorial inquiry. It takes into account research and research projects from undergraduate assignments to postgraduate theses and academic research projects in the area of non-fiction creative writing.

2   Research in writing: Definitions and processes

The Australian Department of Innovation, Industry, Science and Research's OECD-derived definition describes research as 'creative

35

work undertaken on a systematic basis in order to increase the stock of knowledge, including knowledge of man [sic], culture and society'.[4] Much of the work undertaken by creative writers, both inside and outside the academy can, therefore, be classed as 'research' in these terms. Creative writers working in the higher education sector obviously make a contribution to these 'stocks of knowledge' with the content of their scholarly books, articles and theses about writing, but this definition means that creative works can also be assessed as research if they can demonstrate that they also add to these knowledge stocks.

In broad-spectrum terms of making a research contribution, non-fiction writing does not differ markedly from other genres of writing nor, indeed, from other disciplines of the creative arts. This is because writers join the makers of all works of art in their generation of knowledge. Artists of all kinds, including writers, can create this knowledge in two main ways. Firstly, they can, like their colleagues in the humanities and in the sciences, make a discovery that adds to the general stocks of knowledge. This might involve, for instance, the unearthing of a previously lost or unknown document, artefact or fact. This could include the diaries or correspondence of someone of interest, or the detection of an overlooked figure who had made an important contribution in a field, or a piece of new information about an issue of significance. Secondly, as artist and theorist Paul Carter points out, artists can productively reflect on the creative thinking – their working methodologies – that they use when creating their artworks, and the various and progressive iterations of that thinking.[5] This is different from critics and theorists who can, instead, only analyse the final product in terms of content, or describe or rationalise the creative process based on that final outcome or, at most, any extant process evidence (which would include, for example, drafts or the writer's journal entries in the case of creative writing). This is important, as Carter proposes, as artists who work in this way are integrating the craft 'wisdom' that goes into making an artwork with the conscious striving towards knowledge of a researcher. In such a process of creative arts practice-led research, the artist retrieves the 'intellectual work that usually goes missing in translation' during the process of making works of art.[6] These findings contribute to new knowledge when they can demonstrate that they have significance and value in those terms.

In the current university context, creative artists – in this case, writers – who think this way about their creative writing as research similarly strive to enunciate what may be present, but not otherwise articulated, in their art-making processes. But before they can thus describe their research findings, they must engage in a recognisable process of research. In this aspect of their practice, the process non-fiction writers utilise can be described in the same terms as in scientific research, although all the 'steps' below will not necessarily be followed uninterruptedly or consecutively. First, there will be a problem or an issue to be investigated that the writer will seek to identify as clearly as he or she can. Once identified, this is described as the 'research question' (or 'problem') that the writer seeks to examine and, hopefully, solve. The research question is a statement regarding what the researcher wants to write about, and is underpinned by an understanding of why this is important in terms of what new knowledge it will contribute. In order to determine what progress other writers and researchers have already made in the same area, the non-fiction writer will review what these others have already discovered and documented. This part of the research process is usually described as a 'literature review' and will set the new research project in context, provide a foundation for the project to build on and ensure that the same work is not repeated (unless this is a deliberate component of the project). This review might well lead to the writer altering and refining their research question. The writer will then engage in a cyclic process of experimentation and testing the findings of these experiments, in the process evaluating and re-evaluating what they find in this process, and then reporting this in a form that can be validated by others.

In this way, researchers will be engaged in a series of research enquiry cycles. Their findings will be reported in a variety of ways that include the piece of non-fiction writing itself (the creative work) as well as a range of scholarly writings that support, explicate and arise from that artwork. This final product may be an undergraduate essay, or other short work of non-fiction and critical reflection, a (progressively) more sustained and in depth Honours, Masters or Doctoral thesis comprising non-fiction work and exegesis, or a university-based research project with a range of outputs ranging from creative work to formal project acquittal report.

The working methods all writers use have core similarities, but it is important to recognise that not all inquiry a writer undertakes will, however, produce new knowledge, or knowledge of the same value to those 'stocks' cited above. Some of this information may be important to the writer in terms of producing his or her text, but while this reading and other inquiry will increase what the writer him- or herself knows, it will not produce new knowledge for the world at large.

3 Research into non-fiction writing

One of the first tasks for the writer of non-fiction as practitioner-based researcher is that of determining the sub-genre in which he or she is going to be working. This is because this selection will influence and govern the direction of the research activity the writer will engage in, as well as how he or she will report the findings of this research activity. Many sub-genres of writing come under the descriptor of non-fiction. These include life writing such as memoir, biography and autobiography, history, journalism and encyclopedia entries. It also includes a variety of writing including essays classified by their content such as criticism and reviews, and travel, nature, food and true crime narratives. The writer must decide not only which of these sub-genres they want to write in, but also determine which will provide the best 'fit' for the story they want to tell.

This is, however, not as simple as it sounds. Take, for instance, a writer who has the starting point of a childhood memory, something as seemingly simple and unambiguous as a certain family meal eaten on a festive holiday, say, a special birthday lunch. First, he or she must decide what question or problem or issue they wish to answer or explore through writing about this memory. Is it part of a full autobiography of the author, a memoir about family dynamics or becoming a cook, a personal essay about birthdays or aging or the nuclear family, or a piece of food writing about birthday cakes? If the last is chosen, will the focus be on baking, sugar, cookbooks, gender roles in food preparation, homemade versus purchased foods, the development of the author's interest in gastronomy, or the myriad of other subjects that this memory could provide information for? Moreover, will this provide the core component of, say, a 2000-word piece for an undergraduate assignment which can, moreover, be recycled as a magazine article, or part of an 100,000-word doctoral thesis that will be published as a book?

But to take one step back, even the very first choice this writer must make – of working in the non-fiction genre – that unique definition of a genre of writing by what it is not (that is, not fiction) – is not the clear-cut choice it appears. This is despite the fact that the identification of any particular piece of writing as non-fiction (or not) often appears relatively uncontroversial. There are, after all, shelves in bookshops and libraries for fiction, which is usually defined as work that is 'made up' by the author such as novels, short stories and poetry. Almost everything else is non-fiction. In terms of publishers' conventions and readers' expectations, a non-fiction literary work is most generally understood as consisting of a narrative about an event that has actually happened, someone who has actually lived or a material object, place or natural feature which has actually existed. The non-fiction label on such a text, moreover, is seen to be an assurance that the text will contain facts and tell the truth about this event, person or object, place or natural feature. This may, therefore, seem to be the obvious choice for the birthday party narrative.

But are fiction and non-fiction so clearly demarcated from each other as this implies? When he wrote his masterpiece novel in the sub-genre of what has later been defined as 'fact-based fiction' or the 'non-fiction novel', *In Cold Blood*,[7] Truman Capote predicted that what had until then been understood as different, and indeed, parallel literary forms – fiction and non-fiction writing – would eventually merge, 'coming into a conjunction like two great rivers'.[8] The once popular but now rarely used term 'faction' was a later attempt to suggest that these two literary forms could simply be elided into one, as were the post-structural, postmodern assertions that all truth was relative and contextual. Yet, almost fifty years after Capote's groundbreaking work, publishers and readers still understand fiction and non-fiction to be distinct forms. Vicious criticism can, indeed, result when readers feel the boundaries demarking the two genres (of fiction and non-fiction) are being breached. Although there can, moreover, be negative reactions to fictional texts whose writers include non-fiction elements in their work,[9] approbation is most common when ostensibly non-fiction works include fictional passages.[10] Fiction writers who base their work on actual events and/or people can, for example, be charged with exploiting or appropriating others' stories in their work, but this never reaches the level of outcry that results when texts marketed as non-fiction prove to be exaggerated or even wholly fabricated.

This was certainly the case in the furore that surrounded the discovery that memoirs such as James Frey's *A Million Little Pieces*, Margaret B. Jones's *Love and Consequences: A Memoir of Hope and Survival* and Misha Defonseca's *Misha: A Mémoire of the Holocaust Years* were partly or wholly invented. With more than 1.77 million paperback copies sold in the USA in 2005, Frey's sensational memoir of his drug addiction was only bettered in sales that year by JK Rowling's *Harry Potter and the Half-Blood Prince*.[11] However, less than a week after Frey's success made news that was syndicated all over the world, a lengthy report in an investigative online journal, *The Smoking Gun*, revealed that Frey had invented many of the key elements of his narrative. These included dramatic scenes of assaulting a number of policemen, being charged with multiple offences including cocaine possession and serving a three month prison sentence. Instead, police documents and sources have revealed that not only was Frey never charged with assault, no drugs were involved in the matter police questioned him about, and he was released after paying a small (US$733) cash bond.[12]

Similarly, after considerable success, Margaret Jones (real name Margaret Seltzer) confessed that she had completely fabricated the story of her supposed life as a half Native American, half white, foster child and drug-running gang member in a tough part of Los Angeles. Seltzer's memoir was a dual fraud in terms of her identity – she was completely Caucasian, and her life – she grew up with her real parents in an affluent part of the city and had never been a gang member. Belgian born, US-based Defonseca's text was first published in 1997 as a memoir that traced what happened when, as a little Jewish girl, her parents were deported and she walked across Europe trying to find them, hiding with packs of friendly wolves, and killing a Nazi soldier. A bestseller in Europe, it was translated into 18 languages, and was adapted into an Italian opera and a successful French film. After documents were circulated that discredited her story, it was revealed that the author had a different name, was not Jewish (she was Catholic), and had lived in Brussels for the whole war. Strangely, however, her own (real) family story was profoundly moving, as her parents were deported and killed by the Nazis as members of the Belgian resistance.

The problem in these and other such cases in terms of genre and public expectation is that these albeit powerful and, at times, thrilling and moving narratives were presented to the public as memoirs and, therefore, as non-fiction and, by implication, as true as the author could make them, when each was subsequently proven to be in part, or largely, fiction and, therefore, 'made up' by its author. I have written elsewhere of how it is not such practical issues as having to reconstruct, edit or compress dialogue and the other details of life in a written text[13] that is the core issue in such cases, but when the writer steps away from striving for veracity in his or her text. This is the difference between a sincere desire to relay the truth to the best of the writer's ability (conscious as they are of all the obstructions to that objective and the limitations of the tools at hand), and not even trying to relay that truth.

Hybrid descriptors can lead to further confusion and are, moreover, often misused in these discussions. These terms include the 'autobiographical', 'non-fiction' and 'historical' novel for novels based on actual events, and the 'fictional memoir' or 'fictional biography' for novels written in the form of a memoir or biography but where the result is still fiction. On the non-fiction side, there is the (increasingly popular) sub-genre of 'creative nonfiction'. Creative nonfiction uses the creative techniques of fiction, but the result is non-fiction because 'it is necessarily and scrupulously accurate and the presentation of information … is paramount'.[14] But, writers know, and have known for a long time, that the real world cannot be directly rendered into text. The novelist Henry James, for instance, wrote of the difficulty of trying to report the complexity of experience in his books, and this is an even more significant issue for non-fiction authors:

> Experience is never limited, and it is never complete; it is an immense sensibility, a kind of huge spiderweb of the finest silken threads suspended in the chamber of consciousness, and catching every airborne particle in its tissue.[15]

Given the difficulties of representing the intricacies of life in literature with any accuracy, and assertions that the idea of any absolute truth is outmoded, contemporary authors have found that writing non-fiction with these complexities in mind is a challenging task. In attempting to deal with these complexities, they have conducted important research into such issues as defining 'truth'. Their findings on this topic have discussed, for instance, the differences between factual and aesthetic truths, and the ways that authors can signal to their readers how they have dealt with such issues as gaps in their data sets, or conflicting evidence. This is especially important as while readers do have an expectation that non-fiction texts will relay 'the truth', they are also very accepting when authors explain the limitations in both their evidence and their own abilities. In the birthday party memory, for instance, the writer will have some data that represents fairly certain truths – who was present, how old they were at the time, what they were wearing, what food was served, what the weather was like, where the party was held, and so on. There will also be a myriad of issues that are less clear: who said what, for instance, and to whom. Even once this is ascertained, there is the more difficult question of what was meant by what was said, which will, of course, always be a matter of interpretation. The seemingly innocuous 'Happy Birthday', for instance, can be stated with warmth or delivered in a snide and/or ironic fashion, or with a myriad of other intentions falling between these. Even the most banal facts might not be agreed on by all the guests at the party. A photograph could show everyone around the table, but cut off at the waist. What shoes everyone was wearing could be a point of debate, as could be who was the last to leave and other such matters.

Once these kinds of issues are identified, the position the writer will take towards the subject he or she is writing about and the information within that piece is vitally important, and will involve the writer in more research inquiry and praxis. Will, for instance, the writer take a more objective, or a more subjective, stance in relation to the subject and the information they have in front of them? How will they make this clear to the reader? Will they write with a first, second or a third person narrator? Will the work be fully referenced with extensive footnotes relating to the topic? Will this reference list, instead, be implicit in the text of the writing itself, be included as a discursive, even chatty, section at the end, or be formatted as a formal bibliography? While some of these questions will be resolved by following the conventions of the intended publication – a newspaper article will have a very different way of citing source materials than a postgraduate thesis for instance – others will need to be resolved through the research process and may, in turn, direct the most suitable form for publication. Some of this decision-making will not be consciously engaged in, and the choice will seem 'natural', although this will also be based on the writers' own knowledge and intuition.

During this process, writers may experience an uneasy dissonance between the label of non-fiction (producing a true story about the real world) and the process of writing (including research, drafting and editing) that has to be undertaken in order to produce such texts. This is because most writers of non-fiction are aware that they are not mirrors that capture an exact copy of reality in their texts and reflect this back into the world. Even if they do not describe it in these terms, they know, instead, that they are researchers who set out with a question/problem/issue to explore. They then collect and assimilate information about that question or problem or issue, testing the findings they make in terms of genre and sub-genre of the writing produced, and how effective that writing is as art. They may also test boundaries in the course of their experiments. How they embark on this research task is conditioned by what they already know about the question or problem or issue, and what they know about how to find and collect the information they need, and that serves their purpose. They then reflect upon that information in order to find a way to render that information and, nowadays, sometimes the experience of gathering it, into words. Once they have these words in some kind of order – either as a draft, or fragments of a draft – they then edit and re-edit this draft or these fragments until they have a narrative that they believe serves their (non-fiction) purpose. This editing stage may well involve gathering more information, and integrating it with, and testing it against, what they already have. At some time, the writer decides they have enough information, have carried out sufficient editing and rewriting, and they declare their piece is complete, and they submit it to the reviewer, editor, publisher or equivalent. At this time, the information, the way it is assembled as well as the way it is written about, may be questioned, and the writer may need to either gather more information, or express it in a different way. They will always, in this process, be referring back to their research question.

4 Types of research for non-fiction authors

Researching and writing non-fiction can be characterised as a two-fold procedure made up of different, but inseparable, components. These can be defined as the 'non-fiction' (the content) component and the 'writing' (the process) component. In working through this research procedure, the writers' non-fiction words – their writing – are arrived at by focusing the information and data they collect (about the content and about the process) through the prism of their own sensibilities and experience of the world. In this, all writers engage in a research-type process: that is, they cannot progress in any other way but speculate and assume, and build hypotheses about their information and other data, and test and then change and correct their hypothesis, until they have a text that not only answers the problem they set out to solve, but also fits the parameters of their experience and knowledge of the world they are writing about.

At the same time, creative writers know they provide just one source of information among the many available to those seeking information. Bookshops and libraries have books and periodicals on almost every topic, the Internet is bursting with sites and pages, bloggers and the mass media fill our various digital and analogue devices with data. With this range of information sources in mind, writers also know that producing a text that engages the reader is an essential part of the process. That is, writers must not only render the information they have into a form that answers their question or addresses that problem or issue they set out to explore. They must also wrestle the words they come up with into an order that will engage and absorb the reader's interest and fit the publication or other dissemination platform they have in mind – whether this is a full length book, chapter in a book, journal, magazine or newspaper article, encyclopaedia or weblog entry, social media site post, under-graduate assignment or postgraduate thesis. Of course, given today's technological melding of formats and delivery modes, something written for one platform may be easily transformed into text on another, with this melding and morphing sometimes carried out by authors themselves, many times by others.

The process that non-fiction writers undertake has been summa-rised by the prominent critic and much-awarded biographer of James Joyce, Oscar Wilde and WB Yeats, Richard Ellmann, who wrote that, 'biographies will continue to be archival, but the best ones will offer speculations, conjectures, hypotheses'.[16] This statement expresses the disconnect that non-fiction writers often detect between the sources they are using (the enormous, though finite, archive of his-torical facts, real places and material objects, official and personal records and other documents, personal reminiscences and the like that they have at their disposal) and the infinite ways that it is possible to then select from, and express (or, what is often called 'craft') a singular literary object from this archive. It also clearly debunks the commonly held, but clearly impossible, idea that non-fiction writing is a purely objective process, wherein the writer's subjectivity has no part. Of course, the ability to come to such important and influential assertions depends on the writer's experi-ence as a researcher and a writer. Ellmann wrote biographies that were among the most acclaimed of the twentieth century and, he was, moreover, an important critic for some decades. Knowing the field in such depth allowed him to pursue similarly in-depth research into form and content in writing biography.

Aside from research into the genre and sub-genre of the text and related questions, writers will also engage in archival and experiential research. While almost all non-fiction writing will involve these types of inquiry to some extent, whether this will be classed as 'research' in terms of the OECD definition revolves around the question of whether new knowledge has been created, expressed and disseminated in the process.

5 Archival research

Once the above questions of genre are decided, or at least a provisional decision has been made, the non-fiction writer often finds that extensive archival inquiry is required. This is the kind of information gathering that most people mean by the word 'research'. This kind of research is carried out in libraries and archives including art galleries and museums and on the Internet including using databases and a range of open source materials. These online sources may of course include access to works held in libraries and archives around the world. This type of research can involve the writer in locating and consulting books, newspapers, journal articles, manuscripts, official records and published reports, meeting minutes, maps, photographs and other images whether in their actual locations, or gaining access to them online. Before embarking on this quest, the researcher must, first of all, decide what information they need, where to find this, how to access it and, finally, how to process this information. This type of research activity would align with the basic dictionary definitions of research, most of which read along the lines of the 'systematic investigation into and study of materials, sources etc., in order to establish facts'.[17] It may, or may not, however, produce new knowledge. It can be, rather, a matter of writers informing themselves about already known areas of knowledge that they will utilise in order to make their creative work. As Jen Webb and I have written:

To paraphrase an example that has been used in a number of discussions about practice-led research in creative writing: if a playwright is writing a play about the Suffragettes, he or she might be reading about the history of this protest movement, but that is an act of accessing the already existing knowledge that he or she needs to know in order to create the work. Any original contribution to knowledge will be embedded in how this information is presented to the audience in the form of the play.[18]

To follow the above example about the birthday lunch, if the writer is going to concentrate on writing a personal essay about birthdays, with a focus on how these are commemorated around the world, he or she is going to need to know basic information about, for instance, the etymology of the word 'birthday', when the celebration of birthdays became popular and commonplace in the Western world, what different national celebrations have in common and if birthdays are, indeed, celebrated everywhere around the world or not, and so forth. In this research inquiry, the writer is going to have to make choices such as what are useful source materials to pursue, and how long he or she is going to spend on the inquiry. In archival research, writers must constantly calculate what level of detail of information they need and ensure they come away with a record of what they have gathered that is suited to their needs. As Tess Brady has written of her reading for her PhD novel and exegesis:

> I needed to acquire a working, rather than specialist knowledge, not in one area but in a range of areas and disciplines ... With so much information to gather, the writer needs to be able to work quickly, to know the questions to ask and to be able to isolate the essence.[19]

What the author needs to gather in this way, will, moreover, be dependent, again, on their project and what contribution to knowledge it is consciously attempting to make.

In looking for this information, the researcher must also make decisions about the trustworthiness of the information they are gathering. A quick web search may, for instance, reveal a series of answers to the above queries about global celebrations of birthdays, but the writer has to always test the accuracy of this information before they include it in their own work. Just because something is published on the Internet or, indeed, in a book or an article that has found its way to the library or bookshop shelf, does not mean that the information it contains is correct. One of the roles of archival research is for the writer to 'get the details right'[20] and up to date. Archival research also provides an opportunity for the writer to check what they think they know. The central role of this kind of research for writers is widely acknowledged.[21] Samuel Johnson identified that '[t]he greatest part of a writer's time is spent in reading, in order to write; a man will turn over half a library to make one book'.[22] Norman Mailer, who is of great interest in this discussion as he was equally successful as both a fiction and non-fiction author, similarly describes 'reading related books ... [to] absorb reams of facts'.[23]

This kind of research reading to 'absorb facts' is not, however, necessarily going to produce new knowledge in itself. Mailer himself did, utilising this information in his genre boundary stretching work. Alongside the production of clearly identifiable novels, essays and journalistic pieces during the 1960s and 1970s, Mailer developed a hybrid textual form that combined fiction and non-fiction, fusing dramatic narrations of actual events with autobiographical reflection and political commentary. He used this technique to great acclaim in *The Armies of the Night*,[24] winner of both the Pulitzer Prize and the National Book Award, and *Miami and the Siege of Chicago*,[25] which also won the National Book Award in the non-fiction category. *The Armies of the Night* was subtitled *History as a Novel*, and in both this work and *Miami and the Siege of Chicago* Mailer used literary/ novelistic techniques to describe historical events, at the same time autobiographically exploring, and expounding, his own subjective reactions to these events. In 1973, Mailer turned this technique to non-fiction in *Marilyn*, which he described as 'a species of novel ready to play by the rules of biography'.[26] Conceived as a collection of photographs with a brief introduction to be penned by Mailer, the project instead evolved into a dense, meditative examination of not only her life, but also the mythology surrounding Monroe, this narrative being supported by the now-familiar photographic images. An early example of psychobiographical analysis, *Marilyn* allowed Mailer to utilise his novelist's skills to make sense of the contradictions animating Monroe's nature. His aim, as he stated, was to provide 'a literary hypothesis of a *possible* Marilyn Monroe who might fit most of the facts available'.[27]

6 Experiential research

In her suggestion that 'innovative methodologies often appear in fields where conventional sources are unavailable', Sarah Maza includes sources outside the library and archives in her list of the unconventional,[28] but for writers, gleaning information from their own experience of the world is a regularly utilised research methodology. Nadine Gordimer, for instance, describes writers as having 'powers of observation heightened beyond the normal',[29] which they mobilise to read people, events, situations and places by watching, eavesdropping, travelling and, in various ways, attempting to experience, and then understand, that which they wish to represent or evoke in their writing. Writers thus often conduct their own field trips to places that are important in their texts, attempting to locate physical information regarding the present or the past that they are writing about.

As well as the forms mentioned above, writers also experience the world by talking to the people who inhabit it. These conversations may be informal and serendipitous, an unplanned part of everyday conversation. They may, however, also be formally constructed as qualitative research interviews, for which questions are devised and interview scripts followed. These are often recorded in some form and transcripts created from these recordings. In some higher education systems (Australia and UK, for instance), formal ethical clearance must be obtained for such interviews and release forms drafted and signed by participants. Again, the contribution of this 'talk' to the writer's project, and how the project itself is framed, are what defines these activities as 'research' or not.

This experiential research may, again, be material the writer needs, but is not in itself, or productive of, new knowledge. Or, it may be. In reference to his work discussed above, Mailer explains how the data gained from his research (whether from the archives or his experience of the world) was a central part of his authorial decision-making:

> We are the philosophers who are there to make sense of those concentrated if frozen fantasies we pretend to call facts. Someday, may it be, we will say, those old fantasies we *used* to call facts until we learned to unpack them.[30]

Graeme Harper has similarly characterised writers as possessing an 'entirely interrelated creative and critical sense'[31] which, when animated as above, articulates the feedback loop of writing and research that does have the potential to produce new knowledge.

These three types of research inquiry – into writing itself, archival and experiential – are not only key to writer's practice, but they are also never unconnected, each feeding into, and affecting, the other. An Internet search may send the writer to a library to follow up on a lead suggested online or to check some data from an interview against a documentary source. The findings from a conversation that became an ad hoc research interview may need to be read against documented evidence to confirm the names, dates and places mentioned. Something about a historical site, for instance its size or position relative to other sites, mentioned in a document in the archive or even a guidebook, may be need to be confirmed by visiting it in actuality.

7 Conclusion

Non-fiction draws its power from the truths it tells to its readers. The genre similarly draws its popularity from its audience's positive response to the compelling and engaging ways it relays these truths. Readers of literary works classified as non-fiction, while not naïvely believing everything in these texts, read such works with an understanding that they will contain reliable – that is, trustworthy – information. These readers also trust non-fiction writers not to manufacture or alter the truth as those writers understand it, just as these readers trust reputable publishing houses to commission, edit and publish material that is worthy of bearing the non-fiction label.

Although, of course, no author can ever completely represent the intricate complexity of their research findings in writing, writers of non-fiction must nevertheless strive for the highest levels of verifiable accuracy in their work to attract and maintain the trust of their readership. Writers of non-fiction must, therefore, seek an ethical approach to research and writing practice, balancing the limitations of their own abilities and memories with their desire to produce attractive and readable texts. It is when, however, writers reflect on these processes and the resulting work to generate new knowledge, and this is validated as such, that the work moves from the realm of the creative production to that of verifiable research.

Exercises

1 Collect 5 related archival documents that are *not* personal to you.
   a Produce a short non-fiction narrative from these sources.
   b Analyse this narrative in the following terms:
      • What question or problem or issue did you set out to explore in this writing?
      • What has been added to the 'stocks of knowledge' by this work?
      • Is this knowledge in terms of knowledge about writing, or knowledge about the world? Or both?
      • What data would you need to further this research? How you would best obtain this?
      • What ethical issues have arisen in using this information in this way?
2 Repeat this exercise for a set of 5 related archival documents that are personal to you. Then note the differences between these two exercises.

Notes

1 James Frey, *A Million Little Pieces*. New York: N. A. Talese/Doubleday, 2003.
2 Margaret B. Jones, *Love and Consequences: A Memoir of Hope and Survival*. New York: Riverhead Books, 2008.

3   Misha Defonseca, *Misha: A Memoire of the Holocaust Years*. Bluebell, PA: Mt. Ivy Press, 1997.

4   Department of Innovation, Industry, Science and Research (DIISR) *2010 Higher Education Research Data Collection: Specifications for the Collection of 2009 Data*, 2010: 6. http://www.innovation.gov.au/Section/Research/Pages/highereducationresearchdatacollection.Aspx [Last accessed 17 July 2010].

5   Paul Carter, *Material Thinking: The Theory and Practice of Creative Research*. Carlton: Melbourne University Publishing, 2004.

6   Carter: xi–xiii.

7   Truman Capote, *In Cold Blood*. London: Macdonald and Co., 1966 (1989 edn).

8   Truman Capote cited in Rhonda Lieberman 'Double Exposure: Putting the Me into Memoir', *Village Voice* (1 April, 1997) Voice Literary Supplement: 10.

9   Donna Lee Brien, "'Based on a True Story": The Problem of the Perception of Biographical Truth in Narratives Based on Real Lives', *TEXT: Journal of Writers and Writing Programs* 13.2 (Oct, 2009). Online. http://www.textjournal.com.au [Accessed 15 July 2010].

10 Donna Lee Brien, 'The Power of Truth: Literary Scandals and Creative Nonfiction' in Tess Brady and Nigel Krauth (eds), *Creative Writing: Theory Beyond Practice*. Brisbane: Post-Pressed, 2006: 55–63.

11 Reuters, 'Harry Potter Tops Best-Seller List for 2005', *The New York Times*, *nytimes.com* 6 January, 2006. Online. http://www.nytimes.com/reuters/arts/entertainment-arts-books.html [Accessed 15 July 2006].

12 The Smoking Gun reporter, 'A Million Little Lies: Exposing James Frey's Fiction Addiction', *The Smoking Gun*, 8 January 2006. Online. http://www.thesmokinggun.com/jamesfrey/0104061jamesfrey1.html [Last accessed 15 July 2006].

13 See Donna Lee Brien, 'Being Honest About Lying: Defining the Limits of Auto/biographical Lying', *TEXT: The Journal of the Australian Association of Writing Programs*, 6.1 (April, 2002). Online. http://www.textjournal.com.au [Accessed 15 July 2010].

14 Lee Gutkind, *Creative Nonfiction: How to Live it and Write it*. Chicago: Chicago Review Press, 1996: 15.

15 Henry James, 'The Art of Fiction' in William Veeder and Susan M. Griffin (eds), *The Art of Criticism: Henry James on the Theory and the Practice of Fiction*. Chicago and London: University of Chicago Press, 1986: 172; 1st. pub. *Longman's Magazine*, 4 (September 1884): 502–21.

16 Richard Ellmann, *Golden Codgers: Biographical Speculations*. London: Oxford University Press, 1973: 15.

17 Bruce Moore (ed.) *Australian Concise Oxford Dictionary of Current English*. South Melbourne: Oxford University Press, 1997: 1148.

18 Jen Webb and Donna Lee Brien, 'Addressing the "Ancient Quarrel": Creative Writing as Research' in Michael Biggs and Henrik Karlsson (eds)

The Routledge Companion to Reseach in the Arts. Milton Park: Routledge, 2011: 201–2.

19 Tess Brady, 'A Question of Genre: De-mystifying the Exegesis'. *TEXT: The Online Journal of the Association of Writing Programs*, 4.1 (April, 2000). Online. http://www.gu.edu.au/school/art/text [Accessed 15 July 2010].

20 Irena Dunn, *The Writers Guide*. Crows Nest: Allen & Unwin, 2002: 86.

21 Nigel Krauth, 'Learning Writing Through Reading', in Brenda Walker (ed.), *The Writer's Reader: A Guide to Writing Fiction and Poetry*. Rushcutters Bay: Halstead Press, 2002: 167–71.

22 Charles Grosvenor Osgood, ed. *Boswell's Life of Johnson*, abridged ed., avail. *Project Gutenberg*, e-text 1564. 1917. Online. http://www.gutenberg.org [Last accessed 15 July 2010].

23 Norman Mailer, *The Spooky Art: Some Thoughts on Writing*. New York: Random House, 2003: 190.

24 Norman Mailer, *The Armies of the Night*. London: Weidenfeld and Nicolson, 1968.

25 Norman Mailer, *Miami and the Siege of Chicago: An Informal History of the Republican and Democratic Conventions of 1968*. New York: World Publishing Co., 1968.

26 Norman Mailer, *Marilyn*. New York: Grosset and Dunlap, 1973: 20.

27 Mailer, quoted in David Novarr, *The Lines of Life: Theories of Biography, 1880–1970*. West Lafayette: Perdue University Press, 1986: 161.

28 Sarah Maza, 'Stories in History: Cultural Narratives in Recent Works in European History', *The American Historical Review*, 101.5 (December 1996): 1495.

29 Nadine Gordimer, 'Introduction', in *Selected Stories*. London: Bloomsbury, 2000: 4.

30 Mailer, 2003: 308.

31 Graeme Harper, 'Editorial: Buying or Selling? Creative Writing Research in the University', *New Writing: The International Journal for the Practice and Theory of Creative Writing*, 2.1 (2005): 2.

Works cited

Brady, Tess, 'A Question of Genre: De-Mystifying the Exegesis', *TEXT: The Online Journal of the Association of Writing Programs*, 4.1 (April, 2000). Online. http://www.textjournal.com.au [Accessed 15 July 2010].

Brien, Donna Lee, 'Being Honest About Lying: Defining the Limits of Auto/biographical Lying', *TEXT: The Journal of the Australian Association of Writing Programs*, 6.1 (April, 2002). Online. http://www.textjournal.com.au [Accessed 15 July 2010].

—— 'The Power of Truth: Literary Scandals and Creative Nonfiction' in Tess Brady and Nigel Krauth (eds), *Creative Writing: Theory Beyond Practice*. Brisbane: Post-Pressed, 2006: 55–63.

—— '"Based on a True Story": The Problem of the Perception of Biographical Truth in Narratives Based on Real Lives', *TEXT: Journal of Writers and Writing Programs* 13.2 (October, 2009). Online. http://www.textjournal.com.au [Accessed 15 July 2010].

Capote, Truman, *In Cold Blood*. London: Macdonald and Co., 1966 (1989 edn).

Carter, Paul, *Material Thinking: The Theory and Practice of Creative Research*. Carlton: Melbourne University Publishing, 2004.

Defonseca, Misha, *Misha: A Memoire of the Holocaust Years*. Bluebell, PA: Mt. Ivy Press, 1997.

Department of Innovation, Industry, Science and Research (DIISR) *2010 Higher Education Research Data Collection: Specifications for the Collection of 2009 Data* (2010). Online. http://www.innovation.gov.au/Section/Research/Pages/highereducationresearchdatacollection.Aspx [Last accessed 17 July 2010].

Dunn, Irena, *The Writers Guide*. Crows Nest: Allen & Unwin, 2002.

Ellmann, Richard, *Golden Codgers: Biographical Speculations*. London: Oxford University Press, 1973.

Frey, James, *A Million Little Pieces*. New York: N. A. Talese/Doubleday, 2003.

Furia, Philip, 'As Time Goes By: Creating Biography' in Carolyn Forché and Philip Gerard (eds), *Writing Creative Nonfiction*. Cincinnati: Story Press, 2001: 67–84.

Gordimer, Nadine, 'Introduction', in *Selected Stories*. London: Bloomsbury, 2000.

Gutkind, Lee, *Creative Nonfiction: How to Live it and Write it*. Chicago: Chicago Review Press, 1996.

Gutkind, Lee, *The Art of Creative Nonfiction: Writing and Selling the Literature of Reality*. New York: John Wiley and Sons, 1997.

Harper, Graeme, 'Editorial: Buying or Selling? Creative Writing Research in the University', *New Writing: The International Journal for the Practice and Theory of Creative Writing*, 2.1 (2005): 1–3.

James, Henry 'The Art of Fiction' in William Veeder and Susan M Griffin (eds), *The Art of Criticism: Henry James on the Theory and the Practice of Fiction*. Chicago and London: University of Chicago Press, 1986: 165–83; 1st. pub. *Longman's Magazine*, 4 (September 1884): 502–21.

Jones, Margaret B., *Love and Consequences: A Memoir of Hope and Survival*. New York: Riverhead Books, 2008.

Krauth, Nigel, 'Learning Writing Through Reading' in Brenda Walker (ed.), *The Writer's Reader: A Guide to Writing Fiction and Poetry*. Rushcutters Bay: Halstead Press, 2002: 167–71.

Lieberman, Rhonda, 'Double Exposure: Putting the Me into Memoir', *Village Voice*, (1 April, 1997) Voice Literary Supplement: 10.

Mailer, Norman, *Miami and the Siege of Chicago: An Informal History of the Republican and Democratic Conventions of 1968*. New York: World Publishing Co., 1968.

——, *The Armies of the Night*. London: Weidenfeld and Nicolson, 1968.

——, *Marilyn*. New York: Grosset and Dunlap, 1973.

——, *The Spooky Art: Some Thoughts on Writing*. New York: Random House, 2003.

Mantel, Hilary, 'Booker Winner Hilary Mantel on Dealing with History in Fiction', *The Guardian*, 17 October 2009. Online. http://www.guardian.co.uk/books/2009/oct/17/hilary-mantel-author-booker [Last accessed 15 July 2010].

Maza, Sarah, 'Stories in History: Cultural Narratives in Recent Works in European History', *The American Historical Review*, 101.5 (December 1996): 1493–515.

Moore, Bruce (ed.), *Australian Concise Oxford Dictionary of Current English*. South Melbourne: Oxford University Press, 1997.

Novarr, David, *The Lines of Life: Theories of Biography, 1880–1970*. West Lafayette: Perdue University Press, 1986.

Osgood, Charles Grosvenor (ed.), *Boswell's Life of Johnson*, abridged edn, avail. *Project Gutenberg*, e-text 1564. 1917. Online. http://www.gutenberg.org [Last accessed 15 July 2010].

Pearson, M., 'Researching Your Own Life' in Carolyn Forché and Philip Gerard (eds), *Writing Creative Nonfiction*. Cincinnati: Story Press, 2001: 45–9.

Reuters, 'Harry Potter Tops Best-Seller List for 2005', *The New York Times*, *nytimes.com* 6 January, 2006. Online. http://www.nytimes.com/reuters/arts/entertainment-arts-books.html [Accessed 15 July 2006].

Rowling, J. K., *Harry Potter and the Half-Blood Prince*. London: Bloomsbury, 2009.

Smoking Gun reporter, 'A Million Little Lies: Exposing James Frey's Fiction Addiction', *The Smoking Gun*, 8 January, 2006. Online. http://www.thesmokinggun.com/jamesfrey/0104061jamesfrey1.html [Last accessed 15 July 2006].

Webb, Jen and Donna Lee Brien, 'Addressing the "Ancient Quarrel": Creative Writing as Research', in Michael Biggs and Henrik Karlsson (eds), *The Routledge Companion to Research in the Arts*. Milton Park: Routledge, 2011: 186–203.

3   Modelling the Creative Writing Process

Marguerite MacRobert

Chapter summary

Consciously or not, people often model the process of creative writing based on personal experience. This mental construct accounting for how creative writing works then underpins research into the writing process and needs to be examined and compared with other theories on the creative writing process.

Much pioneering research on the cognitive processes of writing was conducted using psychology research methods. One groundbreaking study by Linda Flower and John Hayes developed a complex cognitive process model of the writing process, challenging the idea that writing occurs in sequential stages. Unfortunately, this research was conducted in an artificial laboratory environment, and was not aimed specifically at creative writing. In later research into the lives of renowned creative people, psychologist Mihaly Csikszentmihalyi developed a model of the creative process. My own research used these seminal empirical studies as the foundation for more context-bound interviews with successful publishing novelists in South Africa.

The cornerstone of the Flower and Hayes model was the subprocess of goal setting, similar to Csikszentmihalyi's emergence of problems as a crucial component of any creative process. In my interviews, it emerged that this could indeed be the driving force of the entire creative writing process. This is possibly the place where the world of the writer and the world being created in their fiction are most closely mapped onto one another and could be a primary factor in understanding writer's block. Find the right match between worlds, and you may be able to avoid this dreaded hurdle.

This chapter will discuss research on both the writing process and the creative process that was synthesised to form a conceptual framework for interviews with published novelists in South Africa. Within the traditional framework in South African universities' language departments, creative writing is studied as a product in literature courses, rather than as a process. The focus is on the world created in a text or the socio-political world in which the text is situated. Studying the writing process itself is a relatively new field of enquiry; studying the creative writing process even more so. The interviews conducted with contemporary writers sought to broaden this perspective so that the process of creating textual worlds in a particular context could be investigated. Ways in which these interviews provided insights into altering existing models of the creative writing process, including a new perspective on 'writer's block' and the reiterative nature of creative idea generation and critical judgement, are presented as part of the application of the research methodology.

I   Researching the writing process

In order to learn more about the writing process, including the origination of ideas, how these ideas are translated into writing, reviewed and revised, author and writing teacher Donald Murray[1] maintains that we need to study 'the activity at the workbench in the skull'. In other words, we need to examine not simply the process of developing a product, but also the interaction of 'the inner processes of the person producing this product'.[2] Writing is a cognitive process and getting into someone's skull is not easy, so a good starting point was to examine different methods attempted by other researchers.

A literature survey clarified how many studies on creative writing rely on biographical material on famous authors, or interviews with authors. However, more direct empirical studies of the writing process in general had been conducted primarily in the related field of composition studies.

1.1 Autobiographies and interviews

Works such as Margaret Atwood's *Negotiating with the Dead: A Writer on Writing*,[3] or Gabriel Garcia Marquez's *Living to Tell the Tale*[4] are replete with the personal insights of authors as they put their (writing) worlds under the microscope. However, as books are often designed to entertain as well as inform, they are perhaps likely to highlight the extraordinary at the expense of dull details that might tell us more about how writers actually work. Such material on living authors is invaluable, as you can compare what they tell you in your research to what they write for a public audience. A writer straddles two worlds – public and solitary – and it can be advantageous to study contemporary authors with public profiles who are quoted in a number of newspaper articles and to see them giving public talks. To illustrate the difference, in South African writer Margie Orford's interview for this research, she described writing her first novel as a methodically planned event, where she wrote a synopsis, had it accepted by a publisher, then wrote the novel. At a writers' festival, she had the audience in stitches, admitting to having lied to the publisher about already having written the novel when she submitted her synopsis. When they told her on a Friday that they would like to see the novel on the Monday, she made a frenzied attempt to write a whole novel over a weekend, while her husband urged her to confess. Eventually she said to the publishers, 'I lied', and they said, 'We know.' Nevertheless, it all worked out fine. Both stories are true but one reveals her need to see her process as controlled and methodical as this is what orders her world as a writer and mother of three, while the other demonstrates her ability to entertain, amuse and be simply human in the sometimes chaotic world outside her writing studio.

As with biographies, newspaper and television interviews are in themselves an art form. They can provide deep insights into writer's methods and style, but do not facilitate clear comparison between writers and often focus on content rather than process. The authors interviewed in my study were pleased to discuss process and not content because this was such a novelty. Where interviews do focus on process, there is a challenge typical in studies in the humanities: the fallibility of memory. According to leading writing researchers Flower and Hayes,[5] introspective analysis by writers of their process is 'notoriously inaccurate and likely to be influenced by their notions of what they should have done'. For this reason, protocol analysis evolved to study the cognitive processes at work in real-time as writers compose.

1.2 Protocol analysis

Protocols, borrowed from psychological research methods, are detailed records of a writer's process,[6] including a tape recording of anything the writer says while composing, and the notes, doodles and drafts she produces.[7] In think-aloud protocols, writers are given a topic and asked to write in a laboratory. They are also asked to do any thinking out loud, verbalising everything that occurs in their minds as they write, including false starts, as if talking to themselves.[8] Transcripts, matched to notes and text produced during a session, yield a detailed picture of the composing process. After five years of this research with many writers, both expert and novice, it was possible to construct a sophisticated cognitive process model of writing that is worth any writing researcher's time to study. Their methods permit an examination of that workbench in the skull by capturing 'the flow of thought that would otherwise remain unarticulated'.[9] Above all, their resulting model of the writing process provided a tool for other researchers to think with.

However, this mode of research has the opposite problem to interviews and biographies, as it tends to lean towards 'context stripping' and as such it was challenged by Berkenkotter,[10] who cautioned: 'When researchers remove writers from their natural settings … to examine their thinking processes in the laboratory, they "create a context of a powerful sort, often deeply affecting what is being observed."'[11]

1.3   Naturalistic studies

In an attempt to rectify this, Carol Berkenkotter conducted a naturalistic study by tracking a publishing author's daily writing habits in his habitual writing sessions and settings. This was a groundbreaking first-hand exploration of a writer's world, but the difficulties in replicating this methodology are manifold.

First, a research participant must be found who writes frequently and second, this writer has to be engaged in at least one writing project at the time of the study. This writer has to agree to a new method of work, namely thinking aloud while writing, and allowing someone to record this, while observing his behaviour and taking notes, possibly in his home. Donald Murray, who agreed to participate in this study, felt that this was 'merely a question of turning up the volume knob on the muttering I do as I write' and that 'if there was any self-consciousness in the process it was helpful. I was, after all, practicing a craft, not performing magic'.[12] However, he is accustomed to frequent public speaking and dictates final drafts to his wife. He did not baulk at the invasion of his privacy or interruptions to work time, but he believes that writers as teachers have an 'ethical obligation to write and to reveal our writing to our students' – a sentiment that Imraan Coovadia, a writer-teacher participant in my research, does *not* share.

While pioneering enviable research conditions, it is easy to see why this study remains unique. Beyond the reservations an author might have about an invasion of her (often solitary) world, a researcher could baulk at the money and time required for a study that, over the course of two months, generated over one hundred hours of recordings and involved the mailing of audio-tape dialogues between author and researcher, as well as the correlation of audio material with her observation notes and the drafts he was working on.

Berkenkotter's study did confirm an important point to remember when asking authors about their methods. An author cannot reconstruct everything that he or she does, especially if asked about it too long after the writing, partly because the daily evolving text required all of his mental energy and 'yesterday's page seems like last year's'.[13] In addition, what the writer is actually doing and what he might think he is doing can be different. For example, South African writer Lesley Beake describes as revision some aspects of her writing process which in fact involved generating fresh ideas and planning how to fit these into her existing text.

These findings could lead to a suspicion that all interview-based investigations into the writer's world are, by nature, retrospective. However, privileging one kind of study over another is less helpful than seeing what can be learnt by examining many different kinds of studies to look for points of agreement and divergence.

1.4 Interviewing a number of participants

Psychologist Mihaly Csikszentmihalyi chose to study creativity 'as a process that unfolds over a lifetime'[14] by speaking to 91 respondents and his research provides a counter-balance to the context stripping of Flower and Hayes' study and the individuality of Berkenkotter and Murray's. Furthermore, it places the creative process of writers in the context of other creative individuals, including inventors, and historians, who have made significant creative contributions to their domains.

Csikszentmihalyi posited that it is dangerous to aim for objectivity while discrediting a participant's perceptions of how they go about their work as completely unreliable because they are 'expressions of a bourgeois ideology' or 'a narrative device' in the context of an interview' or even as the opposite of the truth, because the participant is somehow in denial and suppressing reality.[15] It is necessary to listen with 'open skepticism' in order to reach a deeper understanding of the way a creative person experiences and creates their world. While previous studies showed that there is much that an author cannot accurately remember or explain, this is one part of the puzzle; the author's environment and working conditions are another, and the author's own perceptions and explanations are yet another valid part of the whole if we are to attain a truly multi-dimensional understanding of the cognitive process of creative writing. The creative writer is a creator of a particular fictional world in their writing, but, like any other person, they are also creators of their own inner worlds within the context of their identities as fiction writers.

Csikszentmihalyi's research did not uncover one definitive way to describe a universal 'creative process' but he found some common threads which ran across domains and individuals and which he felt might 'constitute the core characteristics of what it takes to [achieve] an outcome the field will perceive as creative'.[16] Thus if we take the perspective of creativity, including writing a poem or novel, as the setting up and solving of a problem, his five-stage model of the creative process could be very useful. He cautions that this model's simplicity could be misleading but, as with Flower and Hayes' model, it could offer a manageable way to conceptualise a complex cognitive process.

2   Synthesis and application

Interviews with authors have been revisited with a fresh approach based on a synthesis of the models developed through the research. How and why writers create their fictional worlds, and how these intersect with the real worlds these people inhabit could then be explored in a more methodical way with a common vocabulary of concepts that would allow for comparison between authors. As Flower and Hayes and Csikszentmihalyi's models are too complex to summarise here, they will be briefly outlined and one key aspect they share will be discussed in relation to examples from the data obtained in this study of South African authors.

2.1   Selecting research participants

For practical reasons of time and cost,[17] only four authors were interviewed, but it is hoped that other researchers in South Africa and abroad will engage with this research and continue to build up a clear picture of the writing process over time across different worlds. As a caveat to the discussion that follows, no generalisations to all writers in all contexts are implied by any comparisons between authors and the other studies mentioned. However, only a bland research project would not note interesting commonalities as well as attempt to account for some equally fascinating differences between authors.

The methodology developed for this study began with a literature review of the studies discussed above. This research formed a conceptual framework for two-hour semi-structured interviews with authors, which were recorded, transcribed and analysed in conjunction with other material available in the popular press, such as blogs, magazine and newspaper interviews and video interviews available on the Internet. The basic questionnaire was the same for each author. However, as much as possible of the authors' writing had been studied, in addition to other published interviews with the authors, before the interviews so that the questionnaire could be personalised to each individual. This proved extremely useful in jogging the authors' memories of particular texts, word choices and such, as well as soliciting the comment from one author that it was polite to have read her books so closely as she had in the past been interviewed by people who had not read her books at all! This reading beyond academic literature also helped to build a picture of the world of South African publishing, where writers struggle to compete for the attention of a very small literature public with the purchasing power to buy books.[18]

The study was by nature not confidential as it would have taken an academic Houdini to perform the convolutions of syntax necessary to cover references to the well-known works of the authors involved. It was, in fact, a small incentive to participate if authors could be promised a modicum of that precious commodity: publicity. A researcher needs to be honest about selection criteria, which are often pragmatic rather than ideal. This research was purposely placed in the context of my home country, so the authors were South African. They also had to have written more than one book, and had to have achieved success in the field in the form of having published their books to some public acclaim.[19] The first author interviewed was Margie Orford, an award-winning journalist, documentary film director and best-selling detective crime novelist whose work has been translated into several languages. She was followed by Imraan Coovadia, an award-winning novelist, essayist and short story writer who teaches creative writing at the University of Cape Town. Next was Lesley Beake, prize-winning writer of over sixty books, mostly aimed at adolescents, and a magazine journalist. Finally, John Van de Ruit was interviewed after just having broken all South Africa's records for book sales and signings. His first book, *Spud*, has been turned into a film featuring actor John Cleese, and has been released in the UK and USA.

2.2 Applying the synthesised model

In essence, Flower and Hayes maintain that the different writing processes in a cognitive process model can function as a writer's tool kit, without constraints as to what order the writer needs to use these tools and with the implication that the use of one tool may necessitate the need for another. For instance, 'generating ideas' may require evaluation, as may writing sentences. And evaluation may force the writer to think up new ideas'.[20]

The power of such a hierarchical process that allows for many embedded sub-processes is its flexibility. It allows us to think of the writing process not in terms of a linear sequence of unique individual stages but as a thinking process that involves multiple embedding and recursion of subprocesses. They point out that 'embedding is a basic, omnipresent feature of the writing process even though we may not be fully conscious of doing it'.[21] When Berkenkotter was studying him, Donald Murray was surprised by the extent of the recursion of subprocesses and their embeddedness, noting that much of what he thought was a revision phase was in fact planning in the sense of reorganising ideas and generating new ones to fill perceived gaps between intention and actual text. This was ratified by the organising mechanisms that Beake, Orford and Van de Ruit demonstrated in their writing notes. Their storyboards and graphs plotting characters' development through different chapters had been written not before the novel was begun but after the first drafts had been completed. They were reviewing what had already been written in order to plan what still needed to be written, altered or left out.

However, Flower and Hayes[22] felt that a theory of composing that only described this embedding would not encompass the true complexity of writing. It would not be able to explain the choices writers make as they invoke particular processes or what makes them decide they need to move on to another. It would also not account for what gives an overall purposeful structure to the act of composing that guides the writer's decisions.

They were able to use the powerful process of goal-setting to account for this feeling of purposefulness when writing because, as they pointed out in an earlier article on the 'cognition of discovery',[23] 'writers don't *find* meanings, they *make* them'. This process of making meaning is a problem-solving process, according to Csikszentmihalyi, who posits that the start of any creative process is the emergence of problems[24] and there seems to be a strong correlation between what he calls problem setting and what Flower and Hayes call goal setting.

A difficulty with remembering the goal-setting process is that once a myriad of problems have been solved satisfactorily most, if not all, the processes used to reach that solution will be forgotten as they are no longer of use to the writer. Despite this fallibility of memory and the fact that the authors interviewed were unlikely to use the terms 'goal setting' and 'problem setting' to describe their activities, angling questions at what they desired to achieve, what problems they needed to solve, and so forth, helped build a picture of some aspects of the goal-setting process. What emerged correlated well with Csikszentmihalyi and Flower and Hayes, but pointed out what both Csikszentmihalyi and Berkenkotter and Murray mention that Flower and Hayes' context-stripped study could not account for, namely how long incubation time for ideas generation can really take. One of the things that surprised Murray about his writing process was how planning can take place throughout his writing. Another surprise was that the incubation time for generating ideas could take far longer than he had initially realised. Ideas can be brewing in the writer's mind for years before actually being put into a piece of writing. Writing does not occur in an isolated chunk of time separated from the rest of a writer's life – even if it may feel this way to a writer.

This makes it decidedly tricky to answer the question 'when does the writing process start?' because writing is characterised as a cognitive process and not simply the physical act of putting words onto paper. There is a tangle of correlation between the world of the writer and the world she is creating in the text that is difficult to unravel

65

and explain. This can be illustrated with an example of one of Csikszentmihalyi's three sources of problems, which happens to also be the most common source of problems for writers in his study and mine: a person's personal life. John Van de Ruit recounted what felt to him like the start of his first *Spud* book in an interview with the *Rapport* newspaper the week after his interview for this research.[25] He was in Zimbabwe, touring with his play, *Green Mamba*, and felt homesick one evening. He felt somewhat as he had in his first year of boarding school when his parents had left him at Michaelhouse for the first time. He could even remember certain scents. At this point he pulled the hotel's writing pad closer to him and wrote the first page of *Spud*. This is a tidy enough scene to report on, but in another interview he spoke of how he had once written a short story on the same theme as *Spud*, before the hotel moment, and he had already penned and acted in a play called *War Cry* dealing with this theme before that. Prior to all three of these writing events, he had completed a Masters Degree in drama with a thesis exploring masculinity in plays and films dealing with boys' boarding schools, such as *The Dead Poet's Society*. Before that, he had attended such a school, which was why he chose this theme for his drama studies in the first place. So when did he formulate the content goal for his book? It is difficult to say. He appears to have been formulating it throughout his adolescent and young adult life. It is an inextricable backdrop to his world.

This corroborates Csikszentmihalyi's point that the 'Aha!' moment so famous in the creative process occurs as a result of a problem brewing in the creative person's mind for some time and then finding a solution so good that it is forced to pop into consciousness. Csikszentmihalyi's study showed this 'Aha!' moment to be the result of hours or more often years of mulling over a particular subject.

The problems that drive what Flower and Hayes term content goals, which in turn drive what Berkenkotter named style goals, are of necessity topics that are intimately bound up with the world view of the writer. Orford decided to become a fiction writer because it allowed her to tell an emotional truth through portraying the intimate spaces between people and the power dynamics these reveal. Her emotional truth is an examination of what she fears most – the violent crime against women and children which is sadly rife in South Africa and which she encountered up close as a journalist. Writing is, for her, a way of examining the *tokoloshe* under the bed (a *tokoloshe* is a feared creature in South African folklore that carries children off in the night). This goal drives her writing process, from her choice of a spare style through to her research methods. She runs writing workshops with dangerous criminals in maximum security prisons and patronises an organisation that supports raped women so that she can get inside the heads of the perpetrators and the victims of the crime she writes about.

South Africa is often described in tourist brochures as 'a world in one country' and there are as many worlds and motivations for creating fictional ones as there are different people in any country. Unlike Orford, Coovadia writes books that all revolve in some way around South African Muslim characters, as he aims to write books that are in some way spiritually representative of South Africa as well as socially and psychologically complex. This may have led to a style goal for his first book, *The Wedding*, in which he captures the idiosyncrasies of the Indian English dialect in his wonderfully comic dialogues (a feat he achieved through following his aunt and mother around with a notebook to catch the cadences of their speech).

Beake left her job as a school teacher under Apartheid, in which the education system was intentionally narrow-minded, racially divided and conservatively Christian (it was, for example, illegal to speak about evolution in your classroom) and has made it her mission as a writer to try to open young minds to the universality of children's experiences, hoping to bridge gaps in a strongly culturally divided society.

Underneath his satirical romp through adolescence, Van de Ruit attempts to depict not only the physical but the emotional violence perpetrated in boys' boarding schools in his generation, as they wrestle with emerging masculinity. Whenever he needs a particular 'emotional quotient', as he describes it, he listens to songs from his teenage years that represent particular moments, such as REM's *Night Swimming*. He succeeded so well getting into the mood for one part of his writing process that he was diagnosed with depression after writing a funeral scene for a boy who dies, even though this was one of the few completely fictional characters in the first book. This is an extreme example of how closely involved in their fictional worlds a writer can become, echoing how Charles Dickens 'cried the whole time his pen-wielding hand was pitilessly doing [Little Nell] in'.[26]

What is important, according to Orford, is that all writing starts from the formulation of a question that will sustain your interest and provide a sense of purpose through sometimes arduous months and even years. The average time it took for a novel to be completed by the full-time writers in this study was eight to fourteen months, but it was much longer for Coovadia, who also works at a university, for obvious reasons. Once the writing has started, Orford has no time for writer's block, and neither did the other authors in this study. Coovadia actually felt that poor initial choice of topic was the only real cause of writer's block – once you had really got going on a topic he did not feel that writer's block ought to happen at all.

This provides some research-based theoretical confirmation that those typical injunctions to 'know thyself' that come standard in creative writing classes and textbooks are probably worthwhile. No one can promise that they will lead to a novel of merit, but they can perhaps guarantee the exploration of a topic that will sustain the interest of the *writer* (never mind any readers for now). They can also perhaps mean there is a possibility of *completing* a novel as it provides the motivation to work on a sustained basis. There must, in other words, be some match between the world of the writer and the world they wish to create in a novel if debilitating writer's block is to be avoided. Csikszentmihalyi stated that 'while it lasts, creative writing is the next best thing to having a world of one's own in which what's wrong with the 'real' world can be set right'[27] and the imaginary worlds that writers create appear to be as necessary to the writer as the physical world they actually inhabit, as they create a 'symbolic refuge' from reality.[28]

2.3 Physical aspects of the writer's world

An unexpected invitation to interview the first participant, Orford, in her home enabled an exploration of another facet of the writers' world: the place where the writing physically happens. This invitation emboldened me to request interviews in the other authors' homes. This was granted, although in Van de Ruit's case it proved easier to interview him while he was on a publicity tour in Cape Town than at his home in Durban. Fortunately his home had been reviewed and photographed recently in a magazine article so it was easy to discuss it with him based on this information. Being able to not simply ask questions about what Berkenkotter and Murray called 'situational variables' – namely the impact of personal life, relationships and physical environment on the writing process – but to actually see where she wrote and to ask questions based on observation, strengthened the research. The other authors all very generously agreed to a request to be interviewed in their writing spaces, and where they could, they showed rough notes as well as computer files. They also patiently answered questions about software and types of pens and pencils used.

Apart from Beake's injunction that her computer is beautiful because 'if you work on something all day, you should work with some pleasure', there was the interesting match between the physical spaces these authors wrote in and what they said about their goals in their writing. Coovadia's study contains a number of decorative items from India and the Orient. He also keeps his work as a novelist physically separated from his work at the University of Cape Town by working at home on his writing and in his office at the university for everything else, just as he believes he should keep his writing process separate from his creative writing students' processes. His drafting process happens entirely on his computer and he does not keep records of his drafts, reflecting perhaps the intransience of the lives his often immigrating and emigrating characters lead.

At a writers' festival, Orford said that she sometimes wishes she were more like the glamorous, single heroine of her thriller series, with her minimalist existence. In reality, Orford has three children, a husband, a dog and a rambling house cluttered with the trappings of family life. In strong contrast to her family home, she had a specially designed writing hut built at the back of her garden, in which she indulges her fantasy of stylish minimalism and a solitary life while she writes, right down to the white laptop which she says she chose mostly for aesthetic reasons. In contrast to Coovadia, Orford writes all first drafts by hand, saying this helps her capture the emotion she seeks. Writing straight onto a computer is for her too cerebral a process. She and Beake prefer writing in the famous mole-skine notebooks popular in South Africa,[29] feeling these are not only convenient for moving around with but also link them in some way with a community of writers and artists.

Van de Ruit says he does not particularly care how his computer looks, and it is his girlfriend who buys him attractive notebooks to write in as on his own he would write on any paper, but he does insist on a new laptop for each new book, as he feels one book 'wears out' a laptop. Perhaps this helps give a sense of keeping each book in a popular series fresh and individual. He does much of his writing on the veranda of his Durban flat, inherited from the grandmother he immortalises as the infamous 'wombat' in his Spud series. These authors all had, in their own ways, an almost ritualistic attachment to their writing spaces and tools, writing there in preference to most other places (except when they needed a break for important reasons) often for particular set times (ranging from a standard work-ing day to mornings or afternoons only). In other words, they had created a physical world in which the tools of their trade were more than simply efficient and easy to work with. They were symbolic of particular aspects of the writing process and of the worlds being created in their fiction; navigation instruments and engineering tools in the exploration and creation of these worlds. The precise relationship between the physical environment where writing takes place, the tools used to translate and store texts and the creative writ-ing process would need to be established through further research. My investigations did reveal that there could be a link in terms of creative writers' personal identities and their need for triggers that help them to enter a particular mental space in order to be able to concentrate.

This intimate meshing of the world of the author, the physi-cal act of a book's creation and the content or style of the book does not mean that novels need or tend to be autobiographical. Orford vowed not to write until she did not need to write about herself. Van de Ruit emphasised that he did not set out to write a memoir even if his book follows a first-person diary format and many of his personal experiences as a teenager. All of these novelists stressed the necessity of transforming raw material – researched, philosophical or autobiographical – into fiction so that it is not too self-aware. This is one of the places where their anticipation of a reader's needs intercepts their own desire to create this other world. Their style goals were often influenced by books they had read, admired and wished to emulate, or the opposite. In contrast, their content goals were apparently not very much influenced by other writers' choices of topics other than superficially. Interestingly, all mentioned a style they particularly wanted to avoid which is rather a cliché in South African literature, as anyone who has studied English literature in this country can testify: long descriptive passages about a farm in the Karoo (a sparsely populated, semi-desert area)!

According to Flower and Hayes' research on composition skills, good writers are constantly evaluating and reformulating their goals as they generate new ideas and organise these ideas into prose. This means that revision as part of the writing process will not only lead to the revision of words on the page or concepts in the writer's mind, but also to an evaluation of the goals that are driving the writing itself. Here it helps to recall the sense writers often describe of writing being a kind of exploration or discovery (this overriding metaphor was only rivalled by a complementary metaphor of writing as practical hard work, like building or plumbing). This leads to something all creative writing teachers will be clamouring to add: being inspired through knowing yourself is not enough. Writing could also be characterised as a craft, and textual worlds need shaping and sharpening into focus if they are to appeal to readers as explorers.

2.4 Revision as a creative process

It is sometimes held in creative writing 'How To' books[30] that revision and editing are the non-creative parts of the writing process, when rational judgement dominates the process. This is the drudgery that happens after the fun of creative ideas generation is over. Csikszentmihalyi pins the blame for writer's block here, saying that the free-flowing discovery process of the evolving text has to be 'monitored by the critical eye of the writer'.[31] This requires the mind to focus on two contradictory goals: 'not to miss the message whispered by the unconscious and at the same time to force it into suitable form'.[32] The first process depends on openness, while the second requires critical judgement, and writer's block can result if this constantly shifting balance is not maintained.[33] It is also exhausting as it requires tremendous concentration.

However, the idea that revision is not enjoyable for writers could be a dangerous misconception. All of the writers in this study said they enjoyed much of the revision process. This is fortunate as it takes up most of their time. It is also happening more or less simultaneously to nearly every other part of the writing process apart from perhaps the subconscious generation of ideas during periods of incubation when, by all accounts, judgement is switched off. The process of revising could also be creative and be driven by the same goal-setting processes, even if in a different way to the mysterious subconscious generation. Revision leads to generation in many ways once the writing process is under way. It is possible that through evaluation and revision a writer spots where more ideas are needed, or new words, characters or better metaphors. If an author feels like laughing during a scene that should make her weep, she could potentially decide this is a better way to get her point across and rewrite the scene to make it even more satirical (in other words, reconsider her style goals as well as content goals). Orford pointed out how polishing your writing at even the mundane level of spelling and punctuation can help you refine the work in other ways – spotting a phrase that clangs where a whisper is desired – or choosing a better word through a slip of the fingers.

It is in revising that many of the exciting challenges of writing might lie, and there is much satisfaction to be derived from finding that perfect solution to a problem. We should remember this when teaching writing, or when embarking on writing ourselves. There is no point casting revision as the villain in the writing process and something to be eschewed until the very end of a creative phase if it is a friendly guiding hand throughout the journey. A writer who does not derive some enjoyment from the revision process could be in the position of a carpenter who is allergic to sawdust.

3   Conclusion

The creative writer has a number of worlds, both fictional and physical to explore and reconcile with one another, as does the researcher of writing. Personal physical spaces that are the creation of writers overlap with the physical constraints of the publishing environment they find themselves in and inner worlds of experience, emotion and imagination. The inner world(s), both past and present, of an individual might find echoes in wider issues in the individual's society and in existing literature, which can be synthesised into unique writing goals for content and style. The researcher of creative writing, within the constraints of his own world, needs to occasionally map out some of these often unchartered territories in ways that can be meaningfully used by other explorers of the process of creative writing. If this is done across countries, demographic groups and disciplines such as composition studies, creative writing research, pedagogy and psychology, it could be possible to build an ever more detailed picture of how creative writing processes work that could be of enormous benefit to both teachers and students.

In South Africa the creative process is often seen as a mystery, and a holy one at that. 'Sacrilege' was a word used by a senior South African English Studies academic to describe this research in one appraisal, as how could anyone conduct an academic study on something as individual and precious as a creative process? All over the world there is a move to examine this mystery, however sacred, not to deconstruct and demystify it necessarily, but rather to seek a better understanding of a phenomenon that is a large part of what an increasingly literate world engages with – writing as a process as well as a product. If a reader's world can be shaped by the worlds present in a text, then it is important to investigate how this world is created at source by writers.

> ### Exercises
>
> - Consider how you might investigate the world of the writer in your own research. The writer could be contemporary and accessible, someone who is already deceased, or even yourself. Brainstorm key questions that really interest you about the writing process.
> - Decide how you could find out more about the writing process of this person or these people in the context of their lives and the society they live in, and investigate the reliability of each source. Write down ways you might use multiple sources to compensate for gaps in reliability in each source.
> - After conducting your research, compare notes from different sources and think critically about what you read about any spontaneous flashes of inspiration – were these entirely spontaneous, or do they represent a distillation over time of some concern in the person's life or wider world?

Notes

1 D. Murray. 'Teaching the Other Self: The Writer's First Reader'. *College Composition and Communication* 33.2 (1982): p. 141.
2 L. Flower and J. R. Hayes. 'A Cognitive Process Theory of Writing'. *College Composition and Communication* 32.4 (1981): p. 367.
3 M. Atwood. *Negotiating with the Dead: A Writer on Writing*. Cambridge: Cambridge University Press, 2002.
4 G. Marquez. *Living to Tell the Tale*. London: Jonathan Cape, 2003.
5 Flower and Hayes, p. 368.
6 Flower and Hayes do not make any distinction between writing fiction or more general prose in the 1981 and other articles where they discuss their protocol research. Topics given to writers in their study varied from creative non-fiction magazine articles to creative essays and academic topics, partly depending on who the research participants were.
7 Flower and Hayes in A. Humes, 'Research on the composing process'. *Review of Educational Research* 53.1 (1983): p. 203.
8 Flower and Hayes, 1981, p. 368.
9 C. Berkenkotter and D. Murray. 'Decisions and Revisions: The Planning Strategies of a Publishing Writer; and Response of a Laboratory Rat: or, Being Protocoled'. *College Composition and Communication* 34.2 (1983): p. 167.

10 Berkenkotter and Murray, p. 156.
11 In this excerpt, Berkenkotter is quoting an essay by Janet Emig.
12 Berkenkotter and Murray, p. 170.
13 Berkenkotter and Murray, p. 170.
14 M. Csikszentmihalyi, *Creativity: Flow and the Psychology of Discovery and Invention*. New York: Harper Perennial, 1997, p. vii.
15 Csikszentmihalyi, p. 17.
16 Csikszentmihalyi, p. 78.
17 The study had limited funding and time in which it could be completed. Four two-hour interviews generated transcripts of over 60 pages that required analysis and cross-checking with the authors. Authors were also chosen in part according to their proximity to Cape Town where I live (which is fortunately one of the two cities mainly involved in publishing in South Africa). This eliminated the need for expensive long-distance travel and related accommodation costs.
18 South Africa is a developing country and according to a government information site (*Education in South Africa*, 2010) illiteracy rates are 'high at around 24% of adults over 15 years old (6- to 8-million adults are not functionally literate). While 65% of whites over 20 years old and 40% of Indians have a high school or higher qualification, this figure is only 14% among blacks and 17% among the coloured population'. This, compounded by poverty and lack of access to bookshops and libraries in rural areas, has an impact on the publishing industry. It means that there is only a relatively small percentage of the adult population able to read books, and many of those able to read do not have the purchasing power to buy books, which can cost more than a day's wage for many. In South Africa, according to Penguin CEO Alison Lowry (in Wilson, 2009), sales of 10 to 20,000 books will make an author a 'bestseller' and when John van de Ruit broke this record, his sales peaked to around 200,000 books. These sales have yet to be matched by any other local author.
19 Space does not permit entering into the usually heated debate on what constitutes 'success' as a writer. Suffice it to say that the aim in this study was as simple and widely accepted a definition as possible (being published by major publishing houses and receiving awards or achieving best-seller status) without getting distracted by questions such as literary merit, biases of the publishing industry and so forth.
20 Flower and Hayes in Humes, p. 376.
21 Flower and Hayes, p. 376.
22 Flower and Hayes, pp. 376–7.
23 Flower and Hayes, p. 21.
24 M. Csikszentmihalyi. *Creativity: Flow and the Psychology of Discovery and Invention*. New York: Harper Perennial, 1997, p. 83.

25 Vorster, A. 'Klein klippie veroorsaaak toe groot rimpeling'. 2009. Online. http:jv.news24.com/Rapport/Gauteng-Rapport/0,,752-798_2533753,00. html [Accessed 30 November 2009].

26 Atwood, p. 38.

27 Csikszentmihalyi, p. 264.

28 Csikszentmihalyi, p. 239.

29 A leaflet in six languages that goes in every Moleskine bears the 'history of a legendary notebook', stating that 'Moleskine is the heir of the legendary notebook used for the past two centuries by great artists and thinkers, including Vincent Van Gogh, Pablo Picasso, Ernest Hemmingway, and Bruce Chatwin. This trusty, pocket-sized travel companion held their sketches, notes, stories, and ideas before they became famous images or beloved books'.

30 Cf. J. Cameron, *The Sound of Paper: Inspiration and Practical Guidance for Starting the Creative Process*. London: Penguin Books, 2004, Keats, F. *Dancing Pencils: Right-Brained 'how to' for Writers and Teachers*. Malvern: umSinsi Press, 1999, Haarhoff, D. *The Writer's Voice: A Workbook for Writers in Africa*. Halfway House: Zebra Press, 1998.

31 Csikszentmihalyi, p. 263.

32 Csikszentmihalyi, pp. 263–4.

33 Csikszentmihalyi, pp. 263–4.

Works cited

Atwood, M., *Negotiating with the Dead: A Writer on Writing*. Cambridge: Cambridge University Press, 2002.

Berkenkotter, C. and D. Murray. 'Decisions and Revisions: The Planning Strategies of a Publishing Writer; and Response of a Laboratory Rat: or, being Protocoled'. *College Composition and Communication* 34.2 (1983): 156–72.

Cameron, J. *The Sound of Paper: Inspiration and Practical Guidance for Starting the Creative Process*. London: Penguin Books, 2004.

Csikszentmihalyi, M. *Creativity: Flow and the Psychology of Discovery and Invention*. New York: Harper Perennial, 1997.

Education in South Africa. [S.A.] Online. http://www.southafrica.info/about/education/education.htm [Accessed 10 August 2010].

Flower, L. and J. R. Hayes. 'A Cognitive Process Theory of Writing'. *College Composition and Communication* 32.4 (1981): 365–87.

Haarhoff, D. *The Writer's Voice: A Workbook for Writers in Africa*. Halfway House: Zebra Press, 1998.

Humes, A. 'Research on the Composing Process'. *Review of Educational Research* 53.1 (1983): 201–16.

Keats, F. *Dancing Pencils: Right-Brained 'how to' for Writers and Teachers*. Malvern: umSinsi Press, 1999.

Marquez, G. *Living to Tell the Tale*. London: Jonathan Cape, 2003.

'The History of a Legendary Notebook'. *2010 Moleskine Diary* [brand information leaflet]. New York.

Murray, D. 'Teaching the Other Self: The Writer's First Reader'. *College Composition and Communication* 33.2 (1982): 140–7.

Vorster, A. 'Klein klippie veroorsaaak toe groot rimpeling'. 2009. Online. http:jv.news24.com/Rapport/Gauteng-Rapport/0,,752-798_2533753,00.html [Accessed 30 November 2009].

Wilson, D. 'Delightful Return to the Wacky World of Spud'. *Tonight*. 2009. Online. http://www.tonight.co.za/general/print_article.php?fArticleId=5048618&fSectionId=351&fSetId=251 [Accessed 23 June 2009].

4   New Modes of Creative Writing Research

Kerry Spencer

Chapter summary

As university creative writing programmes mature, creative writing research has the potential to develop its own new and distinct theoretical frameworks. Non-traditional and interdisciplinary modes of research may help researchers to address the myriad questions creative writers face – questions of process versus product, audience versus profit, quality versus marketability, theory versus output, criticism versus creativity, inspiration versus analysis, etc. This chapter presents the epistemology of statistical market research as a detailed example of one possible kind of 'new' creative writing research and challenges creative writing researchers to construct additional theoretical frameworks by utilising processes of interdisciplinary induction and innovation.

1   Introduction

Creative writers will sometimes go to great lengths when it comes to the research needed for their writing. Novelist Tess Gerritsen says that research has not only led her to 'autopsy rooms', it 'almost got [her] arrested' for trespassing in a hospital.[1] Novelist Kate Flora actually *was* arrested in the name of research.[2] When working on a crime novel, she realised that she 'had never even had a ticket for a moving violation', and her 'obliging police chief' volunteered to send an officer to her house and give her the full experience. When some writers are working on a story, not only do they hit the library, they get on planes, talk to strangers, pretend to be people they're not – they even get arrested.

But if creative writers are so willing to engage in non-traditional research *for* their creative works, why should we be so hesitant to try new modes of research when we are researching *about* creative writing? This chapter presents one example of an 'alternative' approach to creative writing research – the epistemology of statistical inquiry into the creative writing market. This was the 'alternative' approach I used in undertaking my PhD in Creative and Critical Writing – during which I completed both a young adult novel, *Secrets of the Mami Wata*, and a statistically-minded critical response to the process and product of YA fiction writing.

2 How processes of induction can provide new insights

There are innumerable ways to address the question of what makes quality literature. Many approaches traditional to literary theory and the study of literature – the term 'literature' is used in this chapter to describe *texts* while the word 'writing' used to describe the act of *creating* such texts – stem from what are essentially deductive processes. That is, they utilise existing theoretical frameworks to evaluate literature; specific texts are analysed through the lens of general theories, rules, or ideas. When, for example, Susan Knutson looks at story structure through the lens of feminism in her article, 'Protean Travelogue in Nicole Brossard's "Picture Theory": Feminist Desire and Narrative Form',[3] she is essentially making a deductive argument. Likewise, in 'Young Adult Realism: Conventions, Narrators, and Readers', when Catherine Sheldrick Ross compares Young Adult Literature to the Cawelti concept of culturally-centred 'literary formula',[4] she is making a deductive textual evaluation. Structuralism, Modernism, Postcolonialism, Marxism are all examples of existing frameworks of thought that encourage deductive thinking when used to evaluate literature.

The tradition of deductive thinking in scholarly work is strong and far-reaching. In his *Discourse on the Method*, René Descartes says that the real benefit of deduction is that, 'Provided only that one abstains from accepting any for true which is not true, and that one always keeps the right order for one thing to be deduced from that which precedes it, there can be nothing so distant that one does not reach it eventually, or so hidden that one cannot discover it'.[5] The very problem, of course, with deduction can be seen in the clause, 'Provided only that one abstains from accepting any for true which is not true'. Deduction depends utterly upon the truth of the axioms/theories it bases itself upon. If the theoretical foundation is flawed, the logic is flawed and the conclusions may be useless to the writer who wishes to act upon theoretical tenets in a practical creative process. On the other hand, if the theoretical foundation is solid, the conclusions will be equally solid and may, indeed provide practical support to the creative writer.

So while a deductive approach can provide an exceptionally illuminating analysis of *literature*, does it have the same kind of applicability for creative *writing*? Considering the structure of deductive inquiry advocated by Descartes, the answer may simply be 'perhaps'. The ultimate conclusion for any given case rests upon the validity of the fundamental axiomatic foundations of the specific theoretical approach. But with literally thousands of possible deductive approaches available in traditional literary theory, must the creative writer attempt to utilise *all* of them in order to decipher which are the most productive and/or applicable to their own writing?

This approach hardly seems practical.

Indeed, creative writing researchers have advocated the need for creative writing to establish its *own* theoretical approaches – approaches independent from conventional or postmodern literary ones. After all, literary theories are not fundamentally concerned with the *act* of writing, but with its *result*. Mike Harris notes that such 'new' theory might be more process-based, or 'evidential'.[6] That is, it would follow algorithms that are essentially *inductive* in nature – instead of theorising what might make the creative process work, the creative process would be *observed* and theories would stem from the observation. This kind of thinking is intuitive: all epistemologies of thought have their initial origins in observation – in the inductive. It is how new theoretical constructs are created in the first place.

But what would such a process look like in creative writing?

Initially, it could look chaotic. By its very nature, inductive processes require researchers to consider familiar subject matter in an unfamiliar way. Craig R. Nicolson et al., in the article 'Ten Heuristics for Interdisciplinary Modeling Projects', explains the problem this way: 'In the past 100 years, knowledge has become increasingly specialized. This specialization has resulted in tremendous intellectual and technological gains, but it has also led to increasing fragmentation [...] Many of the important issues in society simply cannot be addressed adequately by a single disciplinary perspective'.[7] Instead of attempting to forge an entirely new mode of literary theory on our own, perhaps considering our work within the contexts of *other* fields may be more productive. Indeed, interdisciplinary collaboration has always been essential to establishing new and productive methods of thought – remember Newton and his famous remark in a letter to his rival Robert Hooke, that 'If I have seen a little further it is by standing on the shoulders of Giants'. I would argue that embracing interdisciplinary collaboration is even more essential when attempting to embark upon the inductive creation of a new theoretical framework. Induction, by its nature, requires us to forgo our traditional modes of thought; what better way to do this than to leave our own discipline entirely and seek new perspectives elsewhere?

In approaching my own PhD in Creative and Critical Writing I was drawn to ask how we might work with other disciplines efficiently. Management Professor Gina Colarelli O'Conner (et al.), notes that, 'It is unusual for a team of scholars from different disciplines to work together, not because the need doesn't exist, but because the mechanisms for doing so are not well established'.[8] The process of embarking upon 'new' research methods is wont to cause communication challenges, as well as cognitive ones. But will the end justify the effort? Do inductive and interdisciplinary processes really have a place in creative writing research? I'd argue absolutely.

Indeed, some principles of induction are already embedded in the way we look at our writing. For example, on its website the AWP (Associated Writers and Writing Programs) lists as one of the characteristics of successful writing programs 'extensive literary study.' They justify this characteristic with the argument that, 'One must become an expert and wide-ranging reader before one can hope to become an accomplished writer' (AWP). Is this not a form of induction?

Furthermore, creative writing research *needs* new theoretical frameworks and the advantage of inductive thinking is that it is unencumbered by *past* thinking. It doesn't matter what someone previously *thought* of as rules of good literature, writing can be evaluated based upon what it *is* (currently), not with what was *thought* to be (previously). In this way it can be an incredibly freeing mode of thought.

Potential research projects utilising inductive thinking are limited only by our imagination. Samples of texts from single and multiple time periods could be compared. Samples of texts could be evaluated based upon patterns of theme, language, technique, or geography. Surveys of authorial process could be cross-referenced with perceived 'success' – either in the critical or commercial world. Inductive methodology allows researchers to find *patterns* in wide samples – broadening potential applicability of findings.

And in embracing interdisciplinary action, researchers need not be unduly intimidated by lack of knowledge of inductive processes. That is not to say that applying inductive methodology to creative writing research is without challenges. Traditions of inductive thinking are usually thought to be more suited to scientific thought and the rigorous procedural rules required by induction may seem foreign, if not incompatible, to literary thinking. It was science, after all, not creative industry, that developed some of the primary tenets of inductive thinking. Nevertheless, some of these tenets are worth examining.

Isaac Newton, perhaps the father – or at least one of the fathers – of modern, western induction, outlines some basic rules:

1 Make no guesses. Researchers are to be particularly wary of *a priori* thought – that is, things that *seem* to be true based upon reason

alone. Induction demands that whatever *seems* to be true, you assume *nothing* until you have evidence.[9] This can be difficult as it often requires researchers to set aside even assumptions that seem 'obvious.' For example, it may seem obvious that a well-marketed book will sell better than a non-marketed book; however, this cannot be simply *assumed*, a relationship must be proven and defined before further action is possible. Many seemingly 'obvious' ideas do, indeed, prove true, but researchers may be surprised at the number of 'obvious' ideas that are ultimately proven false through induction.

2 Don't second guess the data. Newton said, 'In experimental philosophy, propositions gathered from phenomena by induction should be considered either exactly or very nearly true notwithstanding any contrary hypothesis, until yet other phenomena make such propositions either more exact or liable to exceptions'.[10] He said that 'this rule should be followed so that arguments based on induction may not be nullified by hypothesis'.[11] The word 'hypothesis' is used in the 17th century sense here – that is, indicating an *a priori* guess or assumption. When the data tells us something, we listen to it and don't let ourselves be distracted by our guesses pertaining to things the data doesn't support. Guesses – or hypotheses – may be useful in the initial phases of defining a research objective, but they are to be strictly avoided in the interpretation of inductively-gleaned data.

3 Pay attention to detail. When Newton performed an experiment on refraction, he did not just consider the light, but the thickness of glass, the presence of shadow, the quality of origin light, the possibility of curved refraction, etc.[12] He would find a way to individually account for *all* possibilities to allow 'gradual removal of suspicions'[13] before coming to any conclusion. Every action at every step of the process must be evaluated and every possible factor that could skew the data must be considered and data must be normalised whenever possible. In addition – and as will be discussed in an upcoming section – researchers must be careful when attempting to identify *causation*, as, fundamentally, inductive inquiry allows us only to identify *correlations*.

By way of an example of what such collaboration could look like, this chapter presents statistical market analysis (of the type used in my own PhD in Critical and Creative Writing) as a mode of considering creative work. Statistical analysis is, by its nature, inductive, and, thus, it allows a clean presentation of a new modality of thought while allowing researchers to consider other possible modalities. Likewise, market research, which is quantitative in nature and, thus, has a natural connection to the statistical, also has large applicability to working creative writers in all genres who often function in a market environment.

3 Statistical inquiry in the creative writing marketplace

When creative writing undergraduate majors express an interest in 'being a writer,' I imagine that most of them do not intend to toil alone for hours a day and then lock away the results never to be seen again. Indeed, most creative writers intend to *publish*.

But the idea of publication introduces a problem that, on the surface, seems to have nothing to do with writing itself: publication is essentially the production of a *product* intended for a *market*. Whether the intended market is large or small – i.e. writing intended for a lay audience in the airport versus writing intended for subscribers to a literary journal – the writing is still a product and the buyers of the product are still a market. Thus, writers who publish are, at least partly, product manufacturers. Whether they publish commercially for the masses, or for smaller literary audiences, they are all constrained at some level by the will of the marketplace – that is, by the laws of supply and demand. These are laws not strictly laws of literature, but of economics – laws more quantitative than poetic. It's a mode of inquiry that is more statistical in epistemology than it is qualitative.

What I wondered, in undertaking my PhD in Creative and Critical Writing, was whether market writing (that is, writing for, and in direct response to, the marketplace) could really be boiled down to statistical norms. Booksellers like Amazon certainly have attempted this. That s, by identifying buying patterns among various individuals in the market, they construct complicated algorithms that are able to predict – sometimes with eerie accuracy – the kinds of books/products that certain buyers are likely to purchase. Simple examples include website highlights and emails noting that 'If you bought [X] you might enjoy [Y]'. But these algorithms can take daunting forms, for example,

$$U_{iqt} = \Gamma_{i,s\{iqt\}} X_{i,q,t-1} + \Phi_{i,s\{iqt\}} U_{iq,t-1} + \varepsilon_{iqt,s\{iqt\}}, \varepsilon_{iqt,s\{iqt\}} \sim MVN(0, \Sigma_{S\{iqt\}})$$

Creative writing researchers, whether graduate students or faculty, and whether engaging in creative work or critical analysis, should not let the daunting nature of such forms inhibit their desire to tackle a statistical market approach. From my experience, the most important tenet to note and absorb is that quantitative measures *may indeed* have applicability to creative works – particularly in an economic/market setting.

The idea may seem distasteful to writers who thrive on creative endeavour; numbers seem the antithesis of creativity. However, because publication (as opposed to writing more generally) is an economic, not strictly creative, process, certain modalities of creativity in an economic setting *can* be evaluated. There are likely similarities between books that sell well in a given market (i.e. a literary market versus a commercial one) and there are similarities between books that do not. Some of these similarities would be internal to the books – like subject matter, overall poetics of writing style, etc. – and some of them would be external – promotion, reviews, bookstore placement, etc. The advantage of a statistical mode of inquiry of the creative writing *market* is that these similarities can be identified. With their identification, creative writers can then make informed decisions about their desired rhetorical and market goals.

4 Epistemology of statistical inquiry

Yet, while creative writers may be somewhat familiar with the concept of the *market*, there are certain terms and tenets of *statistical* inquiry that may unfamiliar. Fundamentally, a statistical analysis involves an inductive methodology that requires a random *sample* to be drawn from within a defined *population*.

Instead of looking at a single book for analysis, or even a set of books that the researchers choose themselves, researchers use a *random* sample of books that are drawn from a very specified population. The sample is then used to determine certain evident patterns that may have a relationship to the overall population. There is no limitation to the types of patterns that can be examined. The limitations of statistical inquiry exist mainly in the initial setup, i.e. in the identification of a population, the process by which a random sample is gleaned and normalised, the overall blindness/objectivity of the procedure, the use of inductive methodology, the quantification of the qualitative, and adherence to caveats about causation versus correlation.

4.1   Population

Identification of a population is a fundamental aspect of statistical inquiry. Do you want to answer questions about young adult fiction? Then you must limit your study to young adult fiction. The same holds for other desired research objectives. In order to statistically study poetry, a population of poetry must be defined. In order to study crime fiction, a population of crime fiction must be defined. By definition, the population consists of *all* objects that adhere to the specified criteria, that is, *All* YA novels, or *all* crime novels, etc.

The definition of population in a specific research inquiry, however, will likely necessitate more narrowing than a simple genre definition. *All* aspects that may affect the desired research aims may need to be defined so that the population can be appropriately limited. These can include, but are not limited to:

- Geography
- Time period
- Language/Culture
- School of thought (e.g. 'postmodernism' or 'impressionism')
- Intended audience
- Market
- Etc.

4.2 Randomised Sampling

Once a population is defined, a procedure must be established to take a random *sample* from within the population for study. Random sampling is a key aspect of valid statistical inquiry because when left to their own devices, *all* researchers are wont to unconsciously assemble samples that confirm their preconceived notions. To paraphrase a statistician-friend of mine, let's say you want to study ice cream. But you only enjoy chocolate ice cream. So you go out and eat 200 kinds of chocolate ice cream and 12 kinds of strawberry ice cream. Can you conclude that all good ice cream is chocolate? After all, you had a sample of *212* flavours of ice cream and the ones you enjoyed were *all* chocolate. Obviously, because the sample wasn't randomly selected, it was skewed towards the initial bias of the researcher. In statistics, what we see depends utterly upon what we look at. Samples that aren't sufficiently random will often be skewed towards the (likely unconscious) biases of the person who compiled the sample.

During my PhD in Creative and Critical Writing I discovered that there were several ways to compile random samples, each with strengths and weaknesses. In what is called by statisticians a 'simple' sample, a researcher may determine the desired size of a sample – say, 200 books (the ideal sample size may be best calculated in consultation with a statistician) – and then from a list of the population – say 2000 books – merely take every tenth book on the list. Thus 'simple sample' essentially means what it says. Rolling of dice or coin flipping are other methods of taking 'simple' samples. The limitation of this kind of sample is that it requires the researcher to have access to the *entire* population and this is not often practical.

Because many populations are not available in easily quantifiable lists, more complicated methods to ensure randomised samples may be necessary. In cases like this, creative writing researchers are best served by seeking interdisciplinary aid; for example, Professors of Statistics are well-versed in alternative ways to establish the relative randomness of samples that cannot be easily randomised. Rather than outline such 'well versed' strategies as if they emerge from within the discipline of creative writing, I note here the help of one of those Professors of Statistics, the Brigham Young University Statistics Professor Dr. Natalie Blades.

4.3 Normalisation/data adjustment

Once a random sample is established, it must be *normalised*. That is, skewing factors that may inhibit your ability to accomplish your research aims must be identified and adjusted for. If, for example, you wish to identify aspects *internal* to a piece of market writing that have a correlation with how well the writing sells, you must account for the most obvious potential skewing factor: the effect of *external* aspects like marketing/promotion. Because well-promoted books may sell more copies than poorly-promoted books – no matter *what* internal characteristics are present – the sample of books must be normalised to account for the effect of the promotion. And although many market-focused writers view the connection between quality and market-success as hazy at best, there is a (relatively) simple statistical method of accounting for the effect of promotion and, thus, separating external sales drivers from internal ones.

The method requires each of the books in the initial sample to be scored for marketing levels and for sales levels. Because marketing/ promotion is a multi-faceted endeavour, a good method for scoring the likely level of marketing is to award a set number of points for the presence or absence of defined marketing-related characteristics. For example, if there is a glowing NY Times review, that may be worth one point. If the publisher paid the author a seven-figure advance and, thus, *must* amp up marketing in order to recoup investment, that may warrant another point. The final point-awarding rubric would likely consist of up to a dozen separate factors and may, indeed, be best constructed with the aid of a statistician.

Once each book in the initial sample has a marketing score *and* a sales score, a statistical exercise can be performed to determine the overall effect that the marketing has on sales. One of the simplest methods of doing this is to calculate what is called a 'Pearson's Relationship Correlation'.[15] Pearson's Relationship Correlation may, in statistical texts, be referred to as 'r,' though here it is referred to as a 'PRC'. A PRC is the extent to which one set of numbers (like marketing scores) tends to increase linearly as the other set of numbers (like sales scores) increases. The actual PRC formula may seem incomprehensible to creative writers, but the PRC calculation is built into many readily available and familiar programs like Microsoft Excel and, thus, should not be an undue obstacle. (Indeed, the fact that PRC calculation functions *are* so readily available in programs familiar to creative writers is part of what makes the method more desirable than other modes of calculating correlation that may yield slightly more accurate measures of association/relationship since they account more fully for non-linear relationships.)

PRC values range from −1 to +1. A score of 0 (or very close to 0) indicates that there is no discernable linear relationship between the two sets of numbers. In the marketing/sales example, a PRC close to 0 would indicate that marketing has no effect on sales – or at least no discernible *linear* effect. The closer the PRC is to one or negative one, however, the more likely that there is a strong linear relationship. In the case of marketing/sales, a negative PRC would indicate that sales decrease when marketing increases while a positive PRC would indicate that sales increase as marketing increases.

Though the PRC is limited in that it only establishes the likelihood of *linear* relationships when other, non-linear, relationships may be present, it is still useful because many non-linear relationships will still result in high PRC's. This is because the method calculates the tendency for one variable to increase or decrease as the other variable changes, and this kind of relationship is also noted in some non-linear patterns. For example, note how even though the dataset in the following figure is obviously non-linear, a linear expression can still note a number of the plot points:

Thus, though it isn't always possible to know the precise nature of a relationship, a high (close to 1 or −1) Pearson's Coefficient often allows us to know that *some* kind of relationship definitely exists while a small (close to zero) Pearson's Coefficient tells us simply that there is no discernable linear relationship.

If we were to run a PRC evaluation of the marketing/sales scores for a sample of books and we got a score of, say, 0.7, this would indicate that there is a strong possibility that there is a linear relationship between marketing and sales. This is important because if there is

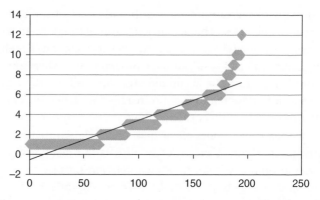

Figure 4.1   High Pearson's relationship coefficients will often spot even non-linear relationships

a strong possibility of relationship, it is moderately easy (especially with programs like Excel which do not require you to *understand* something like a linear regression in order to perform one) to derive a formula expressing the exact nature of the marketing sales relationship. Something like:

$$S = 0.5M + 2$$

As I found in my own PhD work, with this formula in hand I can go back to the sample and then calculate what the sales levels *should* have been for each book, based on their marketing scores plugged into the derived formula, and then I can note how *different* the actual sales were. That is, if observed sales were (S), and this model predicts books with (S) sales to have a marketing score (M), then the book sold either better or worse or the same as predicted by the marketing score (M). The difference between what was predicted and what is observed in an individual case is called the *residual*. You can imagine that knowing this kind of information, along with other kinds of statistical information, has the potential to be very useful to the creative writer thinking about the market. It gives a sales profile on a book, at very least.

Residuals are the numbers then used to accomplish the initial goal of the inquiry which was, in this case, to establish relationships between internal book characteristics and increased sales. (These relationships would also be calculated using the PRC method; the quantification of qualitative elements needed to run a sales/trait PRC is discussed in an upcoming section.) The full list of residuals comprise the *normalised* sample. The way that a sample is normalised will vary depending upon what kind of information the researcher is trying to obtain and, again, consultation with a statistician is fundamentally important.

4.4   Blind research procedure

All researchers are prone to unconsciously project their own ideas upon the outcome of their research. Thus, in a statistical inquiry, it is important to set in place a method that provides objectivity. In the case of examining the internal book qualities that lead to increased sales, the researchers reading the books (and then scoring the presence/absence of applicable book traits) should not know how well a book sold when they are doing the evaluation – that is, the process should be 'blind.' A researcher may have a preconceived notion of what makes a book sell and they may be more likely to unconsciously reinforce those notions if they know that a book is a well-selling book while they are reading it.

True blindness in such research procedures may not always be possible, but the processes should be set up to ensure that they are as blind as *is* possible. Consultation with statisticians, such as my consultation with Dr Blades, can likewise aid in adjusting for unavoidable blindness issues that arise. (Say, by comparing a researcher's evaluation of a control sample to the actual sample and estimating the extent to which a researcher values certain traits over others and, hence, how likely they are to skew the data results; results can then be properly normalised).

The language being used here might seem remote from the most common languages of creative writing; however, essentially what is being analysed are books and readers, and what is being explored is the ways in which the work of a creative writer might consider the market, the kinds of writing decisions that inform the creation of a book, and the possible reactions of publishers and readers of that book.

4.5 Inductive methodology

Statistical inquiry by definition requires the use of an inductive methodology, though it has certain limitations that are unique to statistics. Inductive methodology is, in the basest sense and as noted previously, the opposite of deductive methodology. Instead of using existing models to evaluate a text, a researcher creates new models by first observing patterns within a sample of texts and only *then* beginning to posit theoretical constructs. I'd suggest from my own experience that creative writing researchers wishing to use an inductive *statistical* methodology must do so not by consulting previous theoretical frameworks, but by discarding all previous frameworks and looking directly at *randomised samples* from a defined *population* of writing.

Just as precision is important in non-statistical methods of induction, statistical induction mandates careful control of variables and methodologies. Populations must be carefully defined, samples must be evaluated for skew, linear regressions must be calculated based only on representative data, all lines of logic must be traced back to be evaluated for *a priori* contamination, all assumptions examined for inherent bias, every bit of borrowed theoretical framework must be examined for validity, and so on. Application of inductive statistical ideals into writing research may feel less than artistic, but is nevertheless essential to inductive statistical processes.

4.6 Quantification of the qualitative

Because statistical inquiry is, by nature, quantitative, functioning inside its epistemology requires that creative/qualitative elements be converted to numerical elements. On the face of it, this may also seem like a limitation to creative writers. After all, how do you quantify something like a metaphor? However, quantification is possible in almost any qualitative setting, provided the variables be appropriately defined.

I discovered during my PhD research that one of the simplest ways to appropriately define variables is to utilise a methodology similar to that of someone playing the game '20 questions'. In a

'20 questions' game, players may only ask questions that can be answered 'yes' or 'no'. Most players will find that – even though it may take a few extra questions to arrive at a conclusion – they are able to uncover almost any truth using only yes/no questions.

In a statistical analysis, a similar method is used to convert the qualitative into the quantitative. Questions are assembled in such a way that they can be answered yes/no, true/false, present/absent, etc. And then a quantitative conversion is possible by assigning a value to the yes/no styled questions.

'Yes' = 1
'No' = 0
'True' = 1
'False' = 0
'Present' = 1
'Absent' = 0
etc.

For example, if "first-person' narrative' = 'present', then (1). If 'absent', then (0). If, 'The protagonist is of a non-white race' = 'true', then (1); if 'false', then (0).

The present/absent, 1/0, scoring can be used for almost any independent variable. One can check for the presence or absence of any given plot element, any given poetic element, or any other element that can be identified in a 1/0 manner. The quantitative assignment of one variable for one book may not seem (or be) illuminating, but when you have a collection of a full sample's worth of quantitative scorings, then averages, diversions, and patterns may begin to emerge. You may be able to find that first-person narratives sell better than third person, or you may find that the race of the protagonist affects sales. Statistical inquiry doesn't limit the types of elements that can be addressed, merely the manner in which a researcher is able to ask questions about the elements.

The 1/0 scoring method is one of the simplest means of converting the qualitative into the quantitative, but it is not the only means. Consultation and collaboration with a statistician can broaden your ability to convert the qualitative to the quantitative.

4.7 Causation versus correlation

Finally, statistical measures allow the demonstration of *correlation*, but not *causality* (though they do not necessarily *rule out* causality). For example, say a study discovers that YA books published in the US containing racially offensive subject matter are more likely to sell than books that don't contain offensive material. Does this mean that audiences prefer the racially offensive? Another explanation could be that the racial offensiveness is linked to a third (possibly unknown) factor. For example, perhaps books that contain racially offensive material are more likely to have issues of race as a driving plot factor. Indeed, in taking and evaluating a random sample of 200 YA books from the present US YA fiction market, we find that only approximately five percent of books have a non-white protagonist. Yet, census consultation shows that as many as 44 per cent of the under-18 population is non-white. This demographic skew may favour books that discuss/contain racial elements and, thus, the racially offensive material may not be the *cause* of the increased sales levels, though there *is* a correlation. Even a very strong *correlation* between two variables does not ensure that there is not a third (or fourth or fifth) unknown variable that is the *cause* of the correlation.

Ultimately, interpreting statistical results with regard to the actual creation of creative writing is more complicated than scanning through the lists of traits found to correspond with increased sales and reproducing them verbatim in a creative work. It is the larger patterns that are important for interpretation. As my own statistical advisor, Dr. Natalie Blades, neatly puts it, it's the 'story' the numbers tell that's important.

5 Conclusion: Interdisciplinary methods in creative writing research

The Statistical/Market-based mode of inquiry that I used in my PhD in Creative and Critical Writing seems to me to be just one of *many* possible methods of researching creative writing. For my own part, it certainly was a choice rather than an imposition – that is, I decided to take the approach because it seemed like a useful one for my own writing of young adult fiction. I was able to produce a novel that, at very least, was informed by my increasing awareness of market issues, and publisher considerations, in young adult fiction, and I was able to critically investigate the relationship between a number of ways in which readers were considered and the sorts of choices I made in my own creative writing. Being open to wide interdisciplinary consultation might provide quite a number of other approaches that can contribute to the creation of a new epistemology of creative writing theory.

By way of example, and in the manner of a pilot conclusion, here are just a few more specific fields that seem to me to have a deep potential for interdisciplinary collaboration. This list is drawn from thoughts emerging during my PhD research and the strengths I found in approaching my creative writing with an interdisciplinary sense of critical enquiry:

♦ *Anthropology and Sociology*

Are stories merely products of their cultural environments? How do you know? Marjorie Perloff acknowledges that in much of modern literary theory, there has been a prevailing idea that 'there [is] no such thing as an author, only an author function – no individual talent, only writing as a symptom of the culture it represented'.[16] And while such sentiments may rankle creative writers, perhaps a more productive approach could be found in a collaborative research project with an anthropologist.

Culture, no doubt, does affect writers. But to what extent? Are writers *nothing* but the sum of their culture? Anthropologists and sociologists, experts on culture and cultural expressions, may be able to help creative writing researchers discern where culture ends and where creativity begins – even how the two function together, culture becoming writing becoming culture and so on.

♦ *Neuroscience and Biology*

What happens in the brain of the writer? Does the stereotype of the tortured writer have a biological foundation? These are not necessarily questions we are incapable of answering. For example, Nancy

C. Andreason, author of *The Creating Brain: Neuroscience and Genius*, studied an Iowa Writer's Workshop and, in fact, found connections between creativity and psychological disorder, specifically mood disorders.[17] Fundamentally, all human beings – including most writers – are biological creatures. Phenomena of emotion, creativity, productivity and even transcendence have biological roots in the human brain.

Furthermore, an interdisciplinary collaboration between neuroscience/biology and creative writing could not only lead to enumerable research questions, but could incorporate innovative technologies – such as the functional MRI. Indeed, in March of 2009, *The Journal of Writing Research* published a study that used functional magnetic resonance imaging (fMRI) to uncover the differences in brain activity between children who had spelling difficulty and those who didn't.[18] As daunting as such an endeavour might sound to creative writing researchers, technologies like fMRI may be able to play an even bigger role in the research of creative writing. What exactly is going on in a writer's brain as they write? What about a reader? Is it more important to creativity to activate logical centres of the brain, or emotional ones? Machines like the fMRI may be able to help us answer these questions. Indeed, being aware of technological advances in all kinds of research can ensure that creative writing researchers are making use of all of the possible tools that are available.

Answering questions about neurological/biological roots of creativity becomes not only possible through interdisciplinary collaboration, but filled with potential. What is the difference between the neurochemistry of readers versus non-readers? Can you turn a non-reader into a reader? What makes creativity possible? Is creative writing more language or art? Are there biological predispositions to writing genius? The potential is endless.

♦ *International Studies*

As creative writing can often be a reflection of – or at least be influenced by – a particular society – its morality, sensibilities, logic, values etc. – understanding the way that writing in particular societies differs from that of others is a rich area of potential exploration.

One of the main benefits of collaboration with experts in international study or with international scholars in our *own* fields of research is that it allows us to avoid problems of ethnocentrism. Mark F. Peterson, in an article on international collaboration and organisational behaviour, notes this very strength of international research. International collaboration, he says, 'personalizes tensions about national differences in preferred research approach by bringing these differences within a group of collaborators'.[19]

Another benefit of collaboration in the field of international studies is that of new perspective. In a review of the literature on longitudinal collaboration, Gina Colarelli O'Connor notes that one of the strongest benefits purveyors found is that it can result in 'greater diversity of final theories'.[20] By including different cultural perspectives in our research, we broaden the potential outcomes and applications.

♦ *Computer Science and Software Development*

Collaborating with experts in computing allows many new modalities of research to develop. Examples of such have already been incorporated into literary analysis. *The Canterbury Tales Project*, founded at Oxford University and now headed by the Institute for Textual Scholarship and Electronic Editing at the University of Birmingham, utilises digitisation methods and computer software to both make available Chaucer's manuscripts and to analyse the content of the manuscripts. While such an application may seem more attuned to the study of semi-ancient texts, there could nevertheless be applications to modern creative writing. Computer programs could be used to track textual and behavioural patterns that have applicability not just to the study of writing, but to the study of the *act* of writing.

♦ *Nanotechnology, gene modification, and robotics.*

I'm not sure how you could apply these fields of research to creative writing. But just the idea of trying gets your creative juices flowing, doesn't it?[21]

Applying the same kind of innovation to researching *about* writing as we apply to research *for* our writing suggests that the research potential of creative writing as a research subject is endless. This is a field of research where many other fields of knowledge and inquiry can meet and where creative practice and critical understanding can engage in exchanges before a project, during a project and after a project. There are literal collaborations possible – that is, ways in which the discoveries of other disciplines can directly influence the ways in which creative writing is undertaken. And there are 'meta-phoric' collaborations – that is, ways in which the thinking evident in other research disciplines can inform how we think about, and approach, writing creatively. The statistical/market mode of inquiry that I found useful is just one of the many possible theoretical modalities that promise new discoveries. Ultimately, similarly induc-tive and interdisciplinary methods may allow the full development of a distinctive body of creative writing theoretical constructs. (Even if that means a researcher or two gets arrested in the process!)

Exercises

1   Make a list of ten subjects that you would normally never associate with creative writing. What are the possible connections between writing and these subjects? Is there any way to incorporate ideas or procedures from the subjects into your own creative writing research?
2   I outlined a few possibilities for interdisciplinary collaboration. Can you think of more? Identify one of your possible areas of interdisciplinary collaboration. Next, find an actual (human!) scholar from the other discipline. Initiate a conversation with that person about areas of potential collaboration.
3   How have you used traditional (mostly deductive) and non-traditional (mostly inductive) methods of research for or about creative writing? Identify the strengths and weaknesses of each of these approaches. Have you ever utilised inductive research – either knowingly or unknowingly? Evaluate your experience and discuss new potential ways of approaching creative writing research in an inductive fashion.

Notes

1 Tess Gerritsen, 'Research Almost Got Me Arrested'. 16 June 2009. *Murderati: Mysteries, Murder, and Marketing*. Online. <http://www.murderati. com/blog/2009/6/16/research-almost-got-me-arrested.html> [Accessed 14 January 2010].

2 Kate Flora, 'Please, Ms. Medical Examiner, It's Dark Here in the Morgue. Can you Turn on the Lights?' 6 February 2008. *Writers Plot: A Blooming Good Blog*. Online. <http://writersplot.typepad.com/writersplot/2008/02/ please-ms-medic.html> [Accessed 14 January 2010].

3 Susan Knutson, 'Protean Travelogue in Nicole Brossard's "Picture Theory": Feminist Desire and Narrative Form'. *Modern Language Studies* 27.2/3 (1997): 197–211.

4 Catherine Sheldrick Ross, 'Young Adult Realism: Conventions, Narrators, and Readers'. *The Library Quarterly* 55.2 (1985): p. 174.

5 Rene Descartes, *Discourse on the Method of Rightly Conducting the Reason, and Seeking Truth in the Sciences*. Project Gutenberg: Translation Released 1 July 2008, Part II.

6 Mike Harris, 'Are Writers Really There When They're Writing About Their Writing? And Can We Theorise About What They Say and Do?' *Creative Writing: Teaching Theory & Practice* English Subject Centre, http://www. english.heacademy.ac.uk/ (2009): p. 31.

7 Craig R. Nicolson et al. 'Ten Heuristics for Interdisciplinary Modeling Projects'. *Ecosystems* 5.4 (2002): p. 376.

8 Gina Colarelli O'Connor, 'Managing Interdisciplinary, Longitudinal Research Teams: Extending Grounded Theory-Building Methodologies'. *Organizational Science* 14.4 (2003): p. 353.

9 Isaac Newton, *Newton's Philosophy of Nature: Selections From His Writings*. Ed. H.S. Thayer. New York: Hafner, 1953, p. 45.

10 Isaac Newton, *The Principia: Mathematical Principles of Natural Philosophy*. Berkeley: University of California Press, 1999, p. 796.

11 Newton, 'Principia', p. 796.

12 Newton, 'Nature', pp. 68–70.

13 Newton, 'Nature', p. 71.

14 Alan L. Montgomery et al. 'Modeling Online Browsing and Path Analysis Using Clickstream Data'. *Marketing Science* 23.4 (2004): p. 585.

15 *The American Statistician* Vol. 42, No. 1, 1988, to take one example directly here, provides something of a survey on such 'correlations'.

16 Marjorie Perloff, '"Creative Writing" Among the Disciplines'. *MLA Newsletter* (2006): p. 3.

17 Nancy C. Andreason, *The Creating Brain: The Neuroscience of Genius*. Maryland: Dana Press, 2005.

18 Todd Richards et al. 'Differences in fMRI Activation Between Children With and Without Spelling Disability on 2-back/0-back Working Memory Contrast'. *Journal of Writing Research* 1.2 (2009): 93–123.
19 Mark F. Petersen, 'International Collaboration in Organizational Behavior Research'. *Journal of Organizational Behavior* 22.1 (2001): p. 60.
20 O'Connor, p. 358.
21 As a side note, a database search of interdisciplinary functions of creative writing uncovered an article from the journal *Computers and the Humanities* with the title, 'Electronic Literacy, Critical Pedagogy, and Collaboration: A Case for Cyborg Writing'. Do with that what you will.

Works cited

Andreason, Nancy C. *The Creating Brain: The Neuroscience of Genius*. Maryland: Dana Press, 2005.
AWP. 'Hallmarks of a Successful MFA Program in Creative Writing'. *The AWP Official Guide to Writing Programs*. Online. <http://guide.awpwriter.org/hallmarks/hallmarksgrad.php> [Accessed 19 January 2010].
Descartes, Rene. *Discourse on the Method of Rightly Conducting the Reason, and Seeking Truth in the Sciences*. Project Gutenberg: Translation Released 1 July 2008.
Flora, Kate. 'Please, Ms. Medical Examiner, It's Dark Here in the Morgue. Can you Turn on the Lights?' 6 February 2008. *Writers Plot: A Blooming Good Blog*. Online. <http://writersplot.typepad.com/writersplot/2008/02/please-ms-medic.html> [Accessed 14 January 2010].
Gerritsen, Tess. 'Research Almost Got Me Arrested'. 16 June 2009. *Murderati: Mysteries, Murder, and Marketing*. Online. <http://www.murderati.com/blog/2009/6/16/research-almost-got-me-arrested.html> [Accessed 14 January 2010].
Harris, Mike. 'Are Writers Really There When They're Writing About Their Writing? And Can We Theorise About What They Say and Do?' *Creative Writing: Teaching Theory & Practice* English Subject Centre, http://www.english.heacademy.ac.uk/ (2009): 31–47.
Knutson, Susan. 'Protean Travelogue in Nicole Brossard's "Picture Theory": Feminist Desire and Narrative Form'. *Modern Language Studies* 27.2/3 (1997): 197–211.
Montgomery, Alan L., Shibo Li, Kannan Srinivasan and John C. Liechty. 'Modeling Online Browsing and Path Analysis Using Clickstream Data'. *Marketing Science* 23.4 (2004): 579–95.
Newton, Isaac. *Newton's Philosophy of Nature: Selections From His Writings*. Ed. H.S. Thayer. New York: Hafner, 1953.

—— *The Principia: Mathematical Principles of Natural Philosophy*. Berkeley: University of California Press, 1999.

Nicolson, Craig R., Anthony M. Starfield, Gary P. Kofinas and John A. Kruse. 'Ten Heuristics for Interdisciplinary Modeling Projects'. *Ecosystems* 5.4 (2002): 376–84.

O'Connor, Gina Colarelli. 'Managing Interdisciplinary, Longitudinal Research Teams: Extending Grounded Theory-Building Methodologies'. *Organizational Science* 14.4 (2003): 353–73.

Perloff, Marjorie. '"Creative Writing" Among the Disciplines'. *MLA Newsletter* (2006): 3–4.

Petersen, Mark F. 'International Collaboration in Organizational Behavior Research'. *Journal of Organizational Behavior* 22.1 (2001): 59–81.

Richards, Todd, Virginia Berninger, William Winn, H. Lee Swanson, Patricia Stock, Olivia Liang and Robert Abbott. 'Differences in fMRI Activation Between Children With and Without Spelling Disability on 2-back/ 0-back Working Memory Contrast'. *Journal of Writing Research* 1.2 (2009): 93–123.

Rodgers, Joseph Lee and W. Alan Nicewander. 'Thirteen Ways to Look at the Correlation Coefficient'. *The American Statistician*, 42. 1. (Feb. 1988): 59–66.

Ross, Catherine Sheldrick. 'Young Adult Realism: Conventions, Narrators, and Readers'. *The Library Quarterly* 55.2 (1985): 174–91.

5 The Creative Writing Laboratory and its Pedagogy

Jeri Kroll

Chapter summary

Writers in the academy are researchers within an institutional community whose goal is the production of new knowledge. Asking key questions about the ontology of what I am calling the 'Creative Writing Laboratory' – the *where*, *what*, *why* and *how* of creative writing research – leads to an understanding of the outcomes writers produce and how they are shared with diverse audiences. Exploring parallels between scientific and artistic practice reveals how conventional research definitions can apply to creative knowledge generation and its epistemology. The terms 'local' and 'global' research distinguish between research that only enriches a project and the type that produces transferable knowledge. Especially at postgraduate level, a theoretical framework requires writers to confront their assumptions about knowledge and language as well as suggests appropriate methods for their goals. The dynamic relationship between practice, methodology, theory and artefact that exists can be conceived of as a rhizomatic system (see Deleuze and Guattari), which illuminates conventional, innovative and collaborative projects. An indicative reading of W. H. Auden's poem, 'Musée des Beaux Arts,' reveals the multiple entry and exit points that can aid students at all levels to learn to 'read like a researcher.' In the twenty-first century university, the writing workshop has been crossed with an experimental site to produce a hardy hybrid – the Creative Writing Laboratory – where members research, test hypotheses, innovate and produce results, generating work that contributes to the collective stock of knowledge and culture.

I   Introduction

This chapter explores creative writing in the university as an experimental site where a particular kind of research takes place. Employing the metaphor of the laboratory, it suggests that artistic and scientific practice share instructive similarities. The truism that 'writing is a process of discovery,' often repeated to undergraduates, is literalised, demonstrating that when we conceive of writers not as lone pioneers but as researchers within an institutional community of artists, we can perceive how their common goal is the production of new knowledge.

The ascendance of applied science in the twentieth century in the culture in general and in the university in particular, and the consequent rise of technology, are partly responsible for the laboratory becoming a meme, 'a cultural unit (an idea or value or pattern of behavior) that is passed from one person to another by non-genetic means (as by imitation)'.[1] The laboratory is not only a physical space where we can track patterns of behaviour (the repetition of experiments, for example), but also an educational, social and research nexus where training as well as knowledge production occurs. In particular, the science laboratory is value-laden as the 'gold standard' research site. The arts and humanities have been welcomed as its handmaids, disseminating its findings through explication, adaptation and performance, but are not considered by the sciences as equals in the generation of 'products' valuable to society. How one evaluates research has become a complex procedure in higher education, therefore, with prestige and funding at stake.[2] The creative arts and, in particular, creative writing, argue that they possess their own patterns of behaviour and research practices. This chapter demonstrates how these practices ground not only higher degree and academic research, but also have filtered down to enrich undergraduate teaching.

Let me begin with a scenario to clarify these opposing forces in academia.

1.1 What I am not

I am a creative writer, a researcher and a teacher. What kind of knowledge do I produce? It is easier to answer that by imagining what I am not. Suppose I were a biologist, for example, starting her day at work in the academy. I would enter my office, devote an hour to reading refereed papers over a coffee and editing my latest article, co-authored with four of my colleagues. Finally, I would don a white coat and walk down the hall to my state-of-the-art laboratory, the foundation of my identity. I would greet my team whose members, I sometimes feel, are a collective extension of myself. Like a healthy organism, each body part functions optimally when integrated with the whole. As the head, I ensure that necessary funding flows to sustain us and that, periodically, keen minds join and coalesce, reinvigorating the community. Honours and postgraduate members are offered thesis problems that plug gaps or explore alternate pathways that the central research project throws up.[3] My lab team has achieved good results. The annual research progress report tracks how we have added to the global stock of knowledge and contributed to national priorities. I am well funded for three years and so only need to do minimal teaching. All is right with my world. I have been trained according to its rules, understand its methodologies and can speak its discourse fluently.

1.2 Fade Out. Fade In.

I am now in my own reality, joining a writing workshop of 12 engrossed in a heated conversation about the necessity for theory in their research. They are an odd assortment. If you had populated a story with them, clustered around a tiny café table, ordering them drinks appropriate to their characters in a high-handed authorial way – cappuccinos, short blacks and green teas – your readers would doubt your judgement. Listen to them – their personalities and histories sparking through the dialogue. They come from three countries, half are old enough to be the parents of the others, and four read mostly memoir or fantasy, much to the chagrin of the one poet. If I am head of this group, the master of these apprentices, it is in a very particular way. In one sense I am a mentor, a link between them and the professional world, about which I can provide advice. I also lead the workshop, which is more collaborative and democratic than a science lab might be, although it does ensure that students acquire advanced 'domain-relevant skills',[4] which prepare them for the development of new knowledge, according to some theories of creativity. I can help them grasp what varieties of knowledge their research might involve and which theories might prove compatible with their goals. Their research foci will not necessarily be easy to pin down, as insects preserved for inspection, although this is required for thesis confirmations and grant applications.

There are other differences between these two laboratories. The biology students in the preceding scenario are mostly young white males – standard in the hard sciences in Australia;[5] they finish doctoral work on average much faster than their counterparts in the Humanities. A similar gap between Science and Humanities postgraduates in the United States exists,[6] with the discipline of Biology accounting for the greatest increase in PhDs.[7] Creative writing students at honours and higher degree levels in Australia and the UK tend to come from a more mixed population and, like their peers in the Humanities in general, according to current Australian research, hold themselves to higher standards of originality,[8] which also affects their progress. The writing cohort includes recent graduates, those returning to university after establishing their reputations as authors, or those who have pursued other careers entirely. They are usually supported by scholarships and have sought the university as a research-rich environment where they will be able to nurture their creativity. Mark McGurl's recent book, *The Program Era: Postwar Fiction and the Rise of Creative Writing*,[9] argues similarly that American writing programs 'stepped forward in the postwar period both to facilitate and to buffer the writer's relation to the culture industry and the market culture broadly'.[10] The tension between 'facilitate' and 'buffer' suggests the uneasy relationship between the university and a society interested in readily consumable products rather than pure research. For those trained in the hard sciences, the routes to research and career success are more or less identical. On the surface, then, the only things the creative writing and biology students might have in common are their laptops, their willingness to stay up past midnight to finish an experiment – whether this involves running tests on native amphibians or crafting a story about refugees using only a second-person narrator – and the excess of caffeine and sugar in their systems.

The writing students might work alone or collaboratively, depending on their current projects. They might network with others via the web or other social media platforms, but many will still be isolate practitioners. As university students, however, what they will always do is to come together periodically as a group to present drafts, test and re-test hypotheses, exchange theories and fine tune methodologies in order to validate their critical as well as creative outputs. Then back to the desk, the library, the multimedia studio, the beach – wherever they conduct fieldwork and collect new material before synthesising, writing and revising.

Is there anything else that these students might have in common with their counterparts in the sciences to suggest that they do not, in fact, function on totally different planes? If we dig beneath the surface meaning of revision, we unearth connotative layers that take us to the word's molten core where significations melt and reform. What is signified by revision, that activity that forces us to test and re-test our textual experiments? *Re-Vision*, as Adrienne Rich termed it in her groundbreaking essay for the feminist movement, 'When We Dead Awaken: Writing as Re-vision', incorporates the idea 'of seeing with fresh eyes',[11] seeking new interpretations in order to arrive at new knowledge. For Rich, those insights emanated from taking account of previously ignored data and unearthing still more that had been hidden – the texts of silenced women and minorities in our culture, for example, as well as our personal histories that impinge on what, and how, we create.

Moreover, just as biology students understand basic laboratory procedures, the writing students in my scenario understand how workshops function. They know how to nurture the germ of a tale until it takes root, or to perform (or 'run') standard poetic exercises, until something worthwhile results. They share a community of practice, therefore, as well as an institutional and literary history. They probably share too, with conventional and experimental authors, a 'continuing interest' in 'literary forms as objects of a certain kind of professional research',[12] as McGurl suggests of the heavyweights of postwar American fiction. Finally, once a product exists, these students know how to replicate the revision process, how to re-create, solo and in groups, having been trained in the writerly arts, the techne, from the beginning of their academic careers.

They also have learned that wrestling with problems does more than build up muscle. Skill aided by persistence brings results and provides a sound basis for developing creativity.[13] Those working in the philosophy of science as well as investigating the origins of creativity have discussed over the past forty years a range of similarities between scientific and artistic practice. Thomas Kuhn was one of the first to analyse the non-linear path discovery often took.[14] Paul Davies postulates an aesthetic base for scientific breakthroughs: 'beauty is a reliable guide to truth, and many advances in theoretical physics have been made by the theorist demanding mathematical elegance of a new theory'.[15] The actual Eureka moment, some argue, usually results from nurturing the requisite faculties and skills – that is, from expending perspiration after sufficient training[16] – although this does not discount the necessity for intuition. What the 'Two Cultures,' as C. P. Snow termed the Sciences and the Arts,[17] mean by discovery or invention is still being debated.[18] Artist and critic Paul Carter confronts this verbal confusion by clarifying the possibilities: 'If research implies finding something that was not there before, it ought to be obvious that it implies imagination. If it is claimed that what is found was always there (and merely lost), still an act of creative remembering occurs'.[19] Indeed, discovering, unearthing, remembering, revising, re-perceiving material are all processes involved in creative research.

2 The ontology of the laboratory

2.1 A state of mind

Let us explore this research site, the Creative Writing Laboratory. How different is it from a classroom where students are exhorted to 'read like a writer',[20] an essential form of professional training according to many teachers? In the creative laboratory, team members need to learn an advanced skill – how to 'research like a writer'. I began thinking how appropriate the laboratory metaphor was for creative writing some years ago when I began to explore what occurred in the craft workshop with those students who were eager to experiment and who embraced risk as a necessary part of progress. How did their goals and methods differ from the standard undergraduate concerned primarily with finishing the semester's work and exiting with a passing grade? Both groups had been trained to some extent to split their conscious minds to improve their art: read like a writer; read like your teacher; read like your ideal audience, for example. Both probably shared, as McGurl suggests, that somewhat obsessive focus on the individual symptomatic of certain types of twentieth-century literature, what he calls its 'self-tourism',[21] entrenched in many creative writing classrooms.

As writing as a discipline matured in the 1980s, developing increasing numbers of honours, coursework and research programs, this chronic preoccupation with the self was balanced by a range of influences that began to transform the humanities too – theories of various kinds and a heightened awareness of cultural context. At the same time that the pedagogy and temper of classrooms changed along with the experience of both students and staff, program directors in academia like myself were faced with articulating disciplinary boundaries, as well as methods and goals, to administrators. Researching creativity and innovation, like many of my peers, yielded instructive parallels between art and science. Writers followed a similar practice-led research loop, conducting and replicating experiments, interpreting results, gathering information, before gaining fresh insights and moving on. In both cases, training, skill and persistence worked in synergy with intuition and inspiration on the material at hand. In both cases, researchers were conscious and self-reflexive, motivated to move their projects forward employing rigorous and yet flexible methodologies. From the beginning, however, the additional challenge for creative artists has been to clarify what they conceived of as new knowledge and to explore possible pathways to generate it.

Let us narrow our scope to focus on some basic questions in order to begin understanding this complex concept of creative writing research. We can ask:

Where is the Laboratory?
What do we do there?
Why do we do it?
How do we do it?
What kind of outcomes do we produce?
How do we share them with our peers and the community?

2.2 Where

The Creative Writing Laboratory is any literal space where a writer works, including built environments such as offices, classrooms (home of the workshop), studios, libraries, museums, theatres and any area in the natural environment. The Laboratory also includes the writer's imagination. Advances in psychology, cognitive science and creativity theory have been tracking what occurs during creative production and categorising those stages.[22] Solso, for example, has posited a 'cognitive neuroscience theory of aesthetics',[23] connecting visual artistic creation with the shape of the mind. In particular, the need to survive has been a driving force, but involved in that imperative is the need to test and taste: 'It seems that a fundamental factor in the survival formula is: Attend to focal matters, but also sample exotic things'.[24] The play of creativity that throws up a new project and precedes a planning stage might come from that desire to sample. The most sophisticated science like the most effective art, Solso affirms, does not invent but discovers, 'find[ing] expressions of reality that are compatible with the basic structures of the mind'.[25] The ways in which art and science formulate their 'truths,' therefore, share similar architectural imperatives.

2.3 The what and why of research

The questions of *what, why and how* applied to writers in the Laboratory bring us to the heart of what creative writing research involves and determine the answers to the rest of the questions above. What do we research, why have we begun this exploration in the first place, what form of practice do we choose, what methods do we employ, what theories underpin our choice of method and how do we communicate results to others? As soon as researchers pose questions, they are launched on the research path. Creative writing students might not be aware that they need to ask questions about their practice, but they underpin every challenging project. Implicit questions might lie, for instance, beneath a student's decision to write a detective story in an undergraduate course. Will she follow the rules of the genre, or will she play with them? If she manipulates conventions, why and how will she do this? Will she involve her audience in the game, or will she trick them and then reveal the subterfuge? What agenda lies behind her breaking of the generic contract? And so on.

Questions must be involved in any research endeavour, but all projects do not result in answers that imply new knowledge has been generated, as I clarify shortly. Before distinguishing between what I will call grounding or local research and global research, let me introduce the conventional OECD (Organisation for Economic Cooperation and Development) definition, which applies to 'natural sciences and engineering; social sciences and humanities and inter-disciplinary'; in other words, to all disciplines:

> Any creative systematic activity undertaken to increase the stock of knowledge, including knowledge of man [*sic*], culture and society, and the use of knowledge to devise new applications.[26]

Significantly, a more specific definition of 'experimental development' can also be applied to creative practice:

> Experimental development is systematic work, drawing on existing knowledge gained from research and/or practical

experience, that is directed to producing new materials, products or devices ... or to improving those already produced or installed.[27]

Recent statements from Australia and the United Kingdom expand the boundaries of reportable research for the academy. The *Australian Code for the Responsible Conduct of Research*[28] defines research as 'original investigation undertaken to gain knowledge and understanding'[29] but brings the arts and design more easily under the research umbrella by adding this qualification from the United Kingdom's *Research Assessment Exercise* (RAE) 1998 (reproduced exactly for the 2008 RAE exercise): research also involves the 'generation of ideas, images, performances, artefacts including design, where these lead to new or substantially improved insights'.[30] 'Scholarship*' is included as an item in the RAE list, 'defined as the creation, development and maintenance of the intellectual infrastructure of subjects and disciplines'.[31] All of these definitions refer to the wide range of activities that creative as well as scientific research comprises. The 'discoveries' or developments that result from whatever systematic method researchers employ (as appropriate in their disciplines) must also be available for dissemination to peers and the public. Those 'publicly verifiable outcomes'[32] benefit the culture by suggesting practical applications as well as fostering debate and further research. Creative writing, along with architecture, arts-based social sciences, design and visual and performing arts have been engaged in interpreting the above definitions in order to validate their research practices; it is worth highlighting that these disciplines often produce very different responses.[33]

3 Local and global research: How it shapes new knowledge

Research is both a noun and a verb; it carries a heavy denotative and connotative load. I want to distinguish now between two interpretations of the research process because they cause confusion among students, teachers and those outside the discipline. When they begin a project, writers often research for a local purpose necessary for the writing of the work – this is an internal imperative. On the other hand, they might also research for a purpose external to the work – to generate new knowledge and to benefit others. The first type I call 'grounding' or 'local' research that contributes to a work in the form of specific information, such as facts about milieu, period, people, language, and so on. The second type I call 'global' research that performs beyond the confines of the project. This advanced form of research can make discoveries and it can provide conceptual frameworks for that writing either implicitly or explicitly. In so doing, it communicates to peers and to a broader academic, artistic and global community the value of those concepts; it might also speak to innovations in process or product that the creative work makes.

Take historical novelists, for example, who need to assemble facts in order to make their texts accurate and therefore convincing. This is the *what* of local research. The ease with which writers create another culture because they have immersed themselves in the period (including not only its history but its *Zeitgeist*) contributes narrative authority. This authority functions on the surface of the novel – to give readers pleasure in gaining information – and subliminally – to give readers confidence. They willingly suspend disbelief, feeling that they can offer themselves to the narrative voice because the work understands itself and will yield rewards accordingly.

Global writing research, however, works above that plane. This is where writers 'performing' as researchers make a contribution to knowledge by speaking to that part of the writer and reader's mind that is self-aware. Here they address a public or indeed publics. They might discover, for instance, in the manner of a conventional researcher, documents in an archive that revise our understanding of key historical events. More significantly for creative writing research, they might then take that knowledge, transforming it in the novel in order to suggest how these facts altered a period's ethos. This creative project and whatever critical reflection accompanies it, thus, might 'lead to new or substantially improved insights'.[34] Following research pathways suggested by their identities as practitioners, they might interrogate the product and the process – structure, style, focalisation, for example – arguing that they have moved beyond typical historical fiction conventions to reinvigorate the genre and why that was critical at this point in time.

Global research, which intends to transfer knowledge, accomplishes more than the generation of a satisfying creative work. It involves that work's context within its culture and literary history and might address its mode of production. Reading (or viewing or hearing) a richly inflected artefact of this type is a complex experience, which might begin with an appreciation of its construction and the culture conveyed and develop into a mental dialogue with it. With our hypothetical novel, that conversation might involve the unreliability of historical texts, the silencing of marginalised voices, the slippery nature of language, the role of gender in determining societal structures and other recent concerns of historiography.

In the past, the global research aspect of a work might be described and analysed in a preface, forward, afterword or notes. This type of exposition has a history, the most instructive examples of author statements in the pre-modern era dating from the nineteenth and early twentieth centuries, with Henry James and Edgar Allan Poe on the nature of fiction and poetry being two cases in point.[35] In the twentieth century, prolegomena, notes, afterwords and, indeed, separate essays, interviews and public performances designed to educate readers or to second-guess critics are too numerous to mention, but whatever form the peritextual, paratextual, critical or dramatic authorial voice takes, the intent is to manipulate reader response by inserting the creator's privileged knowledge back into the communication equation.

In an academic context, exposition and argument about the research aspect of creative works take place at undergraduate level in critical commentary. At honours and postgraduate levels in Australia and in some instances in the UK, this kind of discourse appears in its most familiar form in exegeses, critical documents or essays accompanying creative artefacts. Australian author Kate Grenville's research project that earned her a Doctor of Creative Arts at the University of Technology, Sydney,[36] is a noteworthy case. Her award-winning historical novel, *The Secret River*,[37] and her analysis of the research as well as the imaginative journey necessary to write it, *Searching for the Secret River*,[38] demonstrates how both creative and critical thesis components can speak eloquently to an international audience.[39] Of course, no doubt these works did not move straight from the academy into the public arena without revision, but the fact remains that one book was based on the DCA novel and the other on the critical essay. It also demonstrates how beginning with no more plan than a desire to write a family story about an ancestor who had helped to settle the Hawkesbury River and which had hardened into 'a little sealed capsule'[40] – perhaps a non-fiction book, she first thought[41] – can blossom into a fertile project, driven by questions, research, answers and more questions. These activities were complemented by Grenville's habitual working methods as an author in her own version of the practice-led research loop. She began 'writing into the unknown',[42] then 'shifted gear',[43] revised, researched and re-immersed in the work. The entire project resulted in 'the opening of a new set of eyes in my head, a new set of ears',[44] and a contribution to the ongoing debate about how Australian settlement impacted on the Indigenous population. The nature of research, its documentation and the optimal balance between critical and creative work continues to be contested in the academy as stakeholders seek to establish national standards; in fact, research has also been incorporated into creative artefacts self-consciously.[45] The *what* of research, therefore, engages readers on many planes and demands nuanced responses to complex questions.

3.1 The how of research

When we move to consider the *how* and *why* of research in creative writing, the necessity for clarifying methodology and theoretical frameworks becomes clearer. *Why* asks researchers to think about their project's significance, to themselves and to the culture; some writers focus on individual poetics. What will their project add, for instance, to genre, to style, to understanding particular social or ethnic groups? *How* involves what steps will be taken to achieve results. This is the time that theory courts method, or vice versa. They don't have to marry, vowing to be faithful forever; they can co-habit for the natural term of a project and then part ways. Theory requires researchers to confront their assumptions about knowledge and language, often suggesting appropriate methods and forms of discourse.

Theory can, therefore, help to communicate significant findings to others. As Deleuze asserts, theories should not obstruct but rather facilitate: 'a theory is exactly like a box of tools. ... It must be useful. It must function. And not for itself'.[46] Although various theoretical approaches have sometimes misrepresented texts by slavishly 'reading' them according to their agendas – poststructuralism, Marxism, postcolonialism, for example – indulging in 'a sort of willful overlooking',[47] sensitive reading using appropriate theoretical frameworks has also illuminated texts. The truism that 'no text is innocent' can be rephrased as 'no reading is innocent'. Valentine Cunningham's spirited critique of Theory's shortcomings still maintains that understanding how and why we read is critical:

> For what Theory has really brought home is the utterly main function of literature as a shaper of the realities we perceive ... as constructed for us by the texts we know them through, the 'discourses' which make up our personal vision, ideology, sense of things, and are main features of the large 'discourse', or *episteme* (to use another of Foucault's fundamental terms), of our, or any 'time'.[48]

This self-awareness, or self-reflexivity, is equally if not more critical to how and why we write; ergo, 'no writer is innocent.' Writers, like researchers in all disciplines, need to be conscious of the imperatives to be honest about their assumptions and to be clear about how these shape their methodologies.

3.2 New knowledge: Sharing outcomes

Let me summarise the myriad routes to the variety of outcomes creative writing research might involve, especially in graduate study. Then I will turn to how we can share them with peers and the various publics who comprise our audience. Practice-led research is an effective umbrella term because it foregrounds the creative dimension; what inspires a writer to undertake this type of research is the drive to practice, albeit in a specialized way. In academia, that practice leads to creative work that embodies results and, therefore, the writer cannot be wholly separated from the researcher. Writers exploit a variety of methodologies, underpin them by one or more grounding theories, and produce a range of outcomes. How they make those choices is determined by their desired goals.

One common goal is to make practice itself the focus, so that the research, although it produces an artefact – let us say poems – also generates new knowledge about the way in which tonal qualities, for example, can affect a poem's architecture. The poet in this hypothetical case might adapt a technique from another art form, or another language, revivifying a conventional subject or giving voice to a new one. The practice here can be both generator of knowledge – revising or 'devis[ing] new applications'[49] – and the object of study. In short, this new knowledge could not be gained without practice. A second possible goal focuses on the creative artefact itself, exploring how it has modified, developed or advanced the genre, or negotiated with other genres or art forms to engender fresh artistic experiences. The third goal, by exploiting method and theory from one or more art forms as well as other non-artistic disciplines, produces conventional and non-traditional knowledge. The project as an integrated whole makes the contribution to knowledge or culture. This summary oversimplifies the dynamics of practice, methodology, theory and artefact because in any project many of these goals overlap, interact, react and drive the writer on.

The creative product and any documentation comprise outcomes available to the relevant publics, a validation demanded by a conventional research definition. They testify that writers have fulfilled project aims and have demonstrated, analysed, illuminated or performed their practical and theoretical modes. Methodology can involve a mixture of techniques – qualitative, quantitative, depending on need. The work produced, therefore, as arts-based social science and educational inquiry affirms, will not necessarily take the form of 'a linear analytic formula, but a constrained circle of communication'[50] that obviously addresses an audience. Eisner conceives of this research interaction 'as publicly accessible transformations of consciousness'[51] driven 'by both epistemological and political impulses'.[52] So the type of creative product, methodology and research questions impact on how we share new knowledge: conventional print, electronic and/or mixed media, web, stage or screen performance, exhibition, et al. – these and other vehicles have been employed by creative writers.

4 The rhizomatic structure of research and its pedagogy

This analysis of writers in the Laboratory demonstrates how fertile creative writing research is, accommodating both conventional and innovative projects that exploit practical and theoretical strategies. Writers might revive an old style or mix up a new combination by training in the latest technologies; graft one genre onto another in the imaginative hothouse, producing a hardy hybrid; or add controversial matter to a sensitive subject, risking a public explosion – and then monitor the fallout. As researchers, writers must also be responsible for selecting, applying and experimenting on their own and other exemplary creative works in order to discover which theories can produce promising results. In its most innovative form, creative writing research can be, therefore, rhizomatic, in the sense first elaborated in Gilles Deleuze and Félix Guattari's *A Thousand Plateaus*.[53] This complex and provocative work argues for a philosophy that conquers artificial divisions between modes of thought and varieties of knowledge by appealing to the biological concept of the rhizome. What is a rhizome? It is a 'subterranean system' such as those of tubers and bulbs; it also describes interlinked biological systems such as viruses, orchids and wasps.[54] The rhizome has been used as a template for innovative academic and artistic research by a range of critics and artists[55] because it provides such a flexible template for how non-traditional research operates, the research of those disciplines 'on the bleeding edge'[56] of academia or those that have attempted radical renewal.

Writers practicing in cross-disciplinary and hybrid genres might find this conception of research appeals because it invites them to construct and follow pathways that the product and process suggest; the rhizome is, after all, '*a map and not a tracing*'[57] that requires active participation, not regimented adherence to a theory or passive imitation. Further, rhizomatic research seems ideally suited to provide frameworks for collaborative artistic enterprise, where ownership of material by mutual agreement might not be an issue[58] and the ultimate goal is to produce, through 'trans-disciplinary research,' something that '"moves beyond and across what any one discipline offers"'.[59] This drive to integrate is also evident in such degrees as Bachelors of Creative Arts that gather together writing, drama, screen and digital media, for example. The practice-led research loops of action research fit the interactive paradigm of creative research that facilitates this type of collaboration. The research itself can drive the writer's practice and then the practice itself can suggest new research directions, propelling the entire project forward. This fruitful progressive circularity is not a static iteration but a renewal that 'operates by variation, expansion, conquest, capture offshoots'.[60] It is a transitory not eternal return conditioned by the writer's personality, skill and history as well as the project's length, discipline area or areas and scope.

The *Creative Writing Benchmark Research Statement*[61] of the National Association of Writers in Education (UK), which elaborates on the nature, principles and scope of creative writing research, similarly focuses on flexibility[62] and innovation.

> Creative Writing is an investigative and exploratory process. Of the various approaches adopted, some may be called 'situated' or action research; some reflexive; some responsive; some may result from an engagement with 'poetics'; some may adapt or adopt the investigative procedures of other disciplines, where useful.[63]

Students might well feel daunted at this proliferation of choices, which is why teacher/supervisor guidance and peer support is critical. At the higher degree level, students must design and execute a creative product and the critical accompaniment (or clarify how they will integrate the research element), as well as argue for the selection of topic, methodologies and theoretical approach. How, then, might this mutable form of research affect learning; and how might teachers demonstrate it to students, who are concerned with focusing the energy flow?

5   The pedagogy of rhizomatic research

Exploring the multiple inputs and outputs, or entry and exit points, or windows into other bodies of knowledge[64] of this type of exploration is one strategy. As I have argued recently,[65] close attention to a creative work that invites multiple exploratory techniques because of its reflexive, allusive nature, can be rewarding. This approach entails more than a superficial testing of a variety of theories on it; it certainly does not mean to suggest that a choice of reading strategies is arbitrary. It foregrounds the work of art and respects its integrity, at once celebrating its richness and that of the possible modes of discourse that comment on it. I do not have space to offer a comprehensive reading of a sample of poems or novels here, let alone hybrid artefacts, but I will suggest how these readings function to demonstrate approaches to creative research and how they model the way in which writers might train.

Creators inside as well as outside academia benefit by understanding both their art form and their own place as artists within a cultural context. Students too benefit from understanding what creativity theory terms 'historical embeddedness'.[66] Creative breakthroughs can be dependent to some extent on historical and cultural positioning as well as on knowledge of what has already been accomplished in one's art. That broad perspective is what mentors, supervisors or teachers provide to students, offering, in addition to formal instruction, their experience in mapping their own projects and reading programs and, on a higher plane, their careers. Reading and writing are both processes that might begin with a syllabus or a template (based on a genre, for example). To maximise the experience, however, students have to make these processes their own, to internalise texts, to tame, subdue or reshape material so that they find that original insight for themselves in order to own it. This is a logical extension of the original agenda to reform the study of literature charted by Myers in his history of creative writing's incursion into the academy.[67] Experiencing literature 'from the inside'[68] is a precursor to experiencing one's own writing in this way in order the better to understand its dynamics. Eventually, those committed to a deeper understanding of their artform will graduate to researching it. This is where creative writing research can overcome the limitations of self-reflexivity, expanding beyond the personal dimension to reclaim a public space by 'going public' with research results.

Exploring multivocal literary or artistic works that play with audience perceptions, enticing them down one interpretative pathway and then another, taking them below the surface to discover a complex of meanings, can open out the concept of creative research. W. H. Auden's 'Musée des Beaux Arts'[69] is often studied as an exemplar of *ekphrasis*, 'a literary description of or commentary on a visual work of art',[70] but in fact the poem demonstrates much more. The painting to which the poem responds is Pieter Brueghel the Elder's 'Landscape with the Fall of Icarus';[71] Brueghel was a Flemish artist who was skilled at depicting his prosperous world, with its rich farms, dancing peasants, satisfied businessmen and flourishing trading ships. The painting also speaks to the myth of Icarus, the son of Daedalus,[72] the supreme craftsman who designed the Minotaur's labyrinth. Entering the text engages readers immediately, asking them to think about, hear or see more than one historical period, more than one artistic mode, more than one verbal register. Readers have to choose what they will consider in detail first, which door to open.

Following one pathway is not a linear act; others distract readers as they pass. The reading experience becomes a journey akin to a biologist's field trip to a rainforest. The shadowy forest floor, where tunnels lead into fecund darkness; the arboreal network above that sustains epiphytes, lianas, and a profusion of bird life; the canopy from which some animals might never descend – all beg to be explored. Which paths will the biologist follow? The purpose of the expedition and its research orientation will determine choices, just as writers and critics will choose reading techniques based on the questions that they want to pose, the textual type being examined, the cross-section under the microscope and their own creative predilections and memories.

In the case of 'Musée des Beaux Arts,' an unavoidable question must be where is Icarus in the painting and the poem, Icarus the rebellious young man who has plummeted not into the classical world but into Brueghel's sixteenth-century bourgeois civilisation? Do readers hear the voice of the twentieth-century Auden whose biographical trips to a museum on the eve of World War II ground the poem? What is the viewing position of the persona 'reading' Brueghel's paintings? The poem is itself a labyrinth; the reading process is, therefore, a complex negotiation, just as responding creatively to it must be. Twenty-first century students reading Auden 'like a researcher' might find that training in rhetoric, cognitive poetics or new historicism, to name only a few approaches, will open out critical and creative possibilities. At a more advanced level, these approaches might yield new knowledge about the relationship between visual art, poetry and history.

6 Writing students in the laboratory

How does the teaching and supervision of creative writers inter-twine with the way in which writers teach themselves and conduct research? Will a student learn simply by practising under a mentor's direction, much as a lab assistant or team member trains? How can they be encouraged to generate hypotheses that they themselves want to test? It is instructive here to compare a pedagogy of the writer with that of a teacher. Writers have to design an experiment – the project – focus on the problem and generate a theoretical scaffolding to support the methodology, which entails both the forms of practice and the research protocol. Finally, they must set the criteria to determine success. In courses at any level teachers set the knowledge parameters, produce aims and outcomes underpinned by a theoretical understanding of the subject, design modes of delivery, generate exercises and their associated forms of practice and determine the criteria for success.

Both writers and teachers follow, therefore, multiple pathways depending on stated goals, but both, as seasoned practitioners and team leaders, will adjust, modify, adapt and shift if the context in which they function demands it. The class personality often conditions how much emphasis teachers place on one section of the syllabus or another, or whether they generate additional material. At an advanced level, higher degree supervisors know how easy it is for keen students to be distracted by an overload of information and the lure of random searches, so guidance in negotiating the journey can be critical. In Australia, in particular, postgraduate research theses can be compared to a complex ecosystem, where theory, methodology, case studies and creative work interact to produce something new – and that 'something' can take multiple forms – so each aspect needs to be nurtured for what it can contribute to the overall health of the project. Any thesis requires methods that map the body of research, offer a systematic overview, as well as contribute enough detail to allow the project to grow to its potential. Supervisors cannot predict all the hazards or blockages that might impede the creative and critical flow, but they can help students to detour around them. Finding that link, loop or knot that will tie the argument together – or the right voice, style, or image pattern that makes a creative idea evolve and finally coalesce – takes patience and persistence.

What must be clear now is that the writing workshop in its most innovative form has metamorphosed into a twenty-first century incarnation. Perhaps more accurately, and to utilise a biological metaphor, the workshop has been crossed with an experimental site to produce a hardy hybrid – the Creative Writing Laboratory – where members research, test hypotheses, innovate and produce results. As I have argued, practice-led research involves intensive training in subject areas, in skills, in methodology and in theory. Repetition needs to be integrated into any training program. Teachers and supervisors to some extent replicate the master-apprentice dynamic, but this does not simply entail an acolyte sitting at someone's metaphorical feet or imitating their style, as art students often do when they sketch in museums. If universities have become, as Florida argues, 'talent magnets and talent aggregators'[73] in the contemporary world, those 'talents,' whether celebrity writers, best-selling authors or simply practitioners with a respectable publication record, will only prove lastingly influential if they are also educators. They model how they have acquired new skills or knowledge in order o fulfil a vision, or how they have 're-visioned' a project before trekking off into the unknown. Creative writing has its own brand of hermeneutics, therefore; practitioners question and explicate the work of others as well as what they themselves produce in order to generate transferable knowledge. That dynamic drives individual projects forward, encompassing discipline-specific breakthroughs such as developments in form and style as well as interdisciplinary studies of the basis of creativity.

7   Conclusion

In summary, creative writing's proponents have moved from justifying the existence of the discipline as a way to enhance literary studies, to develop communication and technical skills, to aid psychotherapeutic practice and to facilitate creativity[74] to arguing that creative writing itself can be the basis of a legitimate form of research practice. Creative writing has its own varied methods to understand the writing process as well as the results of that process in order to generate knowledge. From another perspective, I suggest that the act of researching as a creative writer has affinities with teaching and supervising the creative writer. In academia, stakeholders form an integrated system where individuals perform on several planes depending on time and need. The various meanings that attach to the word 'research,' as a noun and as a verb, as I have argued, illustrate this complex interaction. Moreover, teachers and students alike will have occasion to exploit both 'local' and 'global' research depending on the nature of their projects and their level of study.

The dynamic relationship between practice, method, theory and artefact also reflects what is happening at the cutting edge outside the university, a natural progression that recognises that the digital age encourages new generations to mix media, performance techniques and artistic vocabularies. Many of the new technologies not only require specialist training but also collaborative practice, asking students to interrogate how they perform as individuals within a group and requiring teachers as representatives of an institution to help them to negotiate practical and ethical pathways. These challenges have forced creative writing to be one of the most self-conscious of the new disciplines. In the twenty-first century, therefore, creative writers in the academy have progressed from interrogating what and why they teach and study to exploring what and why they research in order to contribute to the stock of knowledge and culture.

Exercises

1 **Generating research questions:** Research students often begin with an area of study rather than a project. Generate as many questions as you can about that area and your proposed creative work. Use the preceding discussion of the hypothetical historical novelist as a global researcher for suggestions. Distill your questions into four interlinked ones that give your project focus as well as scope so that you can prepare an outline. Remember to ask: why are you doing this study, how will you do it and what outcomes do you hope to produce?

2 **Reading for research:** Choose an extract from your own creative work or from a key text in your study. How will you 'read' and 'talk' about this extract? What assumptions do you bring to the task and what theory or theories might be appropriate for your own research interests? Your theoretical framework needs to be functional; its purpose is to help you to address why your questions need to be asked and how you will answer them. It will also shape your discourse by suggesting key analytical terms.

Notes

1 wordnet.princeton.edu/perl/webwn
2 The RAE (Research Assessment Exercise) and the ERA (Excellence in Research Australia) are schemes designed by the UK and Australia respectively to audit research output at all government-funded universities. The UK scheme conducts 'an explicit and formalised assessment process of the quality of research' (http://www.rae.ac.uk/aboutus). Undertaken six times since the initial exercise in 1986 and last run in 2008, the 'primary purpose of the RAE 2008 was to produce quality profiles for each submission of research activity made by institutions. The four higher education

funding bodies intend to use the quality profiles to determine their grant for research to the institutions which they fund with effect from 2009–10' (http://www.rae.ac.uk). In Australia various government departments have been auditing or counting research outputs for quality assurance and funding since the 1990s, with the first 'whole of institution approach' (http://www.deewr.gov.au/HigherEducation/Programs/Quality) implemented in 1991. The present government trialled the new ERA system in 2009, focusing on two discipline clusters: Physical, Chemical and Earth Sciences and Humanities and Creative Arts. An official audit of all eight discipline clusters took place in 2010 (http://www.arc.gov.au/era). ERA 'assesses research quality within Australia's higher education institutions using a combination of indicators and expert review by committees comprising experienced, internationally-recognised experts ... ERA will detail areas within institutions and disciplines that are internationally competitive, as well as point to emerging areas where there are opportunities for development and further investment' (http://www.arc.gov.au/era). Since this regime is new, stakeholders cannot predict all of the funding implications as yet, but the audit has been repeated in 2012. New Zealand also has a Performance-Based Research Fund for a similar purpose.

3   See Mark Sinclair, *The Pedagogy of 'Good' PhD Supervision: A National Cross-Disciplinary Investigation of PhD Supervision*, Canberra: Department of Education, Science and Training, 2004, p. 13, Ruth Neumann, *The Doctoral Experience: Diversity and Complexity*, Canberra: Department of Education, Science and Training, 2003, p. 57, Kris Latona and Mairead Browne, 'Factors Associated with Completion of Research Higher Degrees', Higher Education Series, Canberra: Department of Education, Training and Youth Affairs, Higher Education Division, Report No. 37, May 2001.

4   John S. Dacey and Kathleen H. Lennon (with contributions by Lisa B. Fiore), *Understanding Creativity: The Interplay of Biological, Psychological and Social Factors*, San Francisco: Jossey-Bass Publishers, 1998, p. 245.

5   See Latona and Browne, p. 4.

6   Scott Jaschik, 'Ph.D. Completion Gaps', *Inside Higher Ed.* 2008. Online. Available at http://www.insidehighered.com/layout/set/print/news/2008/09/gaps

7   Doug Lederman, 'Doctorate Production Ebbs', *Inside Higher Ed.* 2009. Online. Available at http://www.insidehighered.com/layout/set/print/news/2009/11/20/doctorate. [Accessed 24 Nov 2009], p. 1.

8   Sinclair, p. 24.

9   Mark McGurl, *The Program Era: Postwar Fiction and the Rise of Creative Writing*, Cambridge and London: Harvard University Press, 2009.

10 McGurl, p. 15.

11 Adrienne Rich, 'When We Dead Awaken: Writing as Re-Vision' in

Barbara Charlesworth Gelpi and Albert Gelpi (eds), *Adrienne Rich's Poetry* New York: Norton, 1975, p. 90.

12 McGurl, p. 48.

13 Margaret Boden, *The Creative Mind: Myths and Mechanisms, 2nd edition* London and New York: Routledge, 2004, pp. 1–2.

14 Thomas Kuhn, *The Structure of Scientific Revolutions, second ed. Internationa. Encyclopedia of Unified Science, 2 (2)*, Chicago: University of Chicago Press 1962, 1970.

15 Paul Davies, *The Mind of God: Science and the Search for Ultimate Meaning* London: Simon & Schuster, 1992, p. 175.

16 Boden, pp. 6, 13.

17 C. P. Snow, 'The Two Cultures' in S. Weintraub (ed.), *C. P. Snow. A Spectrum/Science–Criticism–Fiction*, New York: Charles Scribner's Sons, 1956, 1963, pp. 30–3.

18 See James Wayne Dye, 'The Poetization of Science' in M Amsler (ed.), *The Languages of Creativity: Models, Problem-Solving, Discourse*, Newark: University of Delaware Press; London and Toronto: Associated University Presses, 1986, pp. 92–108.

19 Janene Carey, Jen Webb and Donna Lee Brien, 'A Plethora of Policies: Examining Creative Research Higher Degree Candidates and Supervisors', *TEXT Special Issue Website Series No 3*, April 2008, Available at http:// www.textjournal.com.au, p. 7.

20 Francine Prose, *Reading like a Writer*, New York: Harper Collins, 2006.

21 McGurl, p. 16.

22 Margaret Boden, The Creative Mind: Myths and Mechanisms, *2nd edition*, London and New York: Routledge, 2004, and Robert J. Sternberg, 'Introduction' and 'A Three-Facet Model of Creativity' in R. Sternberg (ed.) *The Nature of Creativity*, Cambridge and New York: Press Syndicate of University of Cambridge, 1988, pp. 1–7, 125–47, Robert J. Sternberg, *Wisdom, Intelligence, and Creativity Synthesized*, Cambridge and New York: Cambridge University Press, 2003, and David Edwards, *Artscience: Creativity in the Post-Google Generation*, Cambridge, London: Harvard University Press, 2008.

23 Robert L. Solso, *The Psychology of Art and the Evolution of the Conscious Brain*, Cambridge, London: MIT Press, 2003, p. 254.

24 Solso, p. 256.

25 Solso, p. 257.

26 OECD *Glossary of Statistical Terms* from Research and Development – UNESCO http://stats.oecd.org/glossary [Accessed6 July 2010].

27 OECD *Glossary*.

28 *Australian Code for the Responsible Conduct of Research*, 2006.

29 *Australian Code*, p. 10.

30 *Australian Code*, p. 10.

31 *Research Assessment Exercise (RAE) Guidance on Submissions. Annex B: Definition of research for the RAE* from *RAE 2008*, June 2005. Online. http://www.rae.ac.uk/Pubs/2005/03/rae0305.doc [Accessed 6 July 2010, 1–68], p. 49.

32 Dennis Strand, *Research in the Creative Arts*, Canberra: Department of Employment, Education, Training and Youth Affairs, 1998, p. 32.

33 Until recently in Australia, visual and performing arts and design have not collaborated with creative writing in defining concepts of artistic research. The first government report on research in the Arts (Strand, 1998) excluded Creative Writing. With the formation of a national arts coalition and a push for a national creative arts academy, these divisions are finally blurring.

34 *Australian Code*, p. 10.

35 See Nigel Krauth, 'The Preface as Exegesis', *TEXT*, 6.1 (April 2002). Available at http://www.textjournal.com.au [Accessed April 2002].

36 Kate Grenville, *Searching for the Secret River*, Melbourne: Text Publishing, 2006.

37 Kate Grenville, *The Secret River*, Melbourne: Text Publishing, 2005.

38 Grenville, 2006.

39 *The Secret River* won 'the Commonwealth Prize for Literature and the Christina Stead Prize' as well as being 'shortlisted for the Man Booker Prize and the Miles Franklin Award' (http://www.kategrenville.com/biography). Of course, many students have creative and critical work published either during or after their candidature. The published versions will probably not be identical to the academic versions, especially after editorial intervention.

40 Grenville, 2006, p. 17.

41 Grenville, 2006, p. 14.

42 Grenville, 2006, p. 217.

43 Grenville, 2006, p. 217.

44 Grenville, 2006, p. 221.

45 See Andrew Melrose, 'Reading and Righting: Carrying on the "Creative Writing Theory" Debate', *New Writing: The International Journal for the Practice and Theory of Creative Writing*, 4.2 (2007): 109–17, Carey, Webb and Brien 2008, Camilla Nelson, 'Best Practice? The Problem of Peer Reviewed Creative Practice Research', *TEXT*, 13.1 (2009). Available at http://www.textjournal.com.au/april09/nelson.htm, Hazel Smith and Roger T. Dean (eds), *Practice-Led Research, Research-Led Practice in the Creative Arts*, Edinburgh: Edinburgh University Press, 2009, among many others.

46 Michel Foucault and Gilles Deleuze, 'Intellectuals & Power: A conversation between Michel Foucault and Gilles Deleuze,' 1972, Online. http://www.libcom.org/library/intellectuals-power-a-conversation-between-michel-foucault-and-gilles-deleuze. Identified as 'transcript of a 1972

conversation . . .' 'This transcript first appeared in English in the book *Language, Counter-Memory, Practice: Selected Essays and Interviews by Michel Foucault* edited by Donald F. Bouchard', p. 4.

47 Valentine Cunningham, *Reading After Theory*, Oxford: Blackwell, 2002, p. 75.

48 Cunningham, p. 43.

49 OECD definition.

50 Richard Sigesmund and Melisa Cahnmann-Taylor, 'The Tensions of Arts-Based Research in Education Reconsidered: The Promise for Practice' in Melisa Cahnmann-Taylor and Richard Sigesmund (eds), *Arts-Based Research in Education: Foundations for Practice*, New York and London: Routledge, 2008, p. 233.

51 Siegesmund and Cahnmann-Taylor, p. 239.

52 Elliot Eisner, 'The Promise and Perils of Alternative Forms of Data Representation, *Educational Researcher*, 26.6 (1997): 4–10. http://er.aera.net [Accessed 25 June 2010], p. 4.

53 Gilles Deleuze and Félix Guattari, *A Thousand Plateaus: Capitalism and Schizophrenia* (trans. and foreword Brian Massumi), Minneapolis: University of Minnesota Press, 1987.

54 Deleuze and Guattari, pp. 6, 10.

55 David Cormier, 'Rhizomatic Education: Community as Curriculum', *Innovate*, 4.5 (2008). http://www.innovateonline.info/index/php [Accessed 8 November 2009], Patricia Leavy, *Method Meets Art: Arts-Based Research Practice*, New York, London: The Guildford Press, 2009, Smith and Dean 2009, Jeri Kroll, 'Living on the Edge: Creative Writers in Higher Education', *TEXT* 14.1 (2010): 1–16. Available at http://www.textjournal.com.au/april10/kroll.htm [Accessed April 2010].

56 Cormier, p. 1.

57 Deleuze and Guattari, p. 12.

58 Daniel Mafe and Andrew R. Brown, 'Emergent Matters: Reflections on Collaborative Practice-Led Research' in *Proceedings Speculation and Innovation: Applying Practice-Led Research in the Creative Industries*, 2006. Online. http://eprints.qut.edu.au/6220/ [Accessed May 2012].

59 Crabtree as quoted in Mafe and Brown, p. 6.

60 Deleuze and Guattari, p. 21.

61 *Creative Writing Benchmark Research Statement* of the National Association of Writers in Education (UK).

62 *Creative Writing Benchmark*, pp. 11–15.

63 *Creative Writing Benchmark* 2.5, p. 12.

64 Cormier, 2008, p. 4.

65 Ideas about research discussed in this chapter have been developed over the past decade in several of my essays, most recently in 'Living on the Edge: Creative Writers in Higher Education' (*TEXT* 2010). I have

refined concepts and scope in an effort to produce a functional template for creative writing research. The reading of Auden's 'Musée des Beaux Arts' in that essay demonstrates how a rhizomatic reading of a poem can model various research pathways. My understanding of the poem is indebted to my undergraduate professors, notes in various anthologies and editions of Auden and my own teaching of it for over 35 years.

66 Dacey and Lennon, p. 248.
67 David Myers, *The Elephants Teach: Creative Writing since 1880*, Englewood Cliffs, NJ: Prentice Hall, 1996.
68 Myers, p. 8.
69 W. H. Auden, 'Musée des Beaux Arts' in *Selected Poetry of W. H. Auden*, New York: Vintage/Random House, 1971, p. 49.
70 *Merriam-Webster's Online Dictionary*. Online. www.aolsvc.merriam-webster. aol.com/dictionary/ekphrasis [Accessed October 2009].
71 Pieter Brueghel the Elder, c. 1558.
72 This note appears in 'Living on the Edge': 'All glossaries or commentaries on classical mythology include discussions of the fall of Icarus. Most commentaries on Auden's poem also note the other Brueghel paintings to which the poem alludes.'
73 Richard Florida, *The Rise of the Creative Class: And How it's Transforming Work, Leisure, Community and Everyday Life*, New York: Basic Books, 2002, p. 29.
74 See David Myers, *The Elephants Teach: Creative Writing since 1880*, Englewood Cliffs, NJ: Prentice Hall, 1996, Michelene Wandor, *The Author is Not Dead, Merely Somewhere Else: Creative Writing Reconceived*, Houndmills, Basingstoke: Palgrave Macmillan, 2008, Mark McGurl, *The Program Era: Postwar Fiction and the Rise of Creative Writing*, Cambridge and London: Harvard University Press, 2009.

Works cited

Auden, W. H., 'Musée des Beaux Arts' in *Selected Poetry of W. H. Auden*, New York: Vintage/Random House, 1971: 49.
Boden, Margaret, *The Creative Mind: Myths and Mechanisms, 2nd edition*, London and New York: Routledge, 2004.
Cahnmann-Taylor, Melissa and Richard Sigesmund, eds, *Arts-Based Research in Education: Foundations for Practice*, New York and London: Routledge, 2008.
Carey, Janene, Jen Webb and Donna Lee Brien, 'A Plethora of Policies: Examining Creative Research Higher Degree Candidates and Supervisors', *TEXT Special Issue Website Series No. 3*, April 2008. Online. Available at http://www.textjournal.com.au
Carter, Paul, *Material Thinking*, Melbourne: Melbourne University Press, 2004.

Cormier, David, 'Rhizomatic Education: Community as Curriculum', *Innovate* 4.5 2008. Online. Available at http://www.innovateonline.info/index/php [Accessed 8 November 2009].

Cunningham, Valentine, *Reading After Theory*, Oxford: Blackwell, 2002.

Dacey, John S. and Kathleen H. Lennon (with contributions by Lisa B. Fiore), *Understanding Creativity: The Interplay of Biological, Psychological and Social Factors*, San Francisco: Jossey-Bass Publishers, 1998.

Department of Education, Employment and Workplace Relations (Australian Government), http://www.deewr.gov.au/HigherEducation/Programs/Quality/QualityAssurance/Pages/ImprovingAustraliasHE.aspx [Accessed July 2010].

Davies, Paul, *The Mind of God: Science and the Search for Ultimate Meaning*, London: Simon & Schuster, 1992.

Deleuze, Gilles and Félix Guattari, *A Thousand Plateaus: Capitalism and Schizophrenia* (trans. and foreword Brian Massumi), Minneapolis: University of Minnesota Press, 1987.

Dye, James Wayne, 'The Poetization of Science' in M. Amsler, ed. *The Languages of Creativity: Models, Problem-Solving, Discourse*, Newark: University of Delaware Press; London and Toronto: Associated University Presses, 1986: 92–108.

Edwards, David, *Artscience: Creativity in the Post-Google Generation*, Cambridge; London: Harvard University Press, 2008.

Eisner, Elliot, 'The Promise and Perils of Alternative Forms of Data Representation', *Educational Researcher*, 26.6 (1997): 4–10. Online. Available at http://er.aera.net [Accessed 25 June 2010].

Excellence in Research Australia (ERA), http://www.arc.gov.au/era [Accessed October 2009].

Florida, Richard, *The Rise of the Creative Class: And How it's Transforming Work, Leisure, Community and Everyday Life*, New York: Basic Books, 2002.

Foucault, Michel and Gilles Deleuze, 'Intellectuals & Power: A conversation between Michel Foucault and Gilles Deleuze', 1972. Online. Available at http://www.libcom.org/library/intellectuals-power-a-conversation-between-michel-foucault-and-gilles-deleuze. Identified as 'transcript of a 1972 conversation . . .' 'This transcript first appeared in English in the book *Language, Counter-Memory, Practice: selected essays and interviews by Michel Foucault* edited by Donald F. Bouchard.'

Grenville, Kate, *The Secret River*, Melbourne: Text Publishing, 2005.

——, *Searching for the Secret River*, Melbourne: Text Publishing, 2006.

Jaschik, Scott, 'Ph.D. Completion Gaps,' *Inside Higher Ed*. 2008. Online. Available at http://www.insidehighered.com/layout/set/print/news/2008/09/gaps.

Krauth, Nigel, 'The Preface as Exegesis', *TEXT*, 6.1 (April 2002) Online. Available at http://www.textjournal.com.au [Accessed April 2002].

Kroll, Jeri, 'Living on the Edge: Creative Writers in Higher Education', *TEXT* 14.1 (2010): 1–16. Online. Available at http://www.textjournal.com.au/april10/kroll.htm [Accessed April 2010].

Kuhn, Thomas, *The Structure of Scientific Revolutions, second ed. International Encyclopedia of Unified Science, 2 (2)*, Chicago: University of Chicago Press, 1962, 1970.

Latona, Kris and Mairead Browne, 'Factors Associated with Completion of Research Higher Degrees', Higher Education Series, Canberra: Department of Education, Training and Youth Affairs, Higher Education Division, Report No. 37, May 2001.

Leavy, Patricia, *Method Meets Art: Arts-Based Research Practice*, New York, London: The Guildford Press, 2009.

Lederman, Doug, 'Doctorate Production Ebbs', *Inside Higher Ed.* 2009. Online. Available at http://www.insidehighered.com/layout/set/print/news/2009/11/20/doctorate [Accessed 24 Nov 2009].

Mafe, Daniel and Andrew R. Brown, 'Emergent Matters: Reflections on Collaborative Practice-Led Research' in *Proceedings Speculation and Innovation: Applying Practice-Led Research in the Creative Industries*, 2006. Online. Available at http://eprints.qut.edu.au/6220/ [Accessed May 2012].

Melrose, Andrew, 'Reading and Righting: Carrying on the "Creative Writing Theory" Debate', *New Writing: The International Journal for the Practice and Theory of Creative Writing*, 4.2 (2007): 109–17.

Merriam-Webster's Online Dictionary. Online. www.aolsvc.merriam-webster.aol.com/dictionary/ekphrasis [Accessed October 2009].

Myers, David, *The Elephants Teach: Creative Writing since 1880*, Englewood Cliffs, NJ: Prentice Hall, 1996.

McGurl, Mark, *The Program Era: Postwar Fiction and the Rise of Creative Writing*, Cambridge and London: Harvard University Press, 2009.

Neave, Lucy and Donna Lee Brien, 'Editorial: Creativity and Uncertainty' in *The Creativity and Uncertainty Papers: The Refereed Proceedings of the 13th Conference of the Australian Association of Writing Programs, 2008*. 2008. Online. http://www.aawp.org.au/files/2008–editorial.pdf [Accessed various 2008].

Nelson, Camilla, 'Best Practice? The Problem of Peer Reviewed Creative Practice Research', *TEXT* 13.1 (2009). Online. Available at http://www.textjournal.com.au/april09/nelson.htm

Neumann, Ruth, *The Doctoral Experience: Diversity and Complexity*, Canberra: Department of Education, Science and Training, 2003.

OECD *Glossary of Statistical Terms* from Research and Development – UNESCO http://stats.oecd.org/glossary [Accessed 6 July 2010]. Research definition. Also OECD *Glossary*. Experimental Development definition.

Prose, Francine, *Reading Like a Writer*, New York: Harper Collins, 2006.

Research Assessment Exercise (RAE) Guidance on Submissions. Annex B: Definition of Research for the RAE from *RAE 2008* June 2005 http://www.rae.ac.uk/Pubs/2005/03/rae0305.doc [Accessed downloaded file 6 July 2010, 1–68].

Rich, Adrienne, 'When We Dead Awaken: Writing as Re-Vision' in Barbara Charlesworth Gelpi and Albert Gelpi (eds), *Adrienne Rich's Poetry*, New York: Norton, 1975: 90–1.

Sigesmund, Richard and Melisa Cahnmann-Taylor, 'The Tensions of Arts-Based Research in Education Reconsidered: The Promise for Practice' in Melisa Cahnmann-Taylor and Richard Sigesmund (eds), *Arts-Based Research in Education: Foundations for Practice*, New York and London: Routledge, 2008: 231–46.

Sinclair, Mark, *The Pedagogy of 'Good' PhD Supervision: A National Cross-Disciplinary Investigation of PhD Supervision*, Canberra: Department of Education, Science and Training, 2004.

Slager, Henk and Annette W. Balkema (eds), *Artistic Research* (Lier en Boog Series of Philosophy of Art and Art Theory) Vol. 18, trans. Global Vernunft Amsterdam: Lier en Boog, Editions Rodopi B.V. Amsterdam/New York, 2004.

Smith, Hazel and Roger T. Dean (eds), *Practice-Led Research, Research-Led Practice in the Creative Arts*, Edinburgh: Edinburgh University Press, 2009.

Snow, C. P., 'The Two Cultures' in S. Weintraub (ed.) *C. P. Snow: A Spectrum/ Science–Criticism–Fiction*, New York: Charles Scribner's Sons, 1956, 1963: 30–3.

Solso, Robert L., *The Psychology of Art and the Evolution of the Conscious Brain*, Cambridge, London: MIT Press, 2003.

Sternberg, Robert J., 'Introduction' and 'A Three-Facet Model of Creativity' in R. Sternberg (ed.) *The Nature of Creativity*, Cambridge and New York: Press Syndicate of University of Cambridge, 1988: 1–7, 125–47.

——, *Wisdom, Intelligence, and Creativity Synthesized*, Cambridge and New York: Cambridge University Press, 2003.

Strand, Dennis, *Research in the Creative Arts*, Canberra: Department of Employment, Education, Training and Youth Affairs, 1998.

Wandor, Michelene, *The Author is Not Dead, Merely Somewhere Else: Creative Writing Reconceived*, Houndmills, Basingstoke: Palgrave Macmillan, 2008.

wordnet.princeton.edu/perl/webwn [Accessed June 2010].

6 The Generations of Creative Writing Research

Graeme Harper

Chapter summary

Research through, and in, creative writing offers substantial opportunities for the creation of new knowledge, both for the individual creative writer undertaking that research and for us all, generally. However, choosing to engage in such research is a choice not a requirement of being a creative writer. That said, such a choice could relate to our ability to provide new knowledge on which future generations might build; knowledge for others as well as knowledge for ourselves. Research in creative writing therefore has a relationship to ideals of sustainability. As we determine our methods of approaching creative writing research we are drawn to consider possible avenues of investigation. These avenues are many, and they are varied. In this regard, the clue to modes and methods of research is that creative writing is action. That is, while we can certainly think about it, creative writing cannot exist without us actually *doing* something. How we respond before, during, and after that *doing* incorporates what we currently know, and can incorporate what we seek to find out.

1 Introduction

The ideal of sustainability generates a great deal of discussion here in the early twenty-first century. Environmental sustainability, economic sustainability, societal sustainability, cultural sustainability: the strength of the ideal of sustainability reflects a concern about the ways in which we humans have acted, in the past, and about what we might do to improve the positive impact of our actions. Such discussions are not all borne on moral imperatives, even if the tone of engagement references a morality. However, some of these discussions are entirely pragmatic, supported by negative data about the impact of humans on the world, and on each other, over time. In addition, these discussions are based on our concepts of knowledge, and on what to do with the knowledge we have gained about this world and our role in it.

Might there be a link, then, between this and researching through, and about, creative writing? Could both creative writing and evolving forms of critical engagement with creative writing, relate to engagement with creative writing's future as well as to its present? Indeed, do modes and methods of creative writing research reflect a genuine concern for human engagement with knowledge that can be passed on to future generations?

Answering these questions affirmatively has the potential to produce a few detractors. Some could say such suggestions are far too bold, claim too much; or that they are merely grandstanding for something more sinister, something that itself might impact negatively on creative writing. It has even been said, though with little known intent, that certain recent styles of engagement with creative writing in Higher Education are a form of 'institutionalising of creative writing'. What this means is not entirely clear, given that creative writing has existed in institutions of higher education since institutions of higher education were first founded, and that creative writing, being human action, is in the hands of humans, who entirely form universities and colleges.

Perhaps the fear here is primarily that research explorations in creative writing might not adequately acknowledge the beauty and enjoyment of creative writing, in and of itself. Similar fears are well known throughout the history of the arts – fears, that is, about the arts being undermined, or poorly served, by certain kinds of knowledge, or by certain organisational developments. Sometimes these fears have been configured as an opposition between the sciences and the arts, or between scientific method and the personal ways and means of artists.[1] And yet, to create such an opposition, we'd need to see research as inherently scientific, science as inherently non-artistic, and the arts as inherently weak so that they might fall victim to such opposition. We'd also need to downgrade the presence of human freewill in institutions of higher education, were they to be blamed for 'institutionalising' of creativity.

Suffice it to say, research is not by its nature separate from artistic practice, universities are not inhuman, the arts are not weak, science is not uncreative, and what is being suggested here is not, by those narrow definitions of what this might mean, 'scientific method'. What is being suggested here is the investigation of creative writing, which is brought about by our knowledge of how to do it, by what creative writing is, or by what it might be.

Human involvement in creative writing continues to grow, as it is further encouraged by technological changes that increase our access to creative writing, to discussions about it, and to exchanges regarding it. Creative and critical modes and methods of research reflect a deep interest in creative writing. But it can't be forgotten that engagement in creative writing can occur without any address to what research in creative writing might be, or what it might mean. Engaging in practice-led and critical research in creative writing is a choice, but it is not the only choice.

Here, research considerations in creative writing are going to be considered along four exploratory avenues, under these titles:

1 Creative Writing Habitats
2 The Creative Domain
3 Activities
4 The Artefacts of Creative Writing

By *Creative Writing Habitats* I refer not simply to physical spaces and places but to spaces and places that reflect modes of action and modes of thinking. Habitats can be person-made or natural, created, adapted or adopted. In keeping with the general definition of a 'habitat', such a creative writing habitat is a place *where the creative writer is normally located*. This is not necessarily a home, or any kind of permanent place. Nor, of course, is it necessarily somewhere that is constantly relocated. Likewise, while creative writers might most often be discovered in this habitat, it is not the only place they are to be found. Creative writers can, of course, be highly mobile individuals.

The second term, the *Creative Domain*, recalls a wider set of acts of situating and influence, a domain in this instance being an area of activity over which some human influence is exerted – in this case, creative activity, inclusive of creative writing. The creative domain is made up of activities of creating – humans being creative creatures, and thus engaging naturally in a range of creative activities. The term the creative domain also encapsulates human ingenuity, our ability to approach the world through creative action, and our frequent combining of what is discovered in nature with what we initiate or refine ourselves. Because creative writing combines discovery with initiation and refinement it is directly and considerably related to the human creative domain.

Activities: these have been referred to elsewhere as 'acts and actions'.[2] To simplify this opening exploration, the more general term 'activities' is used. General terms can be useful for grounding initial thoughts, and then further explored to consider their complexities and nuances. In this case, activities involve being active: something is happening, some undertaking of some kind will take place or is taking place, or has taken place. This general sense begins to unearth an area of investigation; more consideration can then follow.

The *Artefacts of Creative Writing*, what are these? Quite obviously some of these are finished works of creative writing; but not all artefacts of creative writing are finished works. 'Artefacts' refers to things produced by humans; in this case, the things produced by humans during their activities of creative writing.

A final, introductory note on the title of this chapter. The word 'Generations' is here to reference generating, originating, producing – that is, *to generate*. A further allusion, however, is to the concept and foundations of what it is to be generative, *generativity*. The developmental psychologist Erik Erikson (1902–94) coined the term 'generativity' in the mid-twentieth century. Stephen J. Whitfield notes that Erikson's discussion of generativity brought about a reshaping of his field 'by focusing on the development of an authentic selfhood rather than the instinctual drives of childhood, on ego rather than on id or superego, on the achievement of maturity through generativity and mutuality'.[3]

Erikson suggested that the middle years of adulthood can see a person working towards betterment of society, a sharing between generations, and that this relates to maturing of outlook and is a preventive measure against stagnation. This is not to say that not wishing to engage in research in creative writing is somehow '*de*generative', inauthentic or immature! Generations, generation, generativity are not intended to be oppositional terms. However, the notion of sharing of knowledge, between us, and between generations, seems an ideal way to consider what lies at the core of development and understanding in creative writing. If generativity can be enhanced by research engagement with creative writing, then this is something directly related to sustainability. Other contributions to sustainability also exist including: a general enjoyment of creative writing, a human connection with the distributed artefacts of creative writing, and an admiration, even a celebration, of aesthetic successes in creative writing. None of this is in opposition to a discussion of the generation and sharing of new knowledge in creative writing. In fact, it forms part of that discussion.

2   Creative writing habitats

A creative writing habitat is the place where a creative writer – you, or any other writer – is most likely to be found, a particular place adopted, adapted or developed by the writer for their creative writing. A creative writing habitat is, most importantly, where the *event* of creative writing takes place. It therefore makes sense that one concern in researching in creative writing is a concern with the formation, attributes and existence of creative writing habitats, with a consideration of the places and the internal qualities of spaces and places where a writer engages in creative writing. This can be considered in a variety of ways.

As a creative writer, you might ask: 'Where am I currently writing and why?' What attributes does this habitat have? How is it configured, or how have I configured this habitat for this particular event of creative writing? In what ways does it relate to the creative writing I undertake or, speculatively, might undertake? Speculating might produce some interesting thoughts. For example, is it possible to construct a creative writing habitat to better support a particular creative writing project? If it is possible, what creative writing activities might then result and how would you critically contextualise them – for your own benefit, or to explore them more generally so as to provide new knowledge about creative writing for others to explore? We could look, say, at remarks such as these from writer Fred G. Leebron, about not forcing himself to write a novel:

> Every morning I sat with a stenographer's notebook (smaller pages that would lead to less pressure to fill them) and wrote. I had about an hour a day. Usually I stole this hour on the commuter train. What the hell, it wasn't writing a novel, now that twenty-four, twenty-five, twenty-six editors had rejected my very first novel. I was just writing.[4]

There are lots of actions here, decisions, things going on; but there is also 'the commuter train'. Leebron presents this in opposition to an earlier section in his discussion where he talks of forcing himself to sit at his desk and write a novel, because a literary agent had said to him: 'I like your stories. . . You need to write a novel.'[5]

The point Leebron makes is that when he forced himself to write, and to 'concentrate' and to exercise 'total control' he was unable to produce the results he desired. We could think here about the nature of creativity and whether control is good or bad, or sometimes contains elements of both. We could consider the notion of creative writing to order – or creative writing *on* order – and whether that is sometimes a useful stimulant to creative writing or entirely unproductive. But we could also consider, interestingly, that commuter train. What roles did it play? Why, and how, did it play those roles?

A considerable amount of work has been done on the lives of creative writers; in particular, their living and working conditions. Critical work has been undertaken on creative writers' daily habits; journals, letters, diaries have been reproduced for publication – at least of those creative writers whose cultural value has been agreed upon by formally recognised critics so as to warrant publishers undertaking such publications. Literary critics focusing on biographical analysis have delved into space and place, macro locations (for example, 'the writers of Hampshire' or 'literary London in the nineteenth century') and micro locations (for example, 'Willa Cather's summer cottage' or 'Kenzaburo Oe's time in Hiroshima'). And yet, the question of researching habitat from the point of view of an individual creative writer's adoption or adaptation of a place or space is not well investigated, as yet, in relation to understanding creative writing habitats themselves.

While it might not be an individual creative writer's inclination to research their habitat there is little doubt, even from the somewhat external viewpoint of a biography, that habitat formation, the function of habitats, modification, revision or variation of space and place, often plays a substantial role in the events of creative writing.

Might a typology of creative writing habitats therefore be developed? Is there merit in a poet exploring the activities of poets in certain places, personal or societal, in order to understand and better develop their own habitat, their own actions within spaces and places? Could a creative writer benefit from comparing the most likely habitats of poets, and the ways these are formed and maintained, and the activities of individual novelists or screenwriters in their most likely habitats?

As creative writing is, among other things, a physical event, investigating physical elements associated with it cannot but be in tune with the general sense of creative writing. But to what end? Creative writing is most often a very individual pursuit, and some creative writers will have little interest in investigating elements of their habitat. However, consider scenarios along these lines:

You decide you're going to write a novel set in Antarctica. It's a contemporary novel, with an historical backdrop. That is, the novel concerns a scientific discovery, and a particular group of modern scientists, but important links to the past occur as discoveries are made in the ice. The novel follows a story of emerging relationships in a disparate group of people, while speaking to themes of loyalty and betrayal, as past and present reveal elements of this theme as the difficult, indeed remote, conditions uncover (literally and metaphorically) truths about human interaction. In brief, that's the novel!

In the first creative writing scenario you cannot afford – 'Absolutely impossible. Having just finished my masters degree, look, I'm flat broke!' – to travel to Antarctica. So you decide that you will read and watch and discuss Antarctica, science, loyalty and betrayal, and quite a deal more, as often and as intensely as you can. Your habitat soon reflects this. Where you write is soon piled with books and print-outs of things about your subject and theme. You watch documentaries, you sit in front of amateur and professional footage, delivered online, you decorate your walls with maps and pictures, you send emails to friendly Antarctic scientists and ask pressing questions. Method and creative writing habitat are this way linked. And you write. The novel is finally completed, to your satisfaction. Add a twist, then: a friend has found a 'work for a discount' cruise to Antarctica, on which you would tend bar on a cruise ship for a discount berth. You could just about afford this, on credit. But the job is already complete, your novel is finished. If you went now, what might happen? You go, or you don't go.

In the second creative writing scenario you can afford – 'No problem at all! Working in that coffee shop had finally paid off!' – to go to Antarctica. So you do. You sail there aboard a scientific vessel, which is also partly a cruise ship – limited number of passengers, adventure tour. It's an eleven-week expedition. You start writing on the way. After all, there are scientists all around you and you get the feeling you'll use parts of this actual journey as adapted, or adopted, parts of your characters' journey. Maybe – though there's plenty to see and it's not easy to spend time on your own, working at your laptop – but maybe you finish the novel in your small but surprisingly well-appointed quarters in the Malmoreton Research Base, wearing a borrowed pair of strangely aromatic salopettes.

Let's add a third scenario. You decide you want to write a novel about human loyalty and human betrayal. There's a sense you have that this theme might be well explored by setting the novel in somewhere remote like, say, Antarctica. But you have never been to Antarctica and you can't afford to go, nor do you particularly want to go. You figure that this is a story in which theme should not be overwhelmed by setting, or creating of character overwhelmed by the truths of reportage. But you know you need time to work on this book, and there are too many distractions at home, it being summer and your house being near the beach so there's always the chance of visitors. So, instead, you take yourself off to what is called 'a writer's retreat'. This is not something you have done before, but for this book it feels the right approach. You stay in a shared house, in the hills. During the day the artists there – there are some writers, some painters, a film-maker – work at their creative pursuits. In the evenings everyone gets together over dinner; the talk is mostly about the hills around you, and the wildlife, and the great feel of the place, though occasionally this talk turns to the work at hand, and you listen to each person in turn and realise everyone is pursuing something unique to them. You finish a good portion of your new novel about loyalty and betrayal, during this three-week retreat. When you arrive home, and in between visits from friends, commenting, 'You have such a great view of the surf from here', you complete your draft, and gradually move the novel towards completion.

The fleshing out of possible event scenarios could continue, of course. None of those mentioned might appear to you to be very likely at all! A creative writer creates their own, personal relationship with space and place. Everyone will thus have their own scenarios. It's the *physicality* of creative writing that is the thing to consider here. Not the only thing; nevertheless, something that has often not been considered. The actions of writing itself, the way in which creative writing is determined (that is, how we know it is happening or has happened) and the relationship between its artefacts and those who might engage with them (that is, in the large part, the readers or audiences) involve recognition of physical action. The attributes of a creative writing habitat are part of that physicality – or, in some cases, virtuality; because, of course, in today's world some creative writing habitats might involve physical action but elements of what would most often would be called 'virtual space'. The associative discussion of action and space/place continues in that case too.

Research methods relating to the impact of physical habitat – whether relatively fixed or relatively fluid locales and attributes – are complex. After all, ask yourself what is the impact of the stack of books beside you while you write, what is the relationship between the space you're writing in and the spaces just beyond it, what difference does it make if you are writing on your laptop or in a notebook, in a room or on a bus? The list could go on. Methods of investigating these things can productively begin in reminding ourselves that creative writing is informed human action; so our own, individual actions offer a productive starting point for investigations. A consideration of how such habitat-related investigations might be part of one project or another, a general mode of creative writing or a specific mode, part of one genre's writing conventions, but not part of another's. All this suggests something that could bring to us further knowledge – personal knowledge as well as broader, subject knowledge – if given some research attention.

3 The creative domain

Because of the vast range of creative endeavours generated by human beings, and recalling the discussion of sustainability, it might be said here that there is enough evidence available to us to suggest we humans are both creative and destructive creatures; that not one of us has lived in this world without impacting on it creatively or destructively in some way.

Concentrating on the element that is human creativity, research in creative writing points us towards some possibilities. An indicative list of research possibilities might run like this list below. However, what perhaps needs recalling briefly here are some key reasons why we might approach creative writing in relation to the wider creative domain.

Firstly, if human beings are by nature creative creatures, then research that *always* deals with creative writing as a separate human practice potentially falsifies its real place in human life. Concentration can most certainly be productive; but failure to engage with the bigger picture (even if only occasionally) can be counter-productive. Secondly, if critical understanding informing creative writing is thought to be an 'area' of investigation are we certain that this epistemological 'grouping' benefits our understanding? If not, then even as a hinterland to specific creative writing research investigations, the creative dimension, domain or component in human life becomes significant. Thirdly, we have seen many investigations of creativity from the point of view of many academic fields, those in the field of Psychology being some of the most well-known. Are we certain, however, that the research undertaken in such fields has yet provided answers to questions in creative writing? If not, then exploring creativity from the point of view of creative writing is, indeed, something creative writers can positively accomplish. And finally, if research methods in creative writing are continually evolving, would we benefit from 'ring-fencing' them now so that creative and critical method in creative writing is highly codified? Surely not.

These are just a few reasons why consideration of the creative domain can inform research in creative writing, and why it might inform your own approach to creative writing. Here are some indicative research questions arising from this:

- What does creative writing have in common with other art practices and what might be learnt about the events of creative writing by considering those other practices?
- How is the evidence of creative practice similar or different between art forms, and how is it understood in these various forms?
- In what ways does human creativity manifest itself generally in our daily lives and how useful, or not useful, is it to a creative writer to consider whether there are identifiable practices, ways of thinking, modes of engagement, whether someone is working in the arts or in the sciences, in commerce or in education, in one culture or in another?
- What role does creative practice play in our knowledge of the world, how we exchange that knowledge between us, or how we use this knowledge to improve our personal understanding?
- Are there modes of engagement with what is around us that could be defined as specific creative modes? For example, if someone was to suggest that creativity is not enhanced by formal patterns of learning, that creative endeavours are better supported by

informal learning, or by unstructured seeking-out, does that suggestion hold water?

- What is a creative act, and what is not a creative act? If it is at all possible to differentiate one from the other, how might this be done? Does doing so offer any new insights? I am reminded here of a comment by anthropologist Stephanie Bunn, who concluded her report on the 2005 annual Association of Social Anthropologists Conference, 'Creative Windows on Creativity', by saying: 'I left almost convinced that creativity is at the heart of all human processes, from talk to movement, dance, building and even growing old'.[6]

Asking these questions draws our attention to the fact that relatively few questions in creative writing are as yet answered, at least from the point of view of undertaking our creative writing. Perhaps these questions never will be answered! But the reasons for considering creative writing more closely, both by doing it and by critically exploring the actions and artefacts produced in doing it from the point of view of being a creative writer, are exactly those reasons to which you'd refer in the area of human knowledge. That is, to find out for your own, personal reasons how this activity takes place – how it is done by you, me, others; how we each might understand it further, in order to be able to pursue our own creative writing more adeptly. But also to increase knowledge of creative writing for cultural reasons – to further understand how creative writers engage with the world, develop their works to reflect something they think, feel, imagine, or have experienced. In all cases, researching through creative writing, developing creative works, and critically considering actions and results in and around what I am calling here 'the creative domain', relates to personal as well as cultural ideals. The human actions that are core to this reflect a combination of individual and societal interests.

4 Activities

Whether you can undertake creative writing without actually *doing something* is not as inane a thought as it might first appear. You'll notice in this chapter that I'm using the term 'creative writing' as a term for actions or a gathering of actions, an event or events. Were I to refer to the things creative writing makes I'd refer to them by their most common artefactual names (for example: novel, short story, poem, script, and so on). The reason for using the term creative writing to refer to actions is perhaps already obvious. Creative writing begins with action. It continues and evolves with, and by, action. Without action creative writing cannot be, it simply does not happen. Some of this action might indeed be the action of the mind, action of a non-material kind. Here potential points of debate arise. Is the engagement and application of the imagination an action? Are the activities of the unconscious an action? Keith Sawyer, an educationalist and psychologist who investigates creativity, says:

> Although many writers talk about a dialogue with the unconscious, this process is very different from our culture's insight myths … A creative text emerges from a long process of hard work, during which the conscious and the unconscious minds are in constant dialogue and during which many small sparks of insight emerge from the unconscious. So although unconscious inspiration plays a critical role, its role can only be understood within the context of these periods of hard work, including the hard work which proceeds each spark, the hard work to elaborate the implications of each spark, and the hard work of weaving these daily small sparks together into a unified work.[7]

Sawyer at least appears to be suggesting work involves action. In which case, he is relating that inspiration and action in creative writing are co-dependent. That idea is not overly controversial. The notion of 'elaboration' seems to be his personal clue to this relationship. Intriguingly, though, words like 'sparks' and 'unified' point us towards something more, but don't quite reach it. More remains unsaid. Of course, Sawyer is looking at the unconscious and I've raised the question of the imagination. Are these the same? The imagination has been called 'the capacity to engage in creative thought'.[8] The choice of the word 'engage' is not at all overwhelmed by semantics. To engage involves *doing something*, some kind of action. Sawyer's reference to 'work' suggests the doing of something too. Thus, in just these two references there's easily identifiable support for the idea that creative writing, involving the imagination and involving the unconscious as well as the conscious, *is* action, but not all these actions will be material actions, some will be actions of the mind.

In researching through undertaking creative writing, and by examining those activities, we are examining human action and the manifestations of human action. The methods of doing this kind of research – this examination of activities and this examination of the evidence of activities – might easily be called 'action research'. However, the term 'action research' has been used in other fields (for example, it is used in a number of areas of social research), and rather than make the discussion plain here the term brings some fairly hefty baggage. To speak more plainly, then, we simply need to say that we approach creative writing actions *as* actions. Possibilities for new discoveries abound. For example, we could:

- undertake an individual consideration of what actions take place from the origination of an idea to the completion (or abandonment) of a piece of creative writing;
- pursue an individual comparative consideration – the composition of one piece of work compared to the composition of another; or the composition of one passage compared to the composition of another;
- initiate a closer examination of our individual actions as they contribute to the overall event in any creative writing. For example, our actions associated with revising or editing, or our actions associated with creating character, or our actions associated with the relationship between form and content in the writing of a poem, or our actions associated with performativity in composing for camera, voice, sound and so on, when writing a film script.

Recalling that creative writing is action might not always focus us on individual research thoughts and research activities. In some cases, we might wish to share our experiences. Experiential knowledge, knowledge derived from our experiences, is naturally highlighted in

Graeme Harper

investigating creative writing. Investigating this can also approach group actions, such as those associated with a culture or those shared between writers working in particular genres or fields. So research here might include:

- comparing how we (eg. a group of creative writers who agree to discuss their work-in-progress) approach the composition of a work on a similar theme or themes;
- in some genre, where collaborative working is more common – say in the writing and production of a screenplay, play, or a piece of digital media – research into how those actions intersect and relate to create individual events associated with one creative writing project or another;
- work on cultural norms of action, establishing what the relationship is between your individual creative writing and the creative writing of those working from similar cultural perspectives. This too could generate new individual and group knowledge.

These suggestions are offered as examples. Given how creative writing proceeds, it makes prefect sense that many areas of research in creative writing can generate investigation of action. However, creative writing also produces evidence of its undertaking, incomplete as well as complete work, complementary works as well as primary works; these can be called the artefacts of creative writing.

5 The artefacts of creative writing

The term 'artefact' refers to objects made by humans. Artefacts can be more or less familiar. The level of general familiarity with creative writing artefacts has a relationship with how creative writing (creative writing being action) is publicly understood and materially represented. This is a productive starting point for thinking about how the artefacts of creative writing have come to occupy public and private positions in our spectrum of human knowledge.

Many commonly used terms relating to creative writing refer to artefacts that have been released into the public realm, and in

147

some point in their history defined by this release. So, for example the non-specialist (that is, here, someone not engaged in creative writing) will generally recognise the terms 'novel', 'short story' and 'poem', and be able to link those terms in some sense to the physical objects to which they refer. The level of recognition naturally differs from culture to culture, and according to levels of education, and is impacted upon by personal interest.

The detailed physical appearance of a 'script' is not so widely recognised, simply because a script tends to be the template for another art form, for a play or a film or piece of webcast or broadcast work, and the wide public recognition of the specifics of a script would suggest a degree of knowledge that is not likely to be present among non-specialists. This is not to suggest that the practice of scriptwriting is any more arcane or any less understandable – but, as a creative writing artefact, a script is somewhat hidden from wide public recognition because it is a template for another art form (e.g. the finished film or play).

Almost certainly, non-specialist recognition of a 'manuscript' or a 'typescript' has a good possibility of relating to a general sense of what these things are, if not necessarily to the event that produced them. Likewise, public recognition of a creative writer's 'diary', or of a 'letter', 'doodle' or 'sketch' offered by a creative writer, would be reasonably high, even if there would be many interpretations of how such things might look generally and to what they might relate in the actual practice of creative writing.

Perhaps less sure, less clearly recognised in the realm of creative writing artefacts, would be 'marginalia', its appearance or its purpose. So it is also that the term 'file', widely used in the electronic age, says little about what is contained within it and how this signification itself would be associated with creative writing is wide open to interpretation and misinterpretation. Similarly, 'correspondence', a common term for archival material from, and relating to, creative writers and creative writing, almost certainly hides more than it reveals.

It will be plain already, even when taking a relatively generic selection of possible evidence, that some of the artefacts of creative writing are publicly exchanged and, in key ways, strongly defined by their public identities. Others are not so strongly defined, or barely defined at all, by public categories. While we might write a novel, it is its public identity that largely defines this evidence of a creative writer having been at work. So, the creative writer might say 'I have finished a novel', and that term is a guide to, or signification of, something that has cultural and societal currency. While a receiver of a novel might not always have a developed definition of 'a novel' to hand, they are likely to know generally how one might physically appear, how a published version of one might be presented to them – even if the thing presented is itself determined by an historically and culturally agreed definition, and that thing does not say a great deal about how it was created.

There are other creative writing artefacts that don't have strong public identities, and these are sources of much knowledge about creative writing. For example, if someone, say a poet, was to say, 'these are the notes I made while writing my last collection,' where would anyone, specialist or non-specialist, begin to contextualise the nature or formation of those notes? Certainly the physical appearance might be recognisable, in some general sense, and these notes could be related to published artefacts. But because these notes represent action, and because the action they represent is now passed, do we know with any certainty what role these notes once played?

The same could be said of such things as 'drafts', 'corrections', 'an email I sent to my friend about the short story I was working on', and so forth. These are not public artefacts – at least not in their making stages – and they may never become public artefacts. However, they are certainly artefacts produced in creative writing, and they are evidence of the event where pieces of creative writing came about, whether the work produced in that event is released now into the public realm or not. These artefacts are as much a part of creative writing as those works that emerge from creative writing and assume public identities. But it is the creative writer whose actions this artefactual evidence represents who is most connected to the purpose, intent and configuration of all those artefacts of creative writing.

Can we truly understand creative writing if it is only the public artefacts of creative writing that are examined? Can we understand it, and gain more knowledge about it, only after its evidence is released from the active involvement of the creative writer? Can we understand it if only works declared 'successful' are examined? And can we gain the best possible knowledge about creative writing if we don't consider the evidence that emerges from our own activities, even if many of those artefacts are our individual writer's artefacts unintended for public release?

In many cases, it will only be the creative writer's own needs that define the notes, the scribbles, the emails, and so on, that are produced during creative writing. Thus in key ways, what better place to look for evidence of creative writing?

None of this is to deny the importance of works released to the public, or to entirely dismiss the knowledge and interpretations of *post-event* critics of creative writing – that is, those who only approach the artefacts of creative writing after they are produced, or from outside the actions of creative writing. However, creative writing is such a combination of human activities that publicly released work can best be approached if it is understood as one element of evidence in a range of artefactual evidence that can be vast, that can even be decidedly idiosyncratic. Some methods of approaching the artefacts of creative writing are these:

- Considering generally what material is generated by you – as a creative writer – when producing your work or works of creative writing. What evidence of practice does the event of creative writing produce for you?
- Looking at the differences, or similarities, between evidence of original ideas, outpourings, notes along the way, and the final works, or works considered by you to be now complete;
- Archival research on other creative writers' artefacts. Because most items that are publicly archived will have been archived for reasons of cultural significance (an idea that can indeed reflect historically prevailing societal conditions), it is likely these artefacts will mostly have been produced by creative writers who have been culturally valued.

Again, these are just a few examples of approaches. Because the artefactual evidence of creative writing is so often spread over private and public realms, how an individual creative writer deals with exploring knowledge about their own events, and the evidence these activities leave behind, can be as individual as the writer themselves. The evidence produced by others, that you might approach, will often be subject to a variety of cultural, societal and economic filters before it reaches you. In addition, there is one school of thought that would suggest that in creative writing, as in many other fields, as soon as an individual is aware that they are considering their activities, and the artefacts produced by these activities, both activities and artefacts will be affected. Perhaps so! These are challenges for us to consider as creative writing continues to develop as a way of exploring what is around us and what is in our imaginations.

6 Not a conclusion

Firmly set conclusions about how a creative writer develops modes and methods of researching through creative writing, and about creative writing, would be magnificent. Or, perhaps, they would not be so magnificent at all! Perhaps they would merely show us that creative writing had little left to explore, little left to achieve. Of course, nothing could be further from the truth.

If the four avenues explored here – 1. Creative Writing Habitats 2. The Creative Domain; 3. Activities and 4. The Artefacts of Creative Writing – generate methods of researching some aspects of creative writing they do so primarily by posing questions, and those questions ask us to consider how best we might answer them. Simple enough, and yet significant in basing research methods in a philosophy of openness to exploring *what works most effectively*. Because creative writing is action, movement, making, then investigative methods also need to *recognise and endeavour to understand human action*. Because creative writing is decidedly individual as well as part of a wider societal and cultural spectrum, research methods are best placed when they show an appreciation of *the potential of individual human knowledge* to contribute to human knowledge generally. And because creative writing produces a wide variety of evidence, both events and results, the pursuit of answers to questions in, and about, creative writing gains veracity when evidence is approached actively in its many varieties.

Practice-led and critical research in creative writing continue to develop, largely in and around our universities and colleges. There is a great deal to explore, investigate and consider, by individual creative writers, by groups of creative writers, and through exchange and discussion. Those undertaking graduate degrees in creative writing are part of this exploration, and the evolution of graduate study in creative writing has contributed enormously to the pursuit and consideration of creative writing.

Being involved in creative writing will never *require* someone to be involved in practice-led or critical investigations in creative writing, just as being a creative writer will never *require* someone to be in university or college. The choice to undertake practice-led and/or critical research in creative writing is only one choice a creative writer might make. Certainly, more than one creative writer would declare that one of the greatest joys of creative writing is that it involves personal choices and comes from us personally. Therefore, perhaps the best way to conclude here is to say something in a decidedly personal register.

I believe researching through, and about creative writing has something significant to do with what Erik Erikson called generativity, meaning that it can offer some knowledge from which future generations will benefit. I don't say this arrogantly; rather, it simply *feels* as if there will be discoveries made by someone conducting practice-led or critical research in creative writing that will add notably to our shared human knowledge. This reference to feeling some might say undermines the research potential that I have outlined; yet, how often is it that human feeling determines thought and that thought then determines action? How important is feeling as a motivator, driver, or orchestrator of action, not always preceded by thought? So, to say it *feels* as if there will be discoveries made is not to weaken the case. Rather, it is to say one element of creative writing – that concerned with feeling – might well be one of the conductive strengths of researching through, and about, creative writing. More tendentiously, I believe practice-led and critical research in creative writing has the ability to produce new knowledge *about* creative writing, and that this new knowledge may be of use to me personally, as a creative writer.

None of this is a declaration that there is only one way, one route, or one research-focused reason to be involved in creative writing. But the sustainability of many human practices is best supported by us approaching them in many ways. Practice-led and critical research in creative writing is one of the ways we can support its future, one of the ways we can contribute to creative writing and one of the ways that creative writing can contribute to our world.

Exercises

1 Are creative events singular or is it possible to look at intersections of activity so that we might consider creative writing as a collection of smaller and larger actions? Consider the patterns of action in creative writing you have recently undertaken. What does this consideration reveal?

2 Observing your creative writing activities can you suggest some you would call 'primary' and some you would call 'complementary'? For example, you might say: 'The physical activity of writing this chapter of my new novel *The Watchmaker* is my primary activity. Complementing this is my reading about the history of timepieces.'

Notes

1 For an interesting discussion of the physical sciences and Sir Isaac Newton and the Romantic Movement, Keats and poetry see Julia L. Epstein and Mark L. Greenberg, 'Decomposing Newton's Rainbow', *Journal of the History of Ideas*, Vol. 45, No. 1, Jan.–Mar., 1984, pp. 115–40.

2 Graeme Harper, *On Creative Writing*, Multilingual Matters, 2010, p. 50.

3 Stephen J. Whitfield, 'Review of Becoming Erikson' in *Reviews in American History*, 28.1, (Mar., 2000): p. 134.

4 Fred G. Leebron, 'Not Knowing', in Frank Conroy, ed., *The Eleventh Draft: Craft and the Writing Life from the Iowa Writers Workshop*, New York: Harper Collins, 1999, p. 53.

The Generations of Creative Writing Research

5 Leebron, p. 52.
6 Stephanie Bunn, 'Creative Windows on Creativity: Association of Social Anthropologists Annual Conference', in *Anthropology Today*, 21.4 (Aug., 2005): p. 23.
7 R. Keith Sawyer, 'Writing as a Collaborative Act', in Scott Barry Kaufman and James C. Kaufman, eds, *The Psychology of Creative Writing*, New York: Cambridge University Press, 2009, p. 175.
8 Roger Scruton, 'Imagination', in David Cooper, ed., *A Companion to Aesthetics*, Oxford: Blackwell, 1995, p. 212.

Works cited

Bunn, Stephanie, 'Creative Windows on Creativity: Association of Social Anthropologists Annual Conference', in *Anthropology Today*, 21.4 (Aug., 2005): 22–3.
Conroy, Frank, ed., *The Eleventh Draft: Craft and the Writing Life from the Iowa Writers Workshop*, New York: Harper Collins, 1999.
Cooper, David, ed., *A Companion to Aesthetics*, Oxford: Blackwell, 1995.
Harper, Graeme, *On Creative Writing*, Bristol: Multilingual Matters, 2010.
Kaufman, Scott Barry and James C. Kaufman, eds, *The Psychology of Creative Writing*, New York: Cambridge University Press, 2009.
Whitfield, Stephen J. 'Review of Becoming Erikson', in *Reviews in American History*, Vol. 28.1 (March 2000): 134–41.

154

7 Forward, Wayward: The Writer in the World's Text, at Large

Katharine Coles

Chapter summary

All writing lives in intertextuality. That being the case, one of the most significant aspects of anyone's creative writing is its relationship with reading. What we read, how we read, for what purposes we read. The kinds of texts we find in the world bridge time and space, offer exchanges between one writer and another, between writers and readers. Researching for content brings about new knowledge just as it does in any other field – in the case of creative writing, of course, that content research might find its way into a poem or story, and that creative work may be a combination of personal voices as well as facts. This kind of research has knowledge value and this knowledge is such that it is certainly worthy of funding by organisations that fund research in and around academe, even if frequently it remains difficult to convince such funders of its value. Knowledge in creative writing is also not necessarily the knowledge found in other fields. It is the knowledge of two minds, that of the writer and that of the reader, actively engaging in exchange and in the kind of understanding that cannot be reduced to the abstract. All this can inform the teaching of creative writing, encourage and support individuality, and contribute to originality in the work that emerges from creative writing workshops and programmes.

1 Text and muse

Many undergraduates bring to my classroom one of two views of the writer. The first is connected to one of two mainstream lines still operative here in the United States two centuries after Wordsworth came onto the scene, so much so that we might think of ourselves as being still in the very long Romantic period. It persists in seeing the writer as one who 'wanders lonely as a cloud' until lightning strikes. She channels God, Nature, or the Muse through her body and imagination onto the page. She says, 'I only write when I'm inspired.'

The second is more explicitly tied to postmodern ideas of artistic making and is rooted in theories about language, but the young people coming into my classes are not necessarily aware of those ties, at least not yet. In this view, which they've developed through constant media exposure, the writer channels not only the muse but also texts of all kinds, language and images as they come to him already in use. A kind of gadfly for intertextuality (I am using the term in Kristeva's sense[1]), he plucks materials from one place and another, remixing them, often without regard for the quality of the source or, any more than the first writer, the quality of his own production. In this age of pastiche, he may be aware that the source of his work is not inside but outside himself and that he is engaging in a specific artistic practice, but he may not. Having not yet considered questions about what art and originality are, or whether they exist as such, he might, like the first kind of writer, think what he's doing is simply what making art is.

Though we may see practitioners in these two camps as ideologically and aesthetically opposed, both position writers as naïfs, not only in relation to themselves and their processes but also in relation to the world. Neither accounts much for intention, consciousness, or awareness that one is making something meant to engage a reader; even less do the camps account for hard labour or the concentrated research so many of us undergo in creating our own work. For the view of the writer as a sort of innocent channeler of experience is not that much different from that of the writer as a channeler of language or an equally intuitive creator of pastiche – the work can, and will, come from anywhere at all.

It doesn't seem odd to me that so many young writers hold one of these views. They may still be blithely unaware that art demands discipline and sustained attention.: the willingness and ability to, as Michael Ventura[2] says, 'sit alone in a room for years', not waiting for lightning to strike but making error upon error, learning to see those errors, and, one hopes, correcting them in one long, sustained series of experiments. Too often in US high schools, art, especially creative writing, which tends to be taught by 'specialists' trained a little in literature and mostly in child development and pedagogy, is taught as having self-expression as its primary goal. Like teaching art in a formulaic, 'paint-by-numbers' way, this approach has the advantage for teachers that it doesn't require them to make aesthetic judgements or teach techniques they may not have mastered. But, as a result, young writers often think of writing as being primarily about the writer rather than about the reader, about creating an experience for oneself and perhaps one's friends rather than about creating a complex experience or expression for an unfamiliar other to enter and take on.

I do find it peculiar that many very good writers I can think of continue to hold these views of the writer into maturity. But writing is a mysterious process the very mysteriousness of which can feel useful or empowering and so become something a writer holds onto. Thus, when we talk about our 'research', even when our work is focused on engaging other texts (and I will take a broad view of textuality in this essay), we can have trouble articulating just what we mean. Yes, intuition, the feeling that seems to lead one stumbling into ideas grander and larger than one's own capacity, is a huge part of any writer's work. But the best intuition is not blind, and it doesn't come from nowhere. It comes through reading and study of texts of all kinds; it is trained, honed, and brought to fruition through work and hard-won technique.

In this, writing is like learning to do anything else. I consider this example from James McMullan's excellent series on learning to draw currently being published on the New York Times web site, NYTimes. com. The particular article it's drawn from, published 24 September 2010, is called 'The Frisbee of Art':[3]

Much of what you are practicing in learning to draw is engaging your fine motor skills in this way, so that the hand moves to do your bidding without a 'controlling' space between deciding to make a particular line and the hand moving to do it. Before this kind of almost simultaneous cooperation between your brain and your hand occurs, you will tend to worry the line out in slow incremental steps. In this hand-eye coordination, drawing is an athletic activity that benefits from practice, like golf or tennis.

Drawing relies on eye and wrist to translate the visible world onto the page. Writing uses eye and mind to make various worlds – textual, historical, intellectual, physical – into imagined ones. This requires practice, which requires the constant action of the mind on those worlds. To rely on intuition as if it were some magical thing, or even to pretend we do, is lazy. Research is what we do to court intuition and to make ourselves ready for when it comes. It is how we improve our equivalent of hand-eye coordination, our discipline.

2   Kinds of texts and how we find them

For the last week, I have been reading a city. Tombs and churches. Ruins and fortresses, paintings and glosses. At the Orto Botanico, the sign outside the glass house tells me it was first 'dressed' in 1800. *Realizzata*, the Italian says. But this, for the moment, is the rare set of words that demands my attention – those that do are mostly not in English, and my own translations are not nearly as charming as this one. I have not been reading, exactly; I have been living on the skins of my eyes, looking and looking.

I am lucky enough to be in Rome. A research grant from the University of Utah paid for my trip. The promised product: poems. I got the grant by promising to engage images, history, and ideas. I argued (and believe) that I needed to make this engagement by putting myself into the presence of certain works of art, *texts*, not through photographs or reproductions but in person – that is, in *context*. This is a pleasure, but it is also a discipline: to make a promise, in the face of all distraction, and travel to keep it, then go home and sit alone in my room repeating and refining my errors for as long as it takes.

All writing, poetry especially but not only poetry, lives in intertextuality. In this, postmodernists are certainly right. Every poem engages some other poem, and through it some body of poems, even if it does so through denial or takes as its overt subject the drinking of a cup of coffee, perhaps while watching sheep browse the meadow next door.

For every sheep in every poem engages all previous poetic sheep. And poetry has over the centuries piled up a large number of them. Then there is the poetry of meadows and pastures, of the specific plants the sheep may be identified as ruminating – maybe only grass, which grows rampant in poetry. Think of Wordsworth, of Whitman, of all that greenery. Think of that word, 'ruminating', which poems are full of, and which leads the poet over her coffee into her own ruminations.

I am not in Italy to engage words and poems, though I can't help doing so. Previous discipline, years of preparation for this and other projects, have conditioned my brain for this, have developed neural pathways that run straight into poetry. In Naples, I visited Virgil's purported gravesite and wrote, of course, a poem, for which I quote Dante quoting the Virgil he invented: *Pay them no mind.* Dante's poem is as much about intertextuality as grudges, politics, and desire. How not? It is about Dante and his own neural pathways.

Before I go, I Google 'intertextuality' + 'poetry'. Google is now something my mind reaches for as automatically as the artist's hand reaches for his pencil. I use it to begin every foray into research, to follow my first intuitions without ever leaving my room. I find essays and posts on poetry and painting, poetry and music, poetry and on-line videos. Hardly anything on poetry and texts, which seems odd in one way but not in another. Poetry and literary prose engage multiple texts inherently by using words. They are so grubby, words, carrying with them every meaning they've ever rubbed against, travelling in a dust storm of usages and implications, like Pigpen from the Peanuts comics. But literary works also engage – as inevitably – other arts as well. Writers work by ear, out of a sense of music. And they work in images, often invoking specific paintings, deploying techniques they learn from looking at art. Like our mosaicists, the ones from Italy, who learnt from the Greeks and adapted what they'd learnt. Or, on the other side, those in Ravenna who learnt from Byzantium. Wherever there is the trading of goods, there is the trading of culture. Those sheep – this poem doesn't exist, mind; I am making it up as we go – invoke a whole history of images, back to the Romans and Greeks. There are a lot of pastoral paintings out there. Our sheep recall their sheep.

So I graze and ruminate, first in my little room with its real windows and its virtual one, and now here. I have an idea that I have to be here, Michael Ventura and my little room notwithstanding, present in these places, seeing what earlier travellers saw and also what they made from what they saw. Google is much, but not sufficient. I am in Italy to see in person its mosaics and frescoes, particularly mosaics and frescoes of animals, and to put myself physically under their sway. It may be a kind of superstition, the feeling I need to do this, but in fact it works. I've been to Venice and Istanbul and, on my own dime in younger days, to Greece and Ravenna. I will finish with Morocco and Lebanon, after a detour to Antarctica on another project. I am pursuing that idea I mentioned, perhaps cockeyed, about how images were traded, along with techniques, across oceans and centuries along the same routes taken by traders in goods. The Greek mosaicists imported to Pompeii and Herculaneum carried in their minds' eyes stores of animals, literal and fanciful. The pictures in their heads and the skill of their hands made them valuable. Was it a Greek artist who lay Neptune into that floor, twisting his legs like eels into fins where feet should be? If so, did he call the god Neptune or Poseidon? Later, someone, *someones*, in Constantinople, Ravenna, Rome will move the human to centre – or, rather, another God, briefly human as Poseidon never could be, who is painted as human but whose divinity is read in signs. A look of endless patience, a raised hand, a halo. I need to be here to know it.

I digress. That's what comes of being here and of letting *here* send me elsewhere – a kind of discipline and a kind of freedom. It can't be that the same artist painted all those fanciful birds on the walls at Herculaneum and Pompeii, can it? They are all in the style of the third period, and 60 odd years is a good long time to work, but there are hundreds. With my iPhone I snap pictures – taking notes. Artists talk to each other across time and space, saying, Look at the way I curl this tail, this wing. Look at what I took and look at what I made. Becoming, together, immortal.

3   If you want to write, read

So we say to young writers. When I was young, I took this to mean I must examine Great Works for their Techniques, which I was then to practice and adapt. And so I read, but as often as not with a kind of dreaming passion, as I hope my students allow themselves to read now, whatever other kinds of discipline I may enforce in class and in papers. Yes, discipline enforced by others helped me harness and focus my attention; then, when something really caught me, I responded by writing poems or stories, not direct responses so much as gestures and echoes, moments of trying on words and rhythms, quirks of syntax or imagery. Did I absorb technique along the way? Of course. Sometimes consciously, always on purpose, the reading and dreaming themselves purposeful. I seethed with jealousy, thought about how to steal, asked, How did that writer do that? Occasionally, I thought I had figured some of it out. Much of what I absorbed I didn't figure out or know how to use until years later, as when Virgil came to me in Naples, channelled by Dante. Give the brain something to chew on, and it will.

Writers do read in conscious ways, to learn technique; more often a writer reads to give the brain something to ruminate over, to create or enrich an interior life and from that to construct voice. Then to deconstruct it, construct it again. We used to talk about young writers 'finding' their voices, as if voices (like Romantic poems) lay hidden inside them somewhere, locked in magic boxes, and if they rummaged around in their own chests long enough they would eventually produce them. It can seem that way when we produce a paragraph or a poem that *feels like it sounds like us*. But really our voices are made up of other voices, voices we've read and absorbed into our sense of 'the literary', of what a story or a poem sounds like, which we at once capitulate to and resist in an effort to find out what *our own* stories or poems sound like. Writers who become really good develop from this process voices identifiably their own, voices you and I would know anywhere. Really strong writers – their voices become part of the great voice from which we all draw, as Eliot and Stevens tell us. Our voices continue to evolve if we work hard and with intention; our reading continues to feed them. I would like to be one of the really strong writers, but the odds are not in my favour.

Still, there is nothing else to do but to read and read (*Draw, Antonio, Draw!* wrote Michelangelo to a student, but he also meant *Look, look!* – and so do I), widely and consciously: Dante, Austen, Burroughs, Yeats, the Flarf poets; Darwin, Einstein, Da Vinci, Levi-Strauss. And we must try not to read only writers who seem to echo voices within us, but to stretch and challenge our ears and minds. I knew little of mosaics and frescos before writing a grant proposal that had to pass muster with art historians. If we imagine, as I do, that 'a voice' is a kind of toolkit, full of hammers and screw-drivers and clever clamps of different sizes – full, that is, of our words and all the different methods we have for putting them happily together – then the more widely we've read the more tools we have in the box and the more likely we are, when we reach in there, to find something useful has come to hand.

The more tools we have, the more language we have, and the more ideas. As we all know, language and ideas cannot be teased apart. If a writer really knows what the space-time continuum is or can understand the new thinking about the sex lives of truffles, if he knows that truffles have sex lives and can use the words that describe them authentically, his landscape of ideas, his reality, is larger than if he doesn't. It really is that simple.

4 Text and content

Is it becoming fashionable again to talk about content as well as about technique? I hope so. Romantic channelling and post-modern grab-bagging relieve us, in a way, of responsibility to content – and also, maybe, to technique. We speak, or mix, and content and tech-nique seem to appear. If we're good, if we have some innate talent or facility, this is true, as far as it goes. Intuition might carry us a long way, even an intuition that is not as disciplined as it might be. But here again, we have to watch ourselves. Garbage in, garbage out, as the saying goes. And, I'd argue, not enough in, with not enough consciousness, not enough out, or not good enough out. If we care about content, if we care about technique, research is how we get to both. Can this be as simple as 'concentrated attention to reality, both of literary worlds and the worlds laid, like our old friend Neptune, at our feet'?

I am not talking about the kind of research a scientist does, or even an historian or literary scholar. Though the scientific method applied in the plodding way we all learnt in secondary school is far from what happens in science, thank goodness, where intuition of the wildest kind has almost a sacred place, or indeed in textual research, what the writer does is still different in kind. Yes, the writer is responsible to the world of facts. They are to her a subordinate kind of content; thus, to find and reveal them may be one goal but is not her ultimate goal. Rather, she works with and through facts to other forms of truth, of knowledge, no less valid. If I run fast and loose with my terms, I wish not to provide an analysis of ongoing epistemological arguments but to say something, I hope, of practical use.

The importance of research is clear for someone writing an historical or science fiction novel. Here, facts are indeed of the highest importance. In order to be merely credible, this writer might have to have place names right or know when the zipper was invented or understand how certain laws of science work. Otherwise, he risks creating some anachronism that jolts the reader out of the text. Perhaps somewhat weirdly, respect for writers in these genres, as long as their work is genre bound, is often nonetheless begrudged by members of grant and tenure committees, even though their own members spend much of their lives pursuing facts. Such research on the part of a writer may be practical but is still not seen as scholarly, in that, while it may unearth facts, it does not always seek to create new knowledge or new interpretations of the facts. Beyond this, committee members from other disciplines might not consider factual research to be part of a writer's work. Rather, they may consider writers to be not people who, as Keats says, engage in 'irritable reaching after fact & reason', but rather inspired magicians. So the poor grant-writing writer lands between a rock and a hard place. If she puts her nose to the grindstone and addresses herself to the hard world of facts, she may be seen as a mere technician. If he writes vague and airy proposals insisting that he must spend March in Italy soaking up atmosphere so that he can spend April in a trance of inspiration, he won't get far either. How do we convince other scholars both that the work we do really is research and that we really are writers in the way they want to imagine us (and, perhaps, in the way we want to imagine ourselves)?

Think of the great works that have necessitated and emerged from historical and factual research. They achieve their greatness, like great works of other genres, including the one we call 'literary', not by piling up facts but by working through facts in the way I spoke of before. Also, I think, by working through texts. When I was writing poems about particle physics, I read everything I could get my hands on – primary texts and, when those made my head hurt, books for the layperson, which I am. I checked facts and details with scientists, including my husband, whose PhD is in physics and who, conveniently, does interdisciplinary work involving the brain and heart, fire and explosions, the universe, and other complex systems, everything that fascinates me. I even revisited my old maths training. And I began a symposium in science and literature that brings scientists and writers together around topics of mutual interest. My excuse was that this would enrich the intellectual community, and I hope it has, but my secret motive was that I wanted to understand how scientists thought about issues and ideas that also mattered to me. I have learnt many practical things and squirrelled away hard facts to last more lifetimes than I have. I reach for them regularly. And when I turn to writing the poems, the epigraphs I choose, the conversations I remember, the books I return to, take me because they are beautiful, both in their concepts and in their words. Their language, like the birds on those ancient walls, becomes a vehicle for dreaming about ideas.

Later, researching a book about my grandparents – he was an explorer, she a wayward flapper – I learnt how to use a plane table and alidade, and I thought about how barometers are real tools and metaphors. I read dry cultural and social histories of Indonesia, the Caribbean, and South America and books on geology and mapping, but also Baedecker's travel guides from the 1920s and 30s; travel memoirs (*Through the Brazilian Wilderness* by Theodore Roosevelt and the equally compelling account of the same journey by Candace Millard, *River of Doubt: Theodore Roosevelt's Darkest Journey*); *Triste Tropiques* by Levi-Strauss; novels, obsessively – Forster and Maugham because, according to the journals, my grandparents were reading them. I stuffed myself with facts, but the books that mattered most also set my dreaming in motion.

Perhaps most importantly, I travelled. For the memoir, to Indonesia and Cuba, where I saw the houses where my grandparents had lived. I stayed in the same bungalow at a remote mountain resort in Java where my grandmother had launched at least one love affair and in the room at the Singapore Raffles where my grandfather first confronted her about her infidelities. I travelled up the Amazon in a small boat and swam with piranhas and pink freshwater dolphins, which, according to legend, lure beautiful women away from their homes. I sat in the corner of the Havana Biltmore Country Club where my mother, at fourteen, received her first kiss and my grandmother danced her way into the final affair that would end her marriage to my grandfather. Through it all, I wore the jade ring her lover had given her.

All this was essential, not just to my 'experience' but to my ability to work intertextually, to move back and forth between, and to make meaning of, the various kinds of texts, written and other, I was engaging. The book, which is long and messy and not yet published, is without question, and unexpectedly, the most intertextual book I have written. I began by thinking I would turn their journals and letters into a narrative, in my words, jazzed up with the 'flavor' I acquired from my reading and travels. But my grandfather wrote, *There is no map. We will make our own.* My grandmother hid her story in and around the edges of her journals, which she used to justify the ways of herself to herself. And they spoke to each other by trading books, sometimes underlined, sometimes annotated. Du Maupassant's *A Woman's Life*, for example. And I found myself refusing to paraphrase them, wanting them to speak as much as possible for themselves. *Burnt Letters* became not just a story of betrayal played out against the backdrop of U.S. economic imperialism but a vehicle for channelling two voices through one sensibility, mine. I picked and chose, bridged and wove, and inserted myself into the narrative, wondering, commenting, judging. When I sat in the night-time garden of that mountain resort on Java, listening to the monkeys call outside the bungalow where my grandmother stayed while falling in love with a Dutch pilot, the voices I used to describe the scene are mine and hers together. They are my content.

5   The importance of losing your way

I am making notes for this essay, standing in the ruins of the Baths of Caracalla typing into my phone. The roof is caved in, but the walls are more or less intact, as are a few of the floors. Mostly the mosaics are propped in fragments against the walls. Here, a human figure riding a beast with the twisted tail of a fish (that tail again). The front of the animal is missing. It could be anything, within certain parameters. Also missing is the rider's rein hand, but not his whip hand. Over here is the head of what I first think is a dog then decide is a bull.

The baths are not on my itinerary. I am here because I want to see one mosaic in a tiny church nearby. This month, the church is supposed to be open today only from 4:30 to 5:30 p.m. When I arrive at 4:35, the door is locked tight. Being here on someone else's money, I don't want to stand and wait. I see, just yards away, the entrance to the baths. I'll spend twenty or thirty minutes in there, I think, then try again.

While I am in the baths, I get some images, some ideas, for the poems I am working on. I see the tail that echoes the Neptune I saw in Herculaneum. I am, serendipitously, doing my research. Thinking about doing my research, I begin to think about this essay, which is underway but stalled, feeling dry and dusty. Until now.

When, a half-hour later, I find the church still locked, I am not dismayed. It is only 5:10; if the caretaker did appear in my absence – I imagine an ancient, bent-backed priest, but who knows? – he didn't stay long.

I might have marked this visit in the 'failed' category. But I don't.

6 Is there help for us?

When I got my assignment, the title of this book was *Research Techniques in Creative Writing*. If it still is, I can so far be seen to have woefully failed to do what I was implicitly asked, to lay out an orderly system by which writers might deploy intertextuality as a research method. I may have been given this assignment because my writing, both poems and prose, is more or less visibly full of Subjects that have, yes, required me to do Research, involving Texts of conventional and other kinds. At times, my poems have been (perhaps irritatingly) festooned with epigraphs.

Order and system have virtues. They give one a clear path to follow both in the work and, perhaps more importantly, in making a compelling case that what writers do is real research and thus deserves institutional support. For the question is, How do we convince the powers-that-be in our various institutions that this is research a) that we need to do, b) that will benefit our institutions, and c) that they therefore need first to fund and second to reward us for having done? Many of our institutions define 'research' in a way that is foreign to us, certainly different than the process I've described as my own. Funds tend to be granted not for what we need (time, travel) but for things that can be enumerated and priced by the piece (post-doctoral students, beakers).

I would argue that the task is not to convince committee members and Deans that what we do is just like what others do (even if what others do isn't quite as they describe it). The task is to help committee members, even those in scientific and scholarly disciplines, understand what we actually do and make a compelling case that it is worthy of support as an activity that generates valuable if not always immediately useful knowledge and also, perhaps, glory for the institution. Relativity, after all, wasn't immediately useful. And most people, even many physicists, have read more Dickens than Newton. But it can be difficult to talk about how art, as valuable as it is, generates knowledge.

We are not like the physicians, who can run experiments that tell us through meticulous comparison that one drug protocol is more effective than another in fighting heart disease; unlike historians, we don't sleuth out the dusty existence of never-before-seen letters that cast new light on the beginning of World War II. Such research represents knowledge in a particular way, as something patently useful. Our knowledge, on the other hand, is generated between two active minds at play: that of the writer, who creates a new world for her own pleasure and the pleasure of others, and that of the reader, who enters into that world, both for pleasure and for the kind of understanding that cannot be reduced to an abstract. The experiment is in one sense repeatable – we are still reading the Odyssey; Dickinson's poems still take the tops of our heads off – but its results cannot be precisely predicted, since they depend entirely on the movement of the new, individual mind coming into the made text and reshaping both the text and itself in the process. It does not claim that its protocol will work in a given way for a given percentage of people a given percentage of the time; it is not directed at the collective but at the individual, over and over again. The experience and knowledge generated from contact with a literary text is *never*, from one encounter to the next, precisely the same knowledge. And it cannot be gotten any other way, cannot be digested for us and re-presented in another form. Thus, it is strangely unmeasurable. Still, it is essential. It helps us develop flexibility, empathy, imagination, the capacity for wonder. It makes us larger inside. It makes us more, and better, ourselves.

Getting support for the book about my grandparents wasn't difficult, probably because it engages topics inherently interesting to academics, including science but also American imperialism and corporate mayhem. I did enough work in advance to develop an extensive bibliography, bibliographies being compelling to academics as well as actually useful to me, but groundwork for the proposal involved mostly reading enough family diaries and letters to give my project, and my prose, spice. These documents gave me enough material to make the case for where I had to go and what I had to see to bring my story to life, to give it the texture of detail.

The Italy/Turkey/North Africa mosaic funds were a different matter, like the funds for the scientific poetry project, for which

I travelled to Kepler's house and Newton's, to anatomical theatres and Linneas's garden – and like also my recently funded National Science Foundation grant to write poems in Antarctica. It's harder to make the case for poems, since they are widely understood to have no utility. In each event, I had to do substantial research before writing the proposals to acquaint myself sufficiently with the histories of the sites I was visiting and what I would find there. For the mosaic project, I had to rewrite the proposal to satisfy an art historian on the panel who wanted me to touch on a specific area in the history of mosaic. This delayed me and made me irritable, since I thought the question itself was irrelevant to my project, but the additional research sent me to useful books and web sites I hadn't come across and gave me vocabulary I didn't have before.

It's also hard, especially with poetry but also with literary prose, to talk about methodology in an honest yet compelling way. A writer can't set up a scientific protocol to be followed precisely, as in the case of testing the effectiveness of one medicine against another; unlike the historian, she may not be trying to find a specific thing, that letter she suspects exists in a given archive. Since she often relies on guided intuition, she might most truthfully write something like, 'I will go to these places. I will stand in them and look, listen, and think hard. I will write poems.' But we can't write this. So we must instead, at least, show intellectual preparedness – that our intuition really has been shaped and guided as much as it can be in advance. Preparation forestalls accusations of mushiness and gives us leeway, I think, to be forthright about the ambiguity of the process and the role of intuition in our work, as well as the impossibility of precisely describing an outcome in advance of achieving it.

I don't want to give the impression that I think other kinds of researchers really are aliens, or that we must be alien to them. Here is where I think honesty about what we do and are might in fact help us. A little earlier, I mentioned a grant from the National Science Foundation, which will be sending me to Antarctica as part of its Antarctic Artists and Writers Program. Space in the programme is very limited, and the proposal was a particular challenge, especially since it was for poetry, not prose, and since the selection committee is always made up of people from across the scientific as well as the artistic disciplines. The most difficult question in the application asked how my project would illustrate and bring attention to Antarctic research programmes, not a goal I generally consider to fall under the purview of poetry. I had arranged partnerships with and letters of support from a museum, an arts council, and a publisher, so I was able to demonstrate that I was labouring to get the work out and noticed. Still, thinking I was killing my chances at a grant, I answered honestly that my poems are not really illustrative, that my primary goal was to write poems of the highest literary quality, and that, as compared to film, photography, and even literary prose, poems don't generally have a broad reach. I went on to say, however, that I wanted to use the poems to 'explore and to reveal the sense that science, like all artifacts of human culture and intelligence, is a fundamentally human endeavor, driven by the humanity and passion of its practitioners'. I believe this and have been meditating on it in my work for some time. The scientists on the panel apparently agreed and embraced this as a worthwhile effort, perhaps even an effort in which they could see themselves.

Which brings me to actual advice for preparing grant proposals:

1 Think about how your work intersects with other disciplines and how you might naturally extend your work to require research in those disciplines.
2 Be prepared to prove, through advance research and preparation, that you are up to the challenges of your project.
3 Generate a clear statement about (a) how literary work contributes to and enhances knowledge and (b) what specific additional knowledge you are creating and/or contributing on the given project. Make sure you define your use of the word 'knowledge' to include the factual, the experiential, and the epistemological. This is easier for some projects than others.
4 Articulate not what you think the travel or research will do for you, personally or as an artist, in terms of enrichment, etc., but, as explicitly as possible, (a) why it is essential to the work, and (b) how the work enhances the mission of the granting body and/or institution.

5 If possible, point out instances in which, in or near your specific area of focus, creative works have influenced thinking in other fields.
6 Be truthful and clear about your research and writing process, acknowledging the role of intuition and chance while emphasising both the work you've done to prepare for this project and your track record and experience in turning research into literary works.
7 Play to your strength: your writing. Do not descend into bureaucratic prose, even if you think it will help your case. You have the chance to demonstrate in the prose of your proposal that you have literary skill and that the members of the committee will actually want to read what you write. Do what you do: engage them, emotionally as well as intellectually.
8 Don't dismiss what other experts have to say. If you are asked to rewrite your proposal to address specific questions, do so thoroughly.
9 Do not try to game the system. There are often smart people sitting on grant committees, and they will know they're being gamed and reasonably object.

I am told that academic funding for creative projects in many countries, including the UK and Australia, is still in its nascency. As a pathological optimist, I encourage writers in countries where the struggle to gain funding is still in early stages to apply for everything they seem to qualify for. We need to make an ongoing case that our work contributes to human and even to academic knowledge. At some point, a committee may be sympathetic and give a writer a grant. Then the proverbial nose is under the tent.

7 Intertextuality and teaching

In the US, creative writing workshops have been criticised for creating a flatness or sameness among their students. If they've done so, this represents not a failure but a success. Most programmes accept and educate both applicants who demonstrate at an early stage imagination, originality, and independence and liveliness of mind and thus relieve us from the responsibility of trying to teach them these things, and applicants who are simply promising. Good programmes won't beat the individuality out of students who arrive with it. Knowledge and skill are hardly inimical to individuality; rather the opposite. No more will they inculcate originality into every student who arrives without its visible sign. But they will enable even the least of them to achieve a level of competence they would not have on their own. Students will learn to construct plausible voices, but not always distinct ones. We can complain about this, but is it really a sign of end times if we actually make people better writers, as we promise to do? That they may become good enough to publish and so irritate others is the proper concern not of teachers but of the publishing industry and critics.

But as teachers we must model and teach original thinking, both to help our best students become at once more disciplined and more free and to give the others a real chance, too. I never know what will break something loose in a student who seems destined to be only ordinary or a little better. Theresa Amabile in her *Creativity in Context: Update to the Social Psychology of Creativity*[4] discusses studies showing that creativity can be modelled and learnt. According to more than one study, students given the chance to work with Nobel Laureates and other exceptionally creative people are more likely to learn to think, work, and judge performance like their mentors and so to work at high levels themselves; in fact, people who have studied and worked with Nobel Laureates are more likely to become Nobel Laureates. Cause-and-effect can be hard to determine, but the evidence is that creativity can be modelled and learnt.

This is good news for us all.

Exercises

I *Let it go and mix it up* (research exploration for writers and their students)

Carry a notebook. Whenever something you read and see in novels, poems, newspapers, magazines, on line, on your iPod music list, etc., attracts your attention, make a note. Remember to engage high and low culture; if you work on line, gather sound and video as well as text and image.

Meanwhile, begin and maintain a lively collection of oddities. For me, these include dictionaries (of saints, angels, art, science, music, mathematics, poetic terms and forms, dances, philosophy, etc.) and other reference books (guides to firearms, field guides); picture postcards; and flash cards from the 'Forgotten English' series.

Put your gatherings in a dedicated folder. When you are ready to work, make a piece comprising bits and pieces from the folder. As you rework, look for connections and links, perhaps using words that crop up in various places or visual images that have echoes in song lyrics, working with disjunction and disunity as well as with unity. Whether the result is electronic or physical (a collage, or an artist's book) include both text and images. In the end, try to produce something that feels serendipitous, not arbitrary – and that, though it's constructed from outside materials, has taken on the shape of your mind and voice.

2 *Mini research project* (research exploration for writers and their students)

Identify a topic of interest – sheep, say. Outline a short-term research project you can undertake over two or three weeks. The project should engage various texts (historical or factual, literary, visual, musical, etc.) and involve at least one field trip. Take notes, attending to both the factual and the lyrical, meditative, and imagistic. From them, create a poem or a prose piece. Avoid going for obvious unity and conclusions. Use white space and links across it to connect ideas, images, and fragments of language.

3 *Aiming to fail* (research exploration for writers and their students)

Plan a piece of writing for which you design a research programme involving a complicated field trip, during which you must perform a series of tasks complex or chancy enough that at least one will probably fail. Find a way to use the failure in the piece.

Notes

1 Julia Kristeva, 'Word, Dialogue and Novel', Trans. Alice Jardine, Thomas Gora, and Leon S. Roudiez. Ed. Toril Moi. *The Kristeva Reader*. New York: Columbia University Press, 1986. 34–61.
2 Michael Ventura, 'The Talent of the Room', *LA Weekly*, 21–7 May 1993.
3 James McMullan, 'The Frisbee of Art', *NYTimes.com*, 24 September 2010. http://opinionator.blogs.nytimes.com/2010/09/23/the-frisbee-of-art/?th&emc=th
4 Theresa Amabile, *Creativity in Context: Update to the Social Psychology of Creativity*. Boulder, CO: Westview Press, 1996.

Works cited

Amabile, Teresa. *Creativity in Context, Update to the Social Psychology of Creativity*. Boulder, CO; Oxford, UK: Westview Press, 1996.
Kristeva, Julia. 'Word, Dialogue and Novel', Trans. Alice Jardine, Thomas Gora, and Leon S. Roudiez. Ed. Toril Moi. *The Kristeva Reader*. New York: Columbia University Press, 1986. 34–61.
McMullan, James. 'The Frisbee of Art', NYTimes.com, 24 September 2010. Online. http://opinionator.blogs.nytimes.com/2010/09/23/the-frisbee-of-art/?th&emc=th
Ventura, Michael. 'The Talent of the Room', *LA Weekly*, 21–7 May 1993.
Weingarten, Roger. 'The Party of the Century' in *The Practice of Poetry*, Robin Behn and Chase Twichell, eds, New York: Harper Paperbacks, 1992.

8 Creative Writing and Theory: Theory without Credentials

Dominique Hecq

Chapter summary

Theory has been dead for well over a decade. But what was/is theory? And what lessons can we learn from its apparent demise? This chapter reassesses the significance of theory for creative writing research. It argues against a favouritism towards any one theory, for there are special affinities between creative writing and certain theories, particularly those underpinned by poststructuralist theories of language. This is partly because creative writers read and research differently from theorists and critics. While many theories highlight the textual specificity of creative writing research, they also highlight that, at its core, the object of creative writing inquiry is twofold, namely *process* and *processor*.

By focusing on the case of psychoanalysis, this chapter argues for a privileging of a 'theory without credentials', one that would disrupt our certainties and thus open up creative possibilities that can in turn be theorised. A psychoanalytic understanding of subjectivity sheds light on the creative process and on the very concept of knowledge production in ways that are not envisioned by other models of subjectivity. Conversely, an examination of writing and research processes can help illuminate and expand on psychoanalytic understandings of subjectivity. Psychoanalysis is useful in that it suggests that both writing and the subject are constructions *in the making*. This has direct pedagogical implications: by grappling with the theory itself, new teaching methods and methodologies arise.

Most of the objections to theory are either false or fairly trifling. A far more devastating criticism of it can be launched
— Terry Eagleton, *After Theory*, p. 11

The most productive locus of mutual illumination for education, writing, and psychoanalysis is the writing subject
— Mark Bracher, *Radical Pedagogy*, p. 17

I am not a poet, but a poem. A poem that is being written, even if it looks like a subject
— Jacques Lacan, *Seminar XI*, p. 9

I Why theory?

Theory is dead. Long live Theory! As a 'moment'[1] imbued with its own momentum, 'Theory' refers to a series of intellectual and cultural developments that began to evolve within the university discourse in continental Europe in the mid 1960s even though the philosophical premises and ideological foundations underpinning it have a much longer history, and indeed, continue into the present well beyond the borders of geography and scholarly disciplines. Theory with a capital T then refers to that period of 'high theory' of the 1960s and 1970s which saw society as the undesirable product of the Enlightenment. Rumours about the death of Theory reach back to the early nineties and were probably initiated by Theory itself. I am speaking in particular of Jean-François Lyotard's prophecy about the death of the 'grand narratives', those large-scale theories and philosophies of the world such as the progress of history, for example.[2] Thinkers as versatile as Pierre Bourdieu,[3] Valentine Cunningham[4] and Terry Eagleton[5] are among those who wrote about this seemingly opportune death, anticipating the richer topos of 'after theory'. Michael Payne and John Schad have considered this state of affairs with some scepticism in their *life.after.theory*.[6] More recently, some commentators have welcomed this passing, damning the 'damaging effects [of] a certain kind of poststructuralist or post-modernist theorising'[7] or the philosophical and aesthetic problems that arise in connection with the appreciation and evaluation of literature, professing theory 'deadly in its consequences'.[8] Others have attempted to 'revive' it in specific areas of critical enquiry.[9] Fascinating though it might be, however, it is not my intention to engage in the ongoing debate about the death of theory, for its arguments are now familiar in both utopian and dystopian forms. My intention is rather to focus on the possible affinities between theory (without the capital 't') and creative writing.

I am struck by the irony of opening a chapter on the possible affinities between creative writing and theory by proclaiming the death of Theory, no less because theory has traditionally encountered some resistance with creative writing teachers, students and practitioners, particularly in English departments. In Australia, Paul Dawson contextualises this resistance in his analysis of the 1990s Literary Studies crisis and explains this resistance in terms of an artificial split between theory and practice, or professional writing and literary criticism, which originated in the advent of creative writing as a series of pedagogic responses to a long[er]-standing crisis in Literary Studies.[10] This resistance has surfaced again and again in the ongoing debate concerning whether creative writing needs to bother at all with theory, a debate that goes back to over ten years ago, that is, before Nigel Krauth and Tess Brady formulated the question at the core of their book: 'Is there a creative writing theory?'[11] As we know, the debate is now exacerbated by creative writing's need to define what research means by comparison and contrast with the 'hard sciences' in the academy and corporate university.

Nonetheless, Dawson's exhortation that 'creative writing needs to answer the critique of authorship and of the category of literature offered by Theory, rather than simply rejecting this critique as unhelpful or deleterious to literary culture'[12] is no less relevant today. This is because writing presupposes 'an active engagement with knowledge producing creative results that *embody* levels of understanding and communication'[13] that require to be *articulated* for the sake of sustenance, expansion and contribution to knowledge. As the third section of this chapter suggests, the knowledge at stake might be of a different order for creative writers, though by no means incompatible with the kind of knowledge as traditionally understood by the discourse of the university. It might indeed fit in quite well within this discourse as 'identities interpenetrate and reflect upon practice'[14] while adhering to imperatives of an ethical or ontological nature.

It is probable, however, that in Practice-led Research or Research-led Practice, two activities that are often complementary,[15] the emphasis is on data creation rather than data collection, where research and practice are reciprocal. For Brad Haseman, 'both the artwork itself and the surrounding practices *are* research'.[16] But as Camilla Nelson points out, one of the major differences between creative writing and 'other disciplines or "interdisciplines" is the premium it places on process'.[17] At the risk of promoting navel-gazing, I would add that, consequently, another major difference is the emphasis on '*processor*'. Thus before even attempting to define what theory, research, knowledge, or methodology might mean for creative writers, I would like to suggest that the object of creative writing inquiry is primarily twofold, namely the *creative process* and the *subject in the process of writing*. Mike Harris offers a clipped definition of the process as 'everything that happens to a work before it is "finished"'. This would include thinking, researching, planning, writing drafts, consciously revising, consciously manipulating the unconscious and being unconsciously driven by it'.[18] What interests me in this *process*, though, is first how one accesses the unconscious and second how one 'consciously' manipulates it. Though I understand that it becomes rather tricky when the *processor* is a collective, as for example in the case of a collaboration, for the purposes of this discussion the processor is merely *the subject writing*. In my view, writing is the least overtly collaborative of all creative acts.

2 What was/is theory?

As a general term, *theory* may be said to be the creative offshoot of the Anglo-American university discourse, for it formally announced its presence in the Anglo-American academy in the 1970s with works by Jonathan Culler[19] and Terry Eagleton.[20] Theory invokes the Critical Theory associated with the Frankfurt School and the work of thinkers such as Walter Benjamin and Theodor Adorno. It also invokes philosophical and psychoanalytic theories of signification associated with varieties of structuralism and poststructuralism emanating from France from the 1960s onwards, the so-called French Theory that has its roots in the work of linguists such as Ferdinand De Saussure and Emile Benvéniste as well as the Prague School. Thus French Theory refers to the work of Barthes, Cixous, Derrida, Foucault, Irigaray, Kristeva, Lacan, Lyotard as well as Deleuze and Guattari, and the relevant philosophical traditions they espouse.

What these theorists have in common is their distrust of the uni-fied human subject and their emphasis on discourse. In different ways and to varying degrees, they argue that all human actions and social formations are related to language and can be understood as systems of related elements. This means that the individual elements of a system only have significance when considered in relation to the structure as a whole, and that structures are to be understood as self-contained, self-regulated, and yet forever self-transforming entities. In other words, it is the structure itself that determines the significance, meaning and function of the individual elements of a system that is therefore unstable. We will see below how Lacan applies this structur-alist approach to our understanding of the human subject and social systems. The case of feminist, postcolonial, lesbian/gay theories, race studies as well as multicultural and class theories is somewhat different, for these are underpinned by forms of Marxism as well as by the intellectual traditions of the Frankfurt School and poststruc-turalism. Today, though, cultural theory has in many ways replaced poststructuralism as the main discourse to which many turn for cross-disciplinary, cross-cultural, multicultural and geohistorical engagements.

The above synopsis would no doubt be familiar to many upper level, honours and postgraduate creative writing students. But the question is how useful an overview of theory is to them, particularly as the conditions that produced the heyday of Theory have faded away. Theory in the twenty-first century has lost the capital T of 'high theory'. It is now multifarious and it often has a thematic or political focus on matters of *identity, ethnicity, transculturation, globalisation* and, increasingly, *sustainability*. This does not mean however, that students should not be exposed to Critical Theory or French Theory. But mere exposure is inadequate. For theory as a body of knowledge to be useful, practitioners need to engage with it at a deeper level. An ideal model would be based on a dialectic between practice and theory that would engage students at an unconscious level, but also make them actively conscious of such dialectic. This would, for example, entail reading, critiquing and responding creatively to theory as well as analysing these creative responses to theory. This, however, presupposes the recognition of, and emphasis on, the reality of the unconscious, that part of the psyche which gives rise to metal phenomena in a person's mind unbeknownst to her. Sigmund Freud[21] and other psychoanalysts have indeed considered the unconscious to play a significant role in creativity. I personally believe that creative writers are particularly sensitive to their own unconscious processes, and further, that unconscious processes themselves play a crucial role in artistic creation.

From my own experience, the theories that are most highly useful to creative writers are those grounded in poststructuralist theories of language, for these enable writers to re-evaluate their ideas about subjectivity, identity, the creative process and communication as well as to re-assess their own writing styles, further develop their craft and formulate their own poetics. Theories grounded in poststructuralist theories of language do alert us to the fact that writing is a *making*, a construction using language, visual images, sound, silence and rhythm, and that the subject itself is a complex construction. Perhaps we need to think more broadly about the meaning of theory and refuse to equate one theory, or set of theories, with the act of theorising itself. For surely theory is not only, as *The New Shorter Oxford English Dictionary* would have it: 'a systematic statement of rules or principles to be followed'.[22] Rather, theory signifies a mode of thought that stems from the particular and reaches out to the generalisable while transferring knowledge from the unknown to the known.

However, for creative writing, there is a difference between theory that *triggers* or *produces* creative work and theory that *informs* creative work. In certain contexts theory can function as a painting can to inspire creativity, but that is not the same thing as having theory that becomes integrated with the work or that functions in a way so as to produce new knowledge. In order to *inform* the creative work and produce new knowledge, theory needs to resonate with the emotions as well as the intellect. In other words, it needs to 'hook up' with something in the unconscious by *immersion* in theory. All readers, including creative writers, construct meaning out of their own conscious and unconscious interests. As readers of theories, we bring to them not only our own understanding but also our unconscious experience that inevitably shapes and determines how we interpret and in turn make use of them. This may be why theories grounded in theories of language are so appealing to creative writers. However, although we are all subject to our own unconscious agendas, it is important to recognise and understand that creative writers read, and therefore think, and research differently. An example is that the creative writer caught in the act of active reading is always on the lookout for writing material. Reading crystallises elements around a question, an obsession, or an affect (a mood, or pre-emotion) – all of which produce effects for both writer and reader, of course.

Research itself, I contend, proceeds from this crystallisation as thoughts are articulated more consciously according to what might be called a methodology of *active consciousness* whereby knowledge emerges from the unknown to the known. New knowledge is thus produced in three steps: inductive, deductive, and retroactive. In other words, new knowledge is produced 'out of sync' from a dialectical process between consciousness and the unconscious. This new knowledge may very well concern concepts and how they evolve by accretion or hybridisation, for example. But as a recent study by Paul Magee suggests, it may just as easily be centred on poetics and issues of style and composition.[23] It may also focus exclusively on *meanings* of language and subjectivity, or indeed on the *making* of language and subjectivity.

3 Theory and pedagogy: The case of psychoanalysis

Psychoanalysis is not a theory. Rather, it is a constant work in progress which draws its insights from the clinic. So, what is called psycho-analytic theory is radically different from both Theory and other theories in that it makes the unconscious its organising concept. The unconscious, however, is largely inaccessible to us. We can only catch glimpses of it in dreams, slips of the tongue or pen, in jokes and in symptoms. We also can access it through self-examination or examination of 'process' as I do with *Out of Bounds*[24] in the last section of this chapter. Although psychoanalytic theory provides the basis for the therapeutic practice of psychoanalysis out of which it emerged, it also provides a structural theory for the construction of subjectivity. As such, it is a 'theory without credentials', one that shakes up our certainties about what theory is and one that disrupts our preconceptions about what the self is. By doing so, it opens up creative possibilities that can be theorised.

By focusing on unconscious processes, psychoanalytic theory has made it possible to analyse the unconscious as well as conscious meanings which contribute to the complexity of our identities and the world in which we live as well as to the question of the very meaning and status of consciousness and language. Jacques Lacan's conceptualisation of the unconscious as the driving force of language is particularly relevant to writers as it demonstrates that language has an integral role in the construction of consciousness and culture. For Lacan, an unconscious sense of lack of being is transformed into unconscious desire – desire being here the *motive* for the subject's relation to the world, thereby 'driving' this subject's destiny. Further, in explaining the unconscious construction of ideology, Lacan shows that language, and therefore discourse, can no longer be seen as neutral and objective.[25]

But how should theory be taught? In order to answer my question I will resort to a favourite story. 'Pierre Ménard, Author of the *Quixote*'[26] is the story of a writer who scrupulously reproduces Cervantes' *Don Quixote* word for word and for whom the text thus reproduced constitutes a new work. By appending his signature to Cervantes' text, Ménard produces a new text. Reproduced in another context, one signifier (a proper name) has a different meaning. The same text thus becomes another text. This story may be allegorical of the act of teaching in the 'hard' disciplines that uphold the discourse of the university whereby knowledge means passing on information. Teaching theory to creative writers is a different tale altogether because 'information and imaginative writing are different forms of knowledge, demanding different skills and wholly different attitudes to language'.[27] For many creative writers, the text is a research statement in itself and the knowledge it gestures towards is often beyond words. This knowledge is in fact intimately related to *the truth of the subject*, that which intimately and exclusively defines our relation to the world as mediated through language. Theory, it seems to me, ought to enable creative writers to articulate this previously unknowable knowledge. It should also enable them to deviate from what might be called a familiar poetics in order to approach new forms of knowledge, or new ways of knowing the world. In order to achieve this, however, as a teacher I can only strive to teach students a relation to language that empowers them by stepping down from the position of master, a position teachers traditionally assume in universities. As Shoshana Felman puts it:

> Psychoanalysis as teaching, and teaching as psychoanalysis, radically subvert the demarcation-line, the clear-cut opposition between the analyst and the analysand, between the teacher and the student (or the learner) – showing that what counts, in both cases, is precisely the transition, the struggle-filled passage from one position to the other.[28]

Drawing on the lessons of psychoanalysis, my teaching is based on a philosophy of ethical desire, that is, a desire for radical difference that effects change through some 'struggle'.[29] This philosophy discards Freudian models of a simple repressed subjectivity, in favour of the

183

Lacanian subject, to allow for an examination of multiple aspects of subjectivity (Symbolic, Imaginary, Real) – all of which struggle for expression in any extended discourse. This is only possible because Lacan refutes the idea that our identity can ever be coherent and authentic. For Lacan, the subject is indeed an imperfect structure comprising three orders. The Symbolic is a universal characteristic of humanity: a group can be said to be human only if it is subordinated to a symbolic structure which is itself articulated in language. In the Symbolic, for example, I am the set of facts written in my passport and these facts are inscribed in the Other, or symbolic network. The Imaginary invokes a set of similarities, that is, a set of projections, identifications and rivalries which govern intersubjective relationships. In the Imaginary, I am the person who gazes in the mirror and hates to see that I look like my mother, the child's specular 'other' *par excellence*. The Real is that which is beyond symbolisation: it is the realm of death and madness that remains hidden from us in the unconscious and is therefore beyond words. In the Real, I speak gibberish or not at all.

Out of my own experience grappling with theory and pedagogy has emerged a form of knowledge which I have called 'interactive narrative pedagogy'.[30] At its core, it is a philosophy of teaching that takes into account the nature of the *relationship* between teacher and student; that is, what Freud defined as 'transference'.[31] However, the dynamics of exchange in a creative writing context is based on narrative interactions that are themselves predicated upon an intricate transferential process: transference *between two subjects* as well as transference *to the work* and *to the institution*. All of these presuppose an understanding of knowledge embodied in behaviours and practices that cannot evade the reality of the unconscious, which is the truth that leaves its trace when we write. All discourses are constructed out of unconscious as well as social or conscious interests. In their gaps and incoherences, they reveal what their creators may have unconsciously disowned or repressed. Thus all writers are 'in transference': texts are invested with unconscious desire before and in the process of writing, and writing bears the mark of this desire. Some of us may in fact actively seek this truth. Students writing under the supervision of an academic, however, are also 'in ransference' with regard to their teacher and to the institution they have chosen. Students, for instance, often feel the need to please teachers while teachers often feel the need to inject knowledge or wisdom in their students. But is this desirable?

Far from claiming to offer a pedagogical paradigm that fits all, believe that analysing the phenomenon of transference may help us understand better the mechanisms and relationships we engage in when we write or discuss our writing.[32] However, because in the university context the teacher/student relationship, like the analyst/analysand relationship is, of itself, artificial, an analysis of transference starts with the teacher's self-knowledge. This, in turn, is bound to empower students.[33] The reflective practice encouraged here is both relevant and useful for all writers as it may foster personal and writerly change. Consider the following questions:

1 What are the formative elements of my systems of knowledge and belief? What is the impact of such identity on my life and work?
2 What are my master signifiers – my ideals and values? Where do these come from?
3 What is my scenario of ultimate fulfillment?
4 What conflicts do I identify in myself? In my work? How is language responsible for these? What causes 'writing block'?
5 Why do I write?

This self-reflection promotes what I have called a 'methodology of active consciousness'. By 'active consciousness', I mean the process of bringing to consciousness what previously lay beneath its surface, namely something pre-conscious or unconscious.[34] The term 'methodology of active consciousness' highlights the active participation in the reflexive method of inquiry which is particular to creative writing research, at least for those of us who describe themselves as 'explorers' rather than 'planners'. The 'explorers' overtly use a 'problem finding style',[35] which means that they don't know what they are doing until they have done it. They start a work with only a question mark, an image, a phrase or even a mere rhythm rather than a plan, and the work emerges from the improvisational act of writing and revising – or not. I write 'overtly', because the so-called 'planners' often diverge from their plan as they write and solve problems. What is common to all writers, though, is that 'there is never a single insight; instead, there are hundreds and thousands of small mini-insights'[36] that happen mostly unconsciously. However, 'the real work starts when many mini insights are analysed, reworked, and connected to each other' consciously.[37] This may happen through *immersion* to theory and self-reflective practice.

4 Theory and creative writing research

For six consecutive years I taught the subject 'Writing the Unconscious' as part of the Master of Creative Writing at the University of Melbourne School of Creative Arts. 'Writing the Unconscious' was a seminar-based subject that explored the implications of theories of subjectivity and the unconscious for writers. Some of the aims of the unit were:

- to explore the nature of writing
- to help students articulate their bond to writing by experimenting with narrative textures, structure, character, point of view and voice
- to help students identify patterns in their creative process
- to encourage students' self-knowledge and boost confidence.

For one semester, we surveyed works from the Modernist period and contemporary postmodern literature along with theoretical writings on the nexus between issues of subjectivity and creative practice using a methodology of active consciousness derived from interactive narrative pedagogy. The course reader included key texts by psychoanalysts and psychoanalytic critics as well as creative works that lent themselves to psychoanalytic interpretation while also highlighting questions of gender, ethnicity, sexuality and power. The seminar was structured according to a tight time-frame and strict protocols so as to encourage symbolic exchanges rather than identifications and rivalries by essentially focusing on the *work* rather than on matters of taste and inter-personal relationships. Activities included discussing creative responses to the set reading, a lecture, a discussion paper, a free-association session, writing, and the workshopping of longer creative pieces.

The lectures aimed at familiarising students with the work of Sigmund Freud, Jacques Lacan, Hélène Cixous, Julia Kristeva, Luce Irigaray, Donald W. Winnicott, Melanie Klein and C. J. Jung as well as fellow thinkers such as Roland Barthes, Gilles Deleuze and Félix Guattari, Jacques Derrida and Slavoj Zizek. Like all other theories, psychoanalytic theory can only represent one among many ways of thinking about the world and even then, there are considerable variations within psychoanalytic theory itself. These thinkers were selected to reflect the variety of ways in which psychoanalysis may be useful to creative writers. Particular texts were chosen to enhance self-reflection, critical engagement and the act of 'hooking up' with something in the unconscious.

The writing exercises for each week drew on key concepts intro-duced in the lecture. In order to respect the rule of free-association as much as possible, these were 'themed' rather than structured. Each writing session would begin with a free-association warm-up. I would say a word – say 'glass', for instance – and then each student would in turn come up with a word as quickly as possible. So 'glass' would prompt 'glitter' from A, to which B would reply 'glare', to which C would say 'beach', and so on. Depending on the theoretical material, the writing tasks were often writing cues, for instance 'in the mirror was nothing more than air on water'. Visual and olfactory cues were also used. For instance, following the lecture 'Sexing the Unconscious', students were asked to write about reproductions of surrealist paintings suggestive of gender issues. Or after discussing 'The Freudian Unconscious: Key Concepts', students were asked to choose from a collection of vials filled with natural oils, spices and condiments and write about the memories one particular scent evoked. The fundamental rule of applied-psychoanalysis in the writ-ing workroom was what became known as 'speed writing'. In other words, the students were instructed NOT to think, but rather to write as quickly as possible about whatever came into their heads. The students did all their work in one single writing-book to emphasise that reading and writing, critiquing and analysing are all integral to knowledge production.

To my surprise, the unit review revealed how obsolete and patronising Freud appeared to many students (both male and female), particularly in 'Creative Writers and Day-Dreaming'.[38] This was no naïve surprise, however, as the individual presentations, the discussions that followed them and the individual conversations I had had with students had led me to believe that Freud was still regarded as the fount of wisdom, albeit to be disagreed with. The most popular thinkers were Lacan, Cixous, Irigaray and Kristeva. Zizek's ideas were received with mixed feelings. Winnicott's concept of the 'potential space'[39] (the intersubjective transitional space between the subject and her environment) proved useful as well; some students made interesting comparisons with Kristeva's concept of the prelinguistic semiotic 'chora'[40] and others pointed out the 'missing link'; that is, language in its volitional, cognitive and cultural dimensions. Though I am aware of my own transference to specific theories and the likelihood of passing on my passions to students, I concluded from their comments that the theories they found most useful were those grounded in poststructuralist theories of language, as these clearly helped them articulate insights gained about their own identity make-up, as well as their own individual creative processes. These insights in turn contributed to their taking risks in terms of subject matter and technique, often consciously devising a 'poetics'. Such *immersion in theory*, combined with free-association and speed writing, as well as the conscious analysis of the creative process, changed some students' style, sometimes in quite dramatic ways. Many students had their final piece published and some have continued researching and publishing.[41]

5   Am I a poem or a case study in ficto-critical mode?

'I am not a poet, but a poem. A poem that is being written, even if it looks like a subject', said Lacan,[42] suggesting a performative connection between himself and the work of poets, and at a broader level of abstraction, between the respective discourses of poetry and theory. This last section will suggest that poetry and theory embody a teleological drive towards the achievement of a greater understanding of aspects of subjectivity. I will reflect back on one of my creative works, *Out of Bounds*,[43] in order to show how it embodies the Lacanian notion of the achievement of self-knowledge through discourse while going beyond his theory of the drives, or unconscious motivations. I will highlight the discrepancy between what I was looking for and what I found, for it is in this gap that the *research* occurred. This research was triggered by the seemingly naïve question at the opening of the book: 'where do words come from?'[44] The process of writing, however, opened up a new way of conceptualising what we call 'voice'.

There is a crucial connection between *lyric* and *process* poetry – with their focus on an almost confessional style of writing – and psychoanalytic theory which probes language for manifestations of the unconscious. Lacan has made the connection overt in his aphorism that 'the unconscious is structured like a language',[45] and he has also stressed that language is, first and foremost, directed at a listener, it is a communicative agent which enables the subject to attain recognition from the other.[46] Both poetry and psychoanalytic theory stress the difficulty of attaining self-knowledge and they both see the 'I' as composed of innumerable layers, many of which are not readily accessible.

Out of Bounds[47] is a sequence of poems in three parts: 'The Gaze of Silence', 'Out of Bounds' and 'The Silence of the Gaze'. It is a double story of dislocation as it retraces the protagonist's experience of physical and psychical exile (including linguistic exile). It draws together the two strands to reveal a subject at pains to re-make herself in a foreign language in a foreign country, a space she reads through the magnifying glass of sexuality, culture, and postcolonial politics. In short it is a quest for self-achievement through a poetry *at play with* psychoanalysis. It is also, psychoanalytically speaking, a fantasy.

What *Out of Bounds* set out to do was to explore the radical otherness of its female protagonist by going beyond what I saw as the limitations of Lacan's ideas about femininity. As a little girl, Isabelle doesn't quite feel 'real'. She doesn't know why, but she feels more like an instrument than a person. The reader learns in part two that she may have been instrumental to the gratification of some priest, for which she was punished by her father. The signifiers father, priest and God become interlinked, and so when, as an adult, she is challenged by a man who makes fun of her writing, indeed makes fun of her *for* writing, she re-experiences a trauma. At that point, she understands that she left her country not out of boredom, as she had previously claimed, but out of fear of losing her mind. She also has an insight into her symbolic enmeshing in language and therefore rejects her Christian name in favour of her *instrumental* name: she rejects 'Is-A-Belle' in favour of 'Viola'. Her new surname, 'Dali', imposes itself on her, in surreal manner. Fear, or rather the anxiety accompanying the trauma Viola Dali relives, robs her of speech, and so she will use writing to learn how to speak again and, ultimately, how to live and love.

As the titles of part one and three suggest, the writing is informed by Lacan's teachings – his theorising of subjectivity and of the organisation of the drives in particular. The poem, however, expands on his theory of the gaze[48] while displacing it on the auditory register, therefore unwittingly expanding on the psychoanalytic understanding of subjectivity. I say 'unwittingly', because it is indeed only retrospectively that I saw what I had done. This was both exciting and constructive.

By using this approach, *Out of Bounds* develops the idea of the Other by speaking of poetry as a way of silencing the malevolent gaze that holds the self captive. The sequential poems then move on to speak of poetry as *singing*, rather than *seeing* the self, as had been the case previously. By changing from the scopic to the auditory register, it highlights that the 'I' is an 'I' *in the making* and that it ends up fully in command of the text when it breaks into song. The poet thus appears in the final sentence of the poem as the conscious, confident controller of her means.

Whenever Lacan uses the term 'discourse' it is in order to stress the fact that speech always implies an interlocutor. For Lacan, the subject experiences the unconscious as 'the discourse of the Other',[49] that part of our desire caught up in a linguistic system which is the moving image of generations of speaking beings. Far from seeing language as transparent in terms of subjectivity, Lacan argues that signifiers are combined in a signifying chain; meaning does not arise in the individual signifier, but in the connection between signifiers. Saussure had admitted that there can occur a shift or sliding in the relationship between signifier and signified.[50] Lacan argues that not only do the two realms never coincide, but that there is an incessant sliding of the signified under the signifier. In order to emphasise this separateness, he introduces a cut into the Saussurean sign, with a new emphasis on the bar as a formula of separateness (S/s). It is precisely this separateness that I sought in the act of writing as is evident in puns, equivocations and surreal images to convey otherness. I used the cut in more obvious ways in the punning across languages inspired by *Finnegans Wake*:[51] '*HiER born hear dad HARE dead la did aah LIP lipping / away law did ha Ding-gong hand lapWing her / M'elle borne la deed ah! Vie oh la … la voix ci lah dit ta!*'.[52] The effect achieved suggests that language itself crosses borders of tongues and being.

Lacan sees the self as an interlocking and dynamic constellation, differentiating between the ego and the subject, the subject of speech and the subject of being, with the former being a fictive creation of the Imaginary, brought into being by the misrecognition of the self in the Mirror Stage (this is me … so like my mother), while the latter partaking of all registers (is this me, Me, ME?). As we saw in the third section of this chapter, Lacan sees both of these facets of the self operating within three orders: the imaginary order of the Mirror Stage, the symbolic order of language and law, and the real order of drives. These three orders are interconnected, providing different perspectives on events in the life of the self.[53] At the core of this complex structure is the horrifying Real beyond words. It is that which Viola stumbles upon twice; firstly, when she re-experiences her trauma and stops speaking,[54] and secondly, when on the brink of madness, she 'hang[s] on to the word word'[55] as if her life depended on it.

Lacan also differentiates between full speech and empty speech: 'full speech is a speech full of meaning. Empty speech is a speech which has only signification'.[56] Lacan in fact associates full speech with the subject and empty speech with the ego. Speech in the field of the ego has the form of *mediation* while speech in the realm of the subject involves *revelation*. This revelation is about reaching the truth of desire; 'speech alone is the key to that truth'.[57] It is here that the connection between the epistemic drives of poetry and theory meet through the creative effect of silence or metaphor.

In particular, it is in this sense of creativity that poetry fuses the discourses of the aesthetic and the psychoanalytic, for speech presupposes the Other, referring to all signification systems that precede the self, and through which the self is able to proclaim its existence and be recognised. *Out of Bounds* both affirms and attempts to refute this by resorting to intra- and interlinguistic puns, thereby ironically acceding to 'full speech' through writing poetry, which would mean that poetry as *revelation* is on the side of full speech. The importance of the Other in determining the difference between the field of the ego and that of the subject with reference to the drives is the focus of the next section as it moves from the scopic (eyes/gaze) to the invocatory (ears/voice) drive in order to seek what a voice might be.

In *Seminar XI* Lacan refers to a funny episode from Sartre's *Being and Nothingness*[58] to illustrate the split between the look and the gaze.[59] The episode is recounted in two steps. First, *I am looking through a keyhole.* Second, *I hear the sound of footsteps in the hallway, I am being looked at.* Thus whereas Sartre is there, *looking through the keyhole,* he is *a pure spectator subject, absorbed by the spectacle, unaware of himself.* He is not *conscious of himself,* and strictly speaking, in this *looking through the keyhole,* he is *nothing.* Second, *I hear footsteps and this makes the gaze of the Other emerge.* It is as though the voyeur wants to capture the subject before he recognises the one who is about to see him. Prior to seeing the person's face, however, he articulates that *I'm being looked at.* The gaze is anonymous, the Other *par excellence.* Sartre then describes the downfall of the subject, who now becomes an object, just like Isabelle in *Out of Bounds,* who, however, is the object of the gaze from the start and only later associates the voice with the gaze, that is when she intuitively names the object she has been all along: 'Viola'. Though Lacan talks about shame at this point, it is more than shame that tips Viola over the edge: it is guilt – she has been interfered with *and also* punished for it. She therefore feels like a criminal, as the French pun on her distorted name, 'Viola Délit' implies (*délit* for crime). Viola is really an abject object.

Jacques Alain-Miller has expanded on Lacan's theory of the split between eye and gaze by transposing it on the auditory register, according to which the voice is split between ear and voice. Miller suggests that the voice as the object cause of desire does not in the least belong to the auditory register – just like the gaze as object cause of desire in Seminar XI is invoked by the noise that surprises the voyeur.[60] However, Miller remains enigmatic as to what the nature of this voice might be. I believe the following passage gives us a clue as to what this nature might be:

> The voice and the eyes and the eyes in the voice.
> Devising lenses. Veering words –
> devouring rows of vowels
> riots of consonants
> clicks of the tongue crystal clear.
> Devoicing voice.
> Vox the fox.[61]

This is the voice of the Other. However, this Other is not the Other of language and the law, but rather of the Other's enjoyment. The voice here echoes the *thingness* of the Real. We are in uncanny territory, a place where the devouring mother is lurking,[62] except that in *Out of Bounds* the devouring one comes in the guise of a priest in vestments, admittedly a strange transformation of the mother in skirts, now also unconsciously identified with the figure of the father. The voice of this seemingly maternal figure of a Father triggers Viola's own terror at the possibility of non-being and non-signification. Why is this so? The voice has become a thing without a body, namely a 'symptom' that exceeds speech's capacity to make sound meaningful.[63] This implies that the voice as object, in psychoanalytic terms, is a registration of a void, an 'antinomy between ear and voice' insofar as it is beyond conscious hearing.[64] It is precisely this registration of a void, this unconscious registration of death, which produces the anxiety that drives Isabelle away from her country of birth to Australia: 'I, Viola *Délit runawry* / running for the life of her / Viola veiling violence evicting the voice running / the vile fox on the run'.[65] What is *new* in this poetic text is that it presents Lacan's concept of the

Name-of-the-Father as a mere scam by foregrounding the lawlessness of the voice of the Other. Exciting, but scary!

Out of Bounds begins with a question and ends in song. Here, poetry is seen as a vehicle in the search for truth of the subject: it is a discourse which, like that of psychoanalysis, probes the *meanings* of language and subjectivity. The 'I' of poetry and the 'I' of Lacanian discourse are coeval in that they are complex, multi-faceted and deeply influenced by their socio-cultural contexts. Both discourses realise the complexity and opacity of the subject, and while realising that full knowledge is probably impossible, poetic discourse alone highlights that the subject is constantly *in the making*.

6 After anxiety: Theory without credentials

The above insights into creative research make a case for a 'theory without credentials', one that disrupts our certainties and thus opens up creative possibilities that can in turn be theorised. These in turn show how *process*, though addressed here in terms of unconscious material brought about consciously and manipulated as such, still needs to be further pursued. I have shown that a psychoanalytic understanding of subjectivity can indeed shed light on the creative process and on the very concept of knowledge production while highlighting that an *analysis of writing processes* can help illuminate, and further, lead to alternative psychoanalytic understandings of subjectivity. I have also shown that unlikely marriages between theories are not only possible, but desirable.

Despite my insistence on the significance of psychoanalysis for creative writing and pedagogy, I would persist against favouring any one kind of theory. As I have revealed, there are indeed affinities between creative writing and various kinds of theories. For instance, many of the methodologies and practices that underpin the work of twentieth-century modernists still echo into postmodern works, including the work of creative writing students. This wide-spread phenomenon can be linked to poststructuralist theories of language. It is nonetheless important to avoid letting any one kind of theory stand in for the act of theorisation itself or for the plurality of theoretical approaches, each one of which has vital and distinctive contributions to make to understanding the interplay between creative writing, theory and knowledge production. I will therefore end with writing tasks which demonstrate that psychoanalysis is a theory without credentials, and yet by virtue of this, opens up countless possibilities.

Exercises

1
  a   Free-associate on the word 'cold'. Write as fast as you can. Do not re-read.
  b   Write a narrative prompted by the following scenario: *You are sitting at your work-station with your back to the open window. You feel a sudden chill.* Write for ten minutes as fast as you can. Do not worry about correct expression.
  c   Reflect upon the relationship between items a and b.
2   Drawing on the previous exercise write a short story (3000–3500 words). When satisfied with your work, put it away for one week.
3   Retrieve all of the above texts and reflect upon the connections and discrepancies between the three. Write about this in your journal. Repeat in a year's time and note new insights.

Notes

1   Ian Hunter, 'The History of theory', *Critical Inquiry* 33.1 (2006), http://www.criticalinquiry.uchicago.edu/33n1/voln1_hunter.htm.   [Accessed 2 February 2010].
2   Jean-François Lyotard, *The Postmodern Condition: A Report on Knowledge*, Minneapolis: University of Minnesota Press, 1984.
3   Pierre Bourdieu, *Pascalian Meditations*, Cambridge: Polity Press, 2000.
4   Valentine Cunningham, *Reading After Theory*, Oxford: Blackwell, 2002.
5   Terry Eagleton, *After Theory*, New York: Basic Books, 2003.
6   Michael Payne and Paul Schad, eds *life.after.theory: Jacques Derrida, Frank Kermode, Toril Moi, Christopher Norris*, London: Continuum, 2003.
7   Gavin Kitching, *The Trouble with Theory*, Sydney: Allen & Unwin, 2008, p. 4.

8   Brian Boyd, 'Theory is dead – Like a Zombie', *Philosophy and Literature*, 30 (2006), p. 294.

9   Stephen Ross, ed., *Modernism and Theory: a Critical Debate*, London and New York: Routledge, 2009, p. 14.

10 Paul Dawson, *Creative Writing and the New Humanities*, London and New York: Routledge, 2005, pp. 160–1; 164.

11 Nigel Krauth and Tess Brady, eds, *Creative Writing: Theory beyond Practice*, Teneriffe: Post Pressed, 2006, p. 14.

12 Dawson, p. 161.

13 Graeme Harper and Jeri Kroll, eds, *Creative Writing Studies: Practice, Research and Pedagogy*, Clevedon: New Writing Viewpoints, 2007, p. 4, my emphasis.

14 Harper and Kroll, p. 4.

15 Hazel Smith and Dean, Roger, eds, *Practice-led-Research, Research-led-Practice in the Creative Arts*, Edinburgh: Edinburgh University Press, 2009.

16 Brad C. Haseman, 'A Manifesto for Performative Research', *Media International Australia: Incorporating Culture and Policy*, 2006. Online. http://wwwemsah.uq.edu.au/mia/issues/miacpl 18.htm [Accessed 2 February 2010], p. 104.

17 Camilla Nelson, 'Research through Practice: a Reply to Paul Dawson', *TEXT* 12.2 (2008), http://www.textjournal.com.au/oct08/nelson.htm [Accessed 20 January 2010].

18 Mike Harris, 'Escaping the Tractor beam of Literary Theory: Notes towards Appropriate Theories of Creative Writing – and some Arguments against the Inappropriate Ones' *TEXT* 13.2 (2009), http://ww.textjournal.com.au/oct09/harris.html [Accessed 2 February 2010].

19 Jonathan Culler, *Structuralist Poetics: Structuralism, Linguistics, and the study of Literature*, Ithaca: Cornell University Press, 1975.

20 Terry Eagleton, *Criticism and Ideology: A Study in Marxist Literary Theory*, London: Verso, 1978.

21 Sigmund Freud, 'Creative Writers and Day-Dreaming', 1908, SE IX, pp. 141–54.

22 Lesley Brown, ed. *The New Shorter Oxford English Dictionary*, Oxford: Clarendon Press, 993, II, p. 3274.

23 Paul Magee, 'Is Poetry Research?' *TEXT* 13.2 (2009), http://www.textjournal.com.au/oct09/magee.htm [Accessed 11 February 2010].

24 Dominique Hecq, *Out of Bounds*, Melbourne: Re.press, 2009.

25 Jacques Lacan, *The Seminar: Book 17. The Other Side of Psychoanalysis*, trans. Russell Grigg, New York and London: Norton, 2007 [1969–70].

26 Jorge Luis Borges, 'Pierre Ménard, Author of the *Quixote*', in *Labyrinths*, New York: New Directions, 1964 [1939].

27 Al Alvarez, *The Writer's Voice*, London: Bloomsbury, 2005, p. 15.

28 Shoshana Felman, 'Psychoanalysis and Education: Teaching Terminable and Interminable', *Yale French Studies* 63 (1982), p. 38.

29 Felman, p. 38.

30 Dominique Hecq, 'Interactive Narrative Pedagogy as a Heuristic for Understanding Supervision in Practice-led Research', *New Writing: The International Journal for the Practice and Theory of Creative Writing* 6.1 (2009): 40–50.

31 Sigmund Freud, *The Interpretation of Dreams*, 1900, SE IV-V, 1900, p. 562.

32 Dominique Hecq, 'To Know or Not to Know', *TEXT* 13 Special Issue 6 (2009), http://www.textjournal.com.au/speciss/issue6/content.html [Accessed 19 January 2010].

33 Mark Bracher's chapter, 'Self-analysis for teachers' is a must for any teacher interested in using a psychoanalytic pedagogy as it offers practical ways in which teachers can chart their own systems of knowledge, see Bracher, 2006, pp. 135–47.

34 Sigmund Freud, 'The Unconscious', 1915, SE XIV, pp. 166–7.

35 Anne Lamott, *Bird by Bird: Some Instructions on Writing and Life*, New York: Pantheon Books, 1994, p. 22.

36 Keith R Sawyer, 'Writing as Collaborative Act' in S. B. Faufman and J. C. Kaufman, eds, *The Psychology of Creative Writing*, Cambridge: Cambridge University Press, 2009, p. 176.

37 Sawyer, 2009, p. 176.

38 Freud, 1908.

39 Donald W. Winnicott, *Playing and Reality*, London: Tavistock, 1971.

40 Julia Kristeva, *Revolution in Poetic Language*, trans. Margarett Waller, New York: Columbia University Press, 1974.

41 For a sample of the writing produced as a result of such immersion in theory, see the award-winning *Things We Didn't See Coming* (Amsterdam, 2009), 'Finding the Angles' (Kofman, 2010), 'Secrets' (Whitting, 2007),'Penis Envy' (Uttig, 2005), 'Vermillon' (Mundell, 2005), and the companion pieces 'Watching Narcissus' and 'Why Does it Hurt so Much? Pain and Stupidity in Creative Work' (Williamson, 2008).

42 Jacques Lacan, *The Seminar: Book 11. The Four Fundamental Concepts of Psychoanalysis*, J. A. Miller, ed., trans. A. Sheridan, Harmondsworth: Penguin, 1971 [1965–6], p. 18.

43 Hecq, 2009, *Out of Bounds*.

44 Hecq, 2009, *Out of Bounds*, p. 16.

45 Lacan, 2006 [1965–6], p. 77.

46 Jacques Lacan, 'The Mirror Stage as Formative of the Function of the I as Revealed in Psychoanalytic Experience' in J. Lacan, *Ecrits*, trans. B. Fink, New York: Norton, 2006 [1949], p. 77.

47 Hecq, 2009, *Out of Bounds*.

48 Lacan, 1971 [1965–6], p. 18.

49 Jacques Lacan, 'The Subversion of the Subject and the Dialectic of desire in the Freudian Unconscious' in J. Lacan, *Ecrits*, trans. B. Fink, New York: Norton, 2006 [1960], pp. 689–90.

50 Ferdinand De Saussure, *Course in General Linguistics*, trans. Wade Baskin, New York: McGill, 1959 [1916].
51 James Joyce, *Finnegans Wake*, London: Faber and Faber, 1939.
52 Hecq, 2009, *Out of Bounds*, p. 43.
53 Jacques Lacan, *The Seminar: Book 1. Freud's Papers on Technique*, trans. with notes by J. Forrester, Cambridge: Cambridge University Press, 1988 [1953–4], p. 113.
54 Hecq, 2009, *Out of Bounds*, pp. 40–2.
55 Hecq, 2009, *Out of Bounds*, p. 25.
56 Lacan, 1976–7, p. 11.
57 Jacques Lacan, *The Seminar: Book 17. The Other Side of Psychoanalysis*, trans. Russell Grigg, New York and London: Norton, 2007 [1969–70], p. 172.
58 Jean-Paul Sartre, *Being and Nothingness*, London: Faber and Faber, 1956.
59 Lacan, 1971 [1965–6], p. 84.
60 Jacques-Alain Miller, 'Jacques Lacan and the Voice' in V. Vorus and B. Bogdan, eds, *The Later Lacan*, New York: State University of New York, 2007, p. 139.
61 Hecq, 2009, *Out of Bounds*, p. 39.
62 Sigmund Freud, 'The Uncanny', 1919, SE XVII, p. 124.
63 Mladen Dolar, *A Voice and Nothing More*, Cambridge: MIT Press, 2006, p. 15.
64 Miller, p. 139.
65 Hecq, 2009, *Out of Bounds*, p. 42.

Works cited

Alvarez, Al *The Writer's Voice*, London: Bloomsbury, 2005.
Amsterdam, Steven *Things We Didn't See Coming*, Melbourne: Sleepers, 2009.
Borges, Jorge Luis 'Pierre Ménard, Author of the *Quixote*', in *Labyrinths*, New York: New Directions, 1964 [1939].
Bourdieu, Pierre *Pascalian Meditations*, Cambridge: Polity Press, 2000.
Boyd, Brian 'Theory is dead – Like a Zombie', *Philosophy and Literature*, 30 (2006): 289–98.
Bracher, Mark *Radical Pedagogy*, New York: Palgrave Macmillan, 2006.
Bracher, Mark *The Writing Cure: Psychoanalysis, Composition, and the Aims of Education*, Carbondale and Edwardsville: Southern Illinois University Press, 1999.
Brown, Lesley, ed. *The New Shorter Oxford English Dictionary*, Oxford: Clarendon Press, 1993.
Culler, Jonathan *Structuralist Poetics: Structuralism, Linguistics, and the Study of Literature*, Ithaca: Cornell University Press, 1975.
Cunningham, Valentine *Reading After Theory*, Oxford: Blackwell, 2002.
Dawson, Paul *Creative Writing and the New Humanities*, London and New York: Routledge, 2005.

Dolar, Mladen *A Voice and Nothing More*, Cambridge: MIT Press, 2006.

Eagleton, Terry *Criticism and Ideology: A Study in Marxist Literary Theory*, London: Verso, 1978.

—— *After Theory*, New York: Basic Books, 2003.

Felman, Shoshana 'Psychoanalysis and Education: Teaching Terminable and Interminable', *Yale French Studies* 63 (1982): 21–44.

—— *Jacques Lacan and the Adventure of Insight: Pyschoanalysis in Contemporary Culture*, Cambridge: Harvard University Press, 1987.

Freud, Sigmund *The Interpretation of Dreams*, 1900, SE IV–V, 1900.

—— 'Creative Writers and Day-Dreaming', 1908, SE IX, pp. 141–54.

—— 'The Unconscious', 1915, SE XIV, pp. 159–215.

—— 'The Uncanny', 1919, SE XVII, pp. 217–56.

Harper, Graeme and Kroll, Jeri, eds *Creative Writing Studies: Practice, Research and Pedagogy*, Clevedon: New Writing Viewpoints, 2007.

Harris, Mike 'Escaping the Tractor Beam of Literary Theory: Notes towards Appropriate Theories of Creative Writing – and some Arguments against the Inappropriate Ones' *TEXT* 13.2 (2009), http://ww.textjournal.com.au/oct09/harris.html [Accessed 2 February 2010].

Haseman, Brad C. 'A Manifesto for Performative Research', *Media International Australia: Incorporating Culture and Policy*, 2006. Online. http://wwwemsah.uq.edu.au/mia/issues/miacpl 18.htm [Accessed 2 February 2010].

Hecq, Dominique 'Interactive Narrative Pedagogy as a Heuristic for Understanding Supervision in Practice-Led Research', *New Writing: The International Journal for the Practice and Theory of Creative Writing* 6.1 (2009): 40–50.

—— 'To Know or Not to Know', *TEXT* 13 Special Issue 6 (2009), http://www.textjournal.com.au/speciss/issue6/content.html [Accessed 19 January 2010].

—— *Out of Bounds*, Melbourne: Re.press, 2009.

Hunter, Ian 'The History of theory', *Critical Inquiry* 33.1 (2006), http://www.criticalinquiry.uchicago.edu/33n1/voln1_hunter.htm [Accessed 2 February 2010].

Joyce, James *Finnegans Wake*, London: Faber and Faber, 1939.

Kaufman, Lee 'Finding the Angles', *Griffith Review* 26 (2010) http://www.griffithreview.com/current-edition.html [Accessed 19 January 2010].

Kitching, Gavin *The Trouble with Theory*, Sydney: Allen & Unwin, 2008.

Krauth, Nigel and Brady, Tess, eds *Creative Writing: Theory beyond Practice*, Teneriffe: Post Pressed, 2006.

Kristeva, Julia *Revolution in Poetic Language*, trans. Margarett Waller, New York: Columbia University Press, 1974.

Lacan, Jacques *Ecrits*, trans. Bruce Fink, New York: Norton, 2006.

—— 'The Mirror Stage as Formative of the Function of the I as Revealed in Psychoanalytic Experience', in J. Lacan, *Ecrits*, trans. B. Fink, New York: Norton, 2006 [1949]: 75–82.

—— 'The Subversion of the Subject and the Dialectic of Desire in the Freudian Unconscious', in J. Lacan, *Ecrits*, trans. B. Fink, New York: Norton, 2006 [1960]: 671–702.

—— *The Seminar: Book 11. The Four Fundamental Concepts of Psychoanalysis* J.A. Miller, ed., trans. A. Sheridan, Harmondsworth: Penguin, 1971 [1965–66].

—— *The Seminar: Book 1. Freud's Papers on Technique*, trans. with notes by J. Forrester, Cambridge: Cambridge University Press, 1988 [1953–54].

—— *The Seminar: Book 17. The Other side of Psychoanalysis*, trans. Russell Grigg, New York and London: Norton, 2007 [1969–70].

Lamott, Anne *Bird by Bird: Some Instructions on Writing and Life*, New York: Pantheon Books, 1994.

Lyotard, Jean-François *The Postmodern Condition: A Report on Knowledge*, Minneapolis: University of Minnesota Press, 1984.

Magee, Paul 'Is Poetry Research?' *TEXT* 13.2 (2009), http://www.textjournal.com.au/oct09/magee.htm [Accessed 11 February 2010].

Miller, Jacques-Alain 'Jacques Lacan and the Voice' in V. Vorus and B. Bogdan, eds, *The Later Lacan*, New York: State University of New York, 2007: 137–47.

Mundell, Megan 'Vermillion', *Meanjin* 64.1–2 (2005), 3–11.

Nelson, Camilla 'Research through Practice: A Reply to Paul Dawson', *TEXT* 12.2 (2008), http://www.textjournal.com.au/oct08/nelson.htm [Accessed 20 January 2010].

Payne, Michael and Schad, Paul, eds *life.after.theory: Jacques Derrida, Frank Kermode, Toril Moi, Christopher Norris*, London: Continuum, 2003.

Ross, Stephen, ed. *Modernism and Theory: a Critical Debate*, London and New York: Routledge, 2009.

Saussure, Ferdinand *Course in General Linguistics*, trans. Wade Baskin, New York: McGill, 1959 [1916].

Sawyer, Keith R. 'Writing as Collaborative Act' in S. B. Faufman and J. C. Kaufman, eds, *The Psychology of Creative Writing*, Cambridge: Cambridge University Press, 2009.

Smith, Hazel and Dean, Roger, eds *Practice-Led-Research, Research-Led-Practice in the Creative Arts*, Edinburgh: Edinburgh University Press, 2009.

Utting, Susie 'Penis Envy', *Blue Dog* 4.8 (2005): 8.

Whitting, Glenice 'Secrets', *Etchings* 3 (2007): 87–93, etchings@ilurapress.com.

Williamson, Caroline 'Watching Narcissus', *Bukker Tillibul* 2 New Series (2008) http://www.ld.swin.edu.au/journal.html [Accessed 18 January 2010].

—— 'Why Does it Hurt so Much? Pain and Stupidity in Creative Work', *Bukker Tillibul* 2 New Series (2008) http://www.ld.swin.edu.au/journal [Accessed 18 January 2010].

Winnicott, Donald W. *Playing and Reality*, London: Tavistock, 1971.

9 Transcultural Writing and Research

Graham Mort

Chapter summary

This chapter will discuss creative writing and its role as a practice-led research discipline in relation to forms of cultural identity. What kinds of research are involved in a postgraduate degree in creative writing and how does an international and transcultural writing community give them a special resonance? How does research in creative writing relate to other forms of academic research and how do its artistic outputs relate to readerships both inside and outside the academy? How can notions of culture help us to understand and locate literary works as manifestations of new understanding or configurations of knowledge?

---

1   Introduction

In writing this chapter, two very different but contrapuntal remarks have guided my thinking. Homi K. Bhaba, describing his work in relation to his own cultural origins, said: 'I ask myself what it would be like to live without the unresolved tensions between cultures and countries that have become the narrative of my life and the defining characteristics of my work.'[1] The photographer Ansell Adams, reaching beyond his own work, said, 'All art is a vision penetrating the illusions of reality'.[2] On the one hand, I was guided by a sense of the enriching possibilities of cultural exchange as defined by a leading intellectual; on the other, I was reminded of the irreducible nature of art, its expressions of the world and of human existence, by a great practitioner.

In the nineteenth century the word 'culture' evolved from denoting an agricultural method to representing a developed state of mind, the intellectual and artistic development of a society, the general body of the arts, even a way of life 'material intellectual and spiritual'.[3] In the twentieth century these definitions took on a strong anthropological inflection that accompanied a move from the colonial to the post-colonial, so that the dominance of western culture gave way to more porous and egalitarian notions of transcultural mobility and hybridity.

In the same period 'indigenous' literatures have replaced classical literatures as the primary focus of study and in the postmodern period, post-colonial literatures and other diverse cultural forms have challenged canonical 'English' texts. In that same modern to post-modern period the growth of literary theory has replaced canonical values of 'taste' or literary judgement with more objective, inclusive and democratic considerations of text and textuality that have led to an emphasis on autonomy, intertextuality, context and culture rather than the aesthetic or literary *quality* of a text or the extent to which an individual author may have realised their intentions through their creative work.

Barthes' famous (sometimes infamous) notion of the 'death of the author'[4] signifies a loss of innocence in our approach to the creative text. The literary text has become a conduit for theoretical discourse that seeks to expand our understanding of human interaction, thought and culture. It has become the subject and object of extensive research from the linguistic to the post-colonial, from structuralism to de-constructivism, from modernism to post-modernism. Yet these fascinating definitions of textuality have been accompanied by a counter-phenomenon: the development of creative writing as an academic discipline in its own right.

Long established in the US, a quantum growth in creative writing has been experienced in the UK in the past 15 years or so. The first MA courses were developed at Lancaster and East Anglia in the early 1980s, leading to the proliferation of undergraduate course and, perhaps most significantly, the recent growth of the PhD in creative writing. Unlike almost any other academic disciplines – apart from Theatre Studies, Visual Arts, Music and related Performance Arts – creative writing finds itself caught between cultures. By this I do not just mean the notion of culture derived from geography, nation-hood, language, ethnicity or religion but the culture(s) of academia itself and the culture(s) of literature-consuming societies beyond.

Of the many cultural boundaries that creative writing negotiates, this may be the most profound. The audiences for creative writing lies both within academia where our works may be the subject of study by literary or cultural scholars and outside where it may be read by the general public. Intersecting with its dual incarnation as an academic discipline and an artform are the exigencies of literary/textual production: the commercial publishing industry and the publishing enterprises supported by Arts Council funding that consider, edit, print, proof, bind, advertise, distribute and then sell literary works.

At my own institution the debate between creative writing and English studies, between theory and praxis, has been a lively one, but it has been accompanied by another phenomenon as our MA by distance learning began to expand rapidly and internationally. This process coincided with the establishment of a new research centre: the Centre for Transcultural Writing and Research (CTWR).[5] This new centre was designed to 're-position' Lancaster in virtual space, de-centring notions of geographical location in favour of virtual location that could form a confluence of emergent transcultural lit-eratures and research projects.

At around the same time, the rather improvised nature of creative writing in the UK academy was being sharply focused by the 2007 Research Assessment Exercise: an evaluation of research outputs upon which Higher Education Funding Council support for each university depends. In many ways this precipitated the coming of age of creative writing at Lancaster and in many other institutions. The rapid growth of creative writing at all levels in the UK acad-emy meant that a 'critical mass' of practitioners now existed who could make a significant contribution to the research profile of their Departments and Faculties.

Such a process continues to throw into relief the position o
creative writing within the academy, not only through the presenc
of individual practitioners but also in the way those practitioner
have to think about the research degrees and the research processe
that are being developed for their students.

2 Pedagogical structures and research

Arts and Humanities Research Council funding for scholarshi₎
carries the expectation that higher degree programmes shoul₍
provide research training. This stimulated a number of develop
ments at Lancaster. The primary outcome was the Virtual Researcl
Environment, derived from the Virtual Learning Environment. Th₍
very existence of an MA by distance learning (or eLearning), mean₍
that we had to create research training by remote means as wel
as by direct methods. To the standard provision of the VLE wer₍
added a series of online research training modules intended to offe₍
basic research functionality to students. They comprised: Postgraduat₍
eLearning, Understanding the Research Context, Scholarl₎
Conventions, Creative and Professional Presentation, Research an₍
Reflective Practice. Within those modules were installed a series o₍
links that led to an extensive web of Internet resources, underpinne₍
by remote access to resources in Lancaster's own university library
We also created a shared space for (scholarly and creative) bool
reviews and a shared conference space where termly work-in-progres₍
(WIP) sessions were to be held.

Following this pedagogic innovation it was decided to use th₍
online modules for all campus MA students as well as those study
ing by distance means. This established a form of 'blended learning'
effectively dismantling the remoteness of distance learning tech
niques and integrating them with direct methods. But the new VL₎
also carried within it the logic of a new distance learning PhD, sinc₍
research training and WIP sessions could now be delivered online
This new programme was enabled through a learning environmen₍
that allowed PhD students to study purely by distance means, by
face-to-face means, or by modulating between the two. The distinc₍

methods of face-to-face supervision and newly realised electronic supervision became fused; formerly separate pedagogic methods became seamless, linking together our off-campus and on-campus students in discussion and critical exchange.

3   Transcultural developments

The effects of transforming pedagogic space/time (since all aspects of the VLE were asynchronous) and the establishment of a virtual platform representing a range of culturally diverse writing projects through the CTWR had another profoundly transformative effect. This might be best explained as a form of 'transcultural resonance'. The existence of online facilities that could allow students from different countries to study at MA and PhD level *and* the establishment of a research centre with powerful representations of transcultural praxis,[6] both answered and created demand among potential students. More and more applications for both the MA and PhD by distance learning began to arrive from 'diasporic' UK citizens, from overseas students and from Anglophone expatriates from various countries. Furthermore, many of their research projects had transcultural elements, exploring aspects of cultural dislocation or tension through their creative writing and related reflective/critical writing.

The relocation of pedagogic space and praxis led to a significant opening up of cultural space in the subsequent two-year period. We now have 40 distance learning MA students and 32 PhD students, of which around 20 are pursuing transcultural research projects. As well as representing transcultural presence within the UK (Nigeria, Uganda, Pakistan), we now have students resident in Italy, the US, the Irish Republic, Malta, Zimbabwe, Nepal, Iran, Bermuda, Japan, Cyprus and Sweden. The resulting international or transnational community of students relates not so much to Lancaster University as an academy in the Northwest of the UK but to Lancaster as a virtual nexus, a meeting place where students from diverse geographical locations can share their creative writing through the medium of the English language.

Another nuance of this 'cosmopolitan' pedagogic space is its obverse: not only can we include students whose lives are defined by movement between political frontiers and their complex cultural conditions, we can also include those fixed in their locations. These include students in places where educational institutions are geographically remote and those who are rooted through circumstances of family commitment, economic restriction, or disability. The cosmopolitanism of these students lies not in actual mobility but in their virtual mobility within the wider international research community at Lancaster.

The susceptibility of creative writing to distance teaching and supervisory methods lies not only in the nature of its 'writerly' transactions and the interaction of reading and composition in pedagogic process but in its relationship with experience, space, time and consciousness. Wolfgang Iser identifies this quality as being the way that a creative text enables the simulation of reality:

> In whatever way, and under whatever circumstances, the reader may link the different phases of the text together, it will always be the process of anticipation and retrospection that leads to the formation of the virtual dimension, which in turn transforms the text into an experience for the reader. The way in which this experience comes about through a process of continual modification is closely akin to the way in which we gather experience in life. And thus the 'reality' of the reading experience can illuminate basic patterns of real experience.[7]

This sense of text as virtual experience with its feedback loop to actual experience, perception and consciousness, is a key formulation in understanding the complex contingencies that contribute to what we have to understand as a research process.

In the post-colonial world, the international readerships for texts in English ensures dialogue (indeed fierce debate) between former colonial and cultural 'centres' and the liberated literatures of former colonised nations that were forged through the exit strategies of colonial powers. When we add the role of English as a globalised *lingua franca* and the action of translation to that dimension, we have a sense of 'world literature' in English that is far from fanciful.

At one level this might equate to the sharing of what Iser defines as 'the basic patterns of real experience': temporal perception, sensory contact, emotional and psychological impulse and process. But creative writing does much more than capture or express such basic human experience and its *qualia*. Creative writing is also a source of human understanding, offering insights into the wider human experience of signification and culture, creating new perspectives and new configurations, experimenting with form while engaging with literary tradition or canonical texts.

In this cultural realm I would argue that creative writing can make an 'original contribution to knowledge' in the long-standing definition of a valid research output. We should also note that this special form of human enquiry or 'research' is also characterised by a dialogic interaction with readers. I will say more about these relationships below.

4 Exploring research concepts

Definitions of research follow an arc in the academy from the 'hard' sciences where new material discoveries segue into the social sciences with their insights into individual and collective human behaviour. Literary research and theory sit within those social sciences, based on library resources and archives as well as published theoretical readings of canonical and contemporary texts.

Creative writing is likely to be grouped within English or other literary groupings such as English and American literature. Yet it is a practice-led discipline, which by its very compositional nature over time is concerned with what is unwritten or in process. Just as creative writing is a dialogic art form engaging readers to realise or 'complete' its texts, so, as a research discipline, it is dialogic in uniting actual textual production with abstract hypotheses or 'theories' of creativity in order to fully realise or complete that process. Theory and practice are intertwined and interdependent, but 'practice-led' implies the primacy of linguistic/literary mark-making.

In order to understand and rationalise the methodologies of creative writing as research, we can identify its stages and components. If we consider the writing of a novel set in a particular historical period, for example, then we might consider research forming three stages: *preparatory* (the exploration of resources); *synthetic/kinetic* (the creation and revision of the text from those resources); and *reflective* (the effort of understanding that creative process and its synthesis of source material). The preparatory process might include archival research, literary research, fieldwork of various kinds and ethnographic research with communities. The synthetic/kinetic process involves the invention of characters, the simulation of location and time and the narration of events bringing character, time and location together. Reflective writing may organise the compositional process into an orderly sequence for the purposes of discussion that can *only be* sequential in writing, but the process itself is unlikely to follow a logical sequence where place precedes character or vice versa. Because our experience of time, place and character is simultaneous, our generation of it through the synthetic working of the imagination is also simultaneous and not – as far as we can identify – consisting of defined stages or sequential inventions. So our convenient model is also perhaps better seen as a series of feedback loops that run simultaneously in related domains within a forward moving compositional/reflective process.

We do know, however, that this process is heuristic, consisting of trial and error, built from discarded ideas, first drafts and false beginnings. In this sense, perhaps the best research model is that of 'action research':

> The practitioner allows himself to experience surprise, puzzlement, or confusion in a situation which he finds uncertain or unique. He reflects on the phenomenon before him, and on the prior understandings, which have been implicit in his behaviour. He carries out an experiment which serves to generate both a new understanding of the phenomenon and a change in the situation.[8]

Though action research is usually based in educational development and team effort, the model fits very well with the nature of creative writing, showing that the kinetic compositional process is a form of phenomenological generation. In creative writing, knowledge is generated through textual production, its content, form and significance *and* through the simultaneous process of reflection that considers aesthetic effect, technique, micro and macro organisational process, anticipation, awareness and accommodation of the reader. When this 'implied' reader enters the process the text 'enters' (or has to be considered as a constituent of) the cultural and (implicitly) transcultural domain.

Part of the compositional process is an implicit engagement with 'the other' in the sense that the unknown reader simultaneously represents the possibility of the familiar/unfamiliar, just as the text represents what may be known/unknown. In a more intimate way, the presence or possibility of the 'other' is what constitutes our sense of self, our sense of difference, of individuality, both as human beings involved in social relations and as writers engaged in literary production that seeks to engage readers and audiences. When we consider this compositional process of testing work against the self *and* anticipating the reader, we begin to understand the 'workshop' method, where work in progress is trialled against the perceptions and understanding of a group of peer writers led by an experienced tutor. The heuristic process that the writer has pursued alone is now placed in a *social* and therefore *cultural* context.

Workshops are designed to place the writing of students in the public domain, to subject it to actual readers rather than implied readers. This is recognition of the fact that our responses to our own writing are encultured and therefore invisibly circumscribed and contingent. Running workshops throughout Africa when working for the British Council brought this home very forcibly: however expert I might have felt about aesthetic or technical aspects of writing, I was a neophyte when it came to its cultural nuances. In the distance learning projects that developed from those workshops a reflective space ('assignment commentary') was designed to encapsulate the creative work, so that a conversation relating to creative practice also incorporates a discussion of linguistic usage, social, historical and political context and cultural practice.

5   Research methods and the transcultural context

In order to consider research methods in creative writing within the academy we have to return to the aims of the 'multi-purpose' creative writing postgraduate degree: attainment of an academic qualification; significant improvement of writing technique; engagement with the publishing industry beyond academia. Separating those aims is not an artificial discrimination but a recognition that those elements are not always co-terminus: creative writing exhibiting serious literary ambition and aesthetic achievement might nonetheless fail to attract a publisher. It could be argued that academia can recognise and reward such aesthetic or literary values in the face of a commercial sector driven by more reductive concerns. The resurgence of small, independent presses in the UK may, indeed, be an expression of this academically driven literary 'counter culture'.

Exploring and defining research methods is essential to the development of creative writing as an academic subject and one that is still establishing some of the fundamental things taken for granted in other subject areas: peer review, pedagogic methods, transparent assessment processes, and interpretations of research that are flexible enough to accommodate method without becoming a reproach to spontaneity and impulse - the penetrative 'vision' that Ansell Adams attributes to art.

It seems essential that MA and PhD programmes provide practical research training in key aspects of academic and research process that will equip a student to understand the context in which they are writing. This encompasses wide reading and the generation of creative writing (poems, stories, novels, scripts, creative non-fiction) and reflective/critical writing that explores their creative outputs in relation to those other creative writers and theorists whose work can enrich our understanding of creative acts. The restoration of intentionality to this process leads to a body of work by successful PhD students that will become the basis for new and stimulating engagement with theory and practice. This will, in turn, synthesise new under-standings while keeping the creative artist within the frame of discourse.

The transcultural development outlined earlier represents an extended research environment that incorporates transcultural dia-logue in the critiquing and shaping of new works. But we should be wary of the uncritical identification of 'culture' as a somehow posi-tivistic or deterministic aspect of human experience or as 'authentic' practices and identities that may be threatened by the new actual and virtual mobilities of populations. Literature is rich in examples of writing that explores such mobilities, challenging the immediate and wider restrictions of social class, religion, sexual orientation, political systems and colonising power.

The cultural space in which we write is not a stable entity with dependable values but constituted from our experience of attempted escape, disappearance, anticipation of new conditions. The choices implied in becoming a creative writer are simultaneously acts of soli-darity, evasion and resistance. Our own 'authentic' voice is subjugated to the polyphony of textual personae that are constantly changing. So the writer's relationship to culture is often one of discomfort, ambivalence, discontinuity, non-belonging, identification, curiosity, disdain, fascination, repugnance, evasion, longing and melancholia. We might argue that the very choices a writer makes on creating a text places them outside of the circumstances that they write about. Or rather, since the act of writing is simultaneously one of reading, the writer 'oscillates' between inner and outer views of experience and of the creative act.

We might think of all writing as inherently transcultural, as form-ing an integument between our personal experience, with all its complexity and contradictions, and that of others. Creative writing is transitive in the sense of connecting, or linking together the different phases of our life experience, moving between and transforming – virtually and actually – aspects of that experience. The effort to understand, express and remake ourselves as culturally inflected individuals creates one of the essential tensions from which new writing proceeds.

6 Reader reception

In the case of the non-verbal arts, transcultural exchange proceed with astonishing facility: in music and the visual arts, for instance where the means of communication can lead to forms of mutual appropriation that are instinctive in their fluidity. In the case of literature, language that communicates and *includes* also *excludes*, so that mobility is contingent upon the sharing of a language or its variants. Language itself can be seen as an accretion and expression of culture, something that places us both within experience through its synthesis and outside it through its ability to reflect upon that experience in the abstract realm of ideas.

Books and other publications – still the primary output and expression of creative writing, though the Internet is rapidly increasing its reach – are also, literally, closed cultural spaces. It is much more difficult to engage in the cultural encounter that is literature than it is to engage with the ambient quality of music, photography, painting, sculpture, design, architecture or fashion. Literature is more specialised, more difficult to access, more contingent upon linguistic and interpretative skills than other forms of cultural expression. But literature is also unique in the range and forms of human experience that it can embody, synthesise and simultaneously discuss through its dialogic structures; through its remarkable method of encryption and decryption, textual space/time can supersede actual space/time, to offer an encapsulating alternative reality.

Reading can be seen as a form of deliberately engaged reverie that reverses the usual hierarchy of human experience. In our everyday experience we engage with the primacy of the actual as it interacts with the involuntary imaginative process of day-dreaming (which is essential to it). But in the process of reading, actuality is deliberately pushed to the edge of the textual/virtual reading experience, so that we engage with the virtual domain at the expense of the actual. Reading a novel on a long train journey recently, I remembered very little of my immediate surroundings and the journey, though I maintained a residual awareness of them. However, I retained vivid memories of characters and places invented by the writer that had only a tenuous basis in reality. In short, I surrendered myself to the virtual realm because culture, with all its material infrastruture, communications, social and political frames, had replaced an insecure and dangerous primal 'nature' as my experiential location.

Through this process, the experience of cultural encounter through writing is deepened beyond aesthetic appreciation towards psychological integration. To become the reader of a text is to activate it: the consciousness of the reader is joined with that of the writer to realise the literary work and it virtuality. The very act of reading mitigates a sense of cultural 'difference' because the process itself is so profoundly participatory: absorption through 'the basic patterns of human experience'.

7   Exploring the research environment

Multiculturalism can be seen on the vertical axis, with the English/British culture at the summit of the totem. My understanding of transculturalism is that it locates itself on the horizontal axis with a consequent democratization of attitude towards the immense diversity of cultural material present in a classroom, in a country or in the world. This new approach suggests that not only should cultures talk to each other as equals but not fear the cross-fertilisation that might occur through that contact.[9]

In this chapter I am concerned with the research environment rather than individual practice and in order to discuss this directly, rather than rhetorically, I would like to return to the provision at Lancaster and its continuing evolution. Here the LUVLE websites with facilities for online research training, informal café exchanges, personal and research profiles, reviews of reading and WIP conferences, offer new possibilities for cultural interaction via personal and creative exchange.

Research carried out with our international body of PhD students (quoted below) in relation to the transcultural interactions through online work-in-progress (WIP) sessions reveals some interesting interpretations of their process and some challenging tensions. Before we consider those, it is worth remembering how the Internet itself has transformed research practice:

> The usage of the Internet has for sure profoundly affected my writing, not only in the ability to get materials which I then use in the writing, but also of being able to exchanging ideas about the social and cultural premise of my story.[10]

In this context, the interactions between students are essentially those between writers and their international readership. In their responses to the research environment four overlapping concerns emerge: language, environment, cultural practice and power relations.

A concern with language, the use of English in an international context, runs throughout the responses with students showing inevitable curiosity about the reach of their own usage in relation to 'the sampling of'[11] an international readership:

> For me the real benefit of transcultural work-in-progress (WIP) sessions is the opportunity to stress test the 'travelability' of my writing. The English language as spoken in Ireland is unique; word order and phrases are different. Much of the English we speak is really Irish that has been translated. So when I write something with colloquial speech – I greatly value the international mini audience the WIP sessions provide.[12]

Those positive sentiments are echoed by a Caribbean student who puts a more complex transcultural interpretation upon them:

> Non-standard variants of English have appeared in our texts as a means of giving voice to a specific region or class. In a couple of cases, we have written our characters speaking different languages; we have written this in English, but using English as a vehicle for different cultural material and sometimes employing altered rhythms to underscore the new cultural landscape. Our WIP colleagues help us to identify obscurity, false notes and the moment when 'explanations' of cultural difference clog the flow of story telling.[13]

The language environment is, then, a testing ground for the language content of the creative writing. That process is encapsulated by the discourse around writing itself, which is also constantly testing language and taking a subtle range of personal and cultural soundings:

> Tone is crucial in linguistic transactions, but it is by no means easy to decipher when one is merely writing. When you suspect that a 'foreigner' on the other end is being sarcastic or ironic, but you are not certain about it, it unsettles the act of communication.

The efficacy of the research environment itself is thus revealed as profoundly contingent upon language usage and the perceptions it triggers in the remote online process of 'negotiated readings' of creative work.

In environmental terms, the WIP exchanges begin to trigger a realisation that the material world – place, space and the things within – is also culturally configured. Discussing the structure his Japanese house, one North American student reflects:

> The crawl space is there, functionally, for ventilation in a humid environment (there are no basements). The space is common practice here, not remarkable, though I thought it might still be resonant or enabling for a poem. Crawling under house was, in the poem, an unmarked premise or entry. It didn't occur to me that it might, and in an on-line session did, itself garner attention. ... I also began to think about how to frame or present the crawl space, and the entering of it, to readers whom, as you say, work in a common language but from very different cultural starting points.[14]

The *effort* of communication required remains a decision for the writer: to what extent they *explain* in their work and to what extent the reader can be trusted to understand or even feel a sense of privilege at the assumption that they will. In other exchanges the materiality that make up our world proved to be subject to different cultural interpretation:

> I remember being quite annoyed when someone passed a comment about lemons in my poem, being 'yellow-bruised'. ... Citrus

trees are very common in Malta and since there are lemon trees in my parents' garden, I know for certain they don't look as artificially yellow as those one buys off a supermarket counter. I'm afraid, at first glance, the comment struck me as downright facile and typically imperialist in its attitude. Later on I was able to regard it more objectively.[15]

It is fascinating, even alarming, to see how quickly the object under discussion becomes a potent metonym for much wider cultural and historical issues!

The particularities of the material environment begins to define how human beings behave within it, what, in a quotidian sense, we might call 'cultural practice':

One of the aspects of this process that I have noted and given thought to is how working in a transcultural environment asks me and requires me to make culturally specific practices in the place I live, which is Japan, understandable and accessible to, and appropriately impacting on, readers in other places. By cultural practices, I mean elements of everyday life, be it architecture or a type of vegetation, which naturally find their way into a stretch of writing, but which might be unfamiliar or ring differently to people in a different place.[16]

In this interpretation of cultural practice we see the benefits of the transcultural research environment as stimulating reflection on habitual actions, especially those that have become assimilated to the extent that they no longer seem situated or remarkable. They become visible only in the conscious attempt to assimilate them into the temporal structure of a transcultural work that will be received by a diverse and curious readership.

The temporal and historical dimension also informs discussion of the fourth and most complex area of concern for students. Crudely expressed, this is a division between the established 'cultural confidence' of students from the US and the UK (or England) in relation to the emergent, sometimes tentative, sometimes fiercely defiant attitudes of post-colonial writers. One English student who draws heavily upon US culture in his work argues that as writers, 'we sit on the periphery of our societies and therefore share the role of outsiders' but he also recognises that goals and cultural difference relate to cultural and economic context:

> Maybe this links to a key cultural difference – the confidence that comes from being part of a global superpower, the home of the largest film and publishing companies and having a massive, inwards looking media. Whereas my fiction takes influences from outside my own world (using many American sources), theirs reflects in.[17]

That sense of the confidence underwritten by superpower status and its implied insularity prompts another student to question whether English and North American students 'also perceive each other as coming from different *cultures* as well as different *nations*?' But for a North American ex-patriot resident in Sweden, the identification of culture with national identity is itself issue:

> I will honestly say that, as an American, I am often uncomfortable in intercultural discussions because the assumption is that everyone knows and understands my culture on an intimate level (when in fact they understand it only as it is shaped by the media to which they have access) and that my role in such discussions is often expected to be one of the passive student: question for the sake of gathering information, not to challenge or debate. I resent the stereotypes imposed upon me and I feel invisible as an individual voice.

A final crosscutting inflection of this cultural debate comes when a student reflects upon writing about the presence of sub-cultures within dominant cultures and their relationship to transcultural understanding:

> Subcultures also have an interesting place in our work and in the WIP forums. One of my peers is writing about her involvement in the Hare Krishna movement. This world is utterly foreign to me. As I try to navigate her recreation of that world – with its customs, traditions, and terminology – I am gaining a broader

understanding not only of this one particular subculture, but also of human culture as a whole.

So, at a point where I was tempted to generalise about the beneficial effects of the transcultural research environment these student responses have provided a sobering reality-check – returning me, in effect, to the reflexivity of action research principles. While there is clear evidence that the environment helps students to 'grow as a reader' and to analyse the form and content of their work in relationship to their readership, there is also evidence of historical tension, miscommunication and perceived inequities of power in relation to language and cultural practice that are being worked through in 'beneficial' but 'often painful' ways.

8   Conclusions

In order to discuss the research methods of any academic discipline we have to consider the epistemological framework to which that research is intended to contribute. In the case of the stem cell scientist this will be to understand the way in which specialised cells replicate, migrate and are able to repair specific sites in the human body. The literary scholar approaches the extant text and tries to understand it within a discursive framework that includes politics, sexual identity, history, culture, language and structure in relation to literary theories. The creative writer may draw upon all those areas to make new work: so science fiction (to invoke genre) draws upon areas of scientific process that provide a narrative framework, while texts in science, literary theory and literature offer information, context, theoretical perspectives, stylistic antecedents and examples that they may consider as more or less relevant and useful.

The creative writer is unlikely to be able to create new knowledge in the way that a scientist can – based upon new and observable phenomena – which partly explains our residual discomfort with the research culture of the academy. They may find a new and 'original' synthesis of source material and writing technique and they may contribute to the public understanding of other forms of research (new technology, for instance) through anticipation of its social effects. Such work is unlikely to include the mathematical modelling of scientific phenomena or detailed computer projections of process, but will find generalised ways to express the fine detail of scientific matters. The work itself is 'original' in the sense that it is the product of an individual writer: even if it is contingent upon earlier work or highly derivative it will still show some of this quality. Its originality might even lie in its elision of certain literary/technical qualities – characterisation, description, dialogue or the evocation of spatial context. In the case of the lyric poem, it may attempt to evade any specific context of space or time.

Setting aside the preparatory and contributory research that underpins a new book of poems, a novel or a play script, we can understand the epistemological system that the creative writer contributes to as being one of social, political, cultural and personal *affect*. In a generative process where fantasy, fabulation, distortion and invention play a necessary part, we can see that creative writing process can never map easily onto other social scientific or scientific models. However formal our starting points, the synthesis of new writing will always involve the deliberate distortion of data or contextual research in order to create the illusory fabrication of space/time that is a work of art. And this epistemological tissue is value laden, depending on the immense subjectivity of human experience across cultures for its significance. Yet, to choose on example, post-colonial literature in the hands of Chinua Achebe, Ngugi wa Thiong'o or Mehmood Darwish has exposed the psychological, political, social and cultural effects of colonialism every bit as much as the social scientific analysis of Edward Said, Albert Memmi or Franz Fanon.

The transcultural activity of a creative writing community within an academic research environment is an inevitable result of twenty-first century mobilities and the new technologies of education that can work across geographical and political borders through a common language medium. Through its collaborative learning and research processes such a community exemplifies the contribution of creative writing to human knowledge and understanding, since cultures themselves are constantly evolving and hybridising. Such cultural dynamism will always precipitate new creative works. The maturation of creative writing within the academy allows a nuanced analysis of its practice-led research, allowing formal methods to be identified in compositional process, showing innovation in literary form, but also foregrounding the finished/unfinished form itself, the synthesis that, like Lorca's notion of *duende*,[18] fuses elements into a passionate or visionary whole. The 'knowledge' resulting from this is felt as well as understood, apprehended as well as experienced, anticipated as well as precipitated: sometimes it evades definition or explanation, reaching beyond the materiality and language it is constituted from towards the numinous, towards its own dissolution.

This artistic affect is essentially synthetic and aesthetic, constituting the unique nature of creative writing. To shy away from this affective quality in favour of demonstrable or measurable 'outcomes' on a social scientific scale is to evade the key significance of literature. The debate about forms of research in creative writing is an essential one in its foundation as an academic discipline and is being accompanied by a growing body of successful PhD theses that constitute a new discourse of praxis. The influence of creative writing practitioners on research council peer review colleges and internal university committees will grow, so that our contribution to academic culture will be made increasingly from within its institutions – and by definition, we are articulate advocates for our own core values. The success of creative writing in the academy, its use of new learning technologies and its ability to recruit significant numbers of research students across cultures will confirm it as an essential element in the Arts and Humanities. Just as English replaced Classics as a discipline, we may find that the presence of creative writing in an increasingly internationalised academy leads to a new concept of literary studies in English and one in which practice plays a central and catalytic role.

Exercises

1   Culture is an encapsulating web of personal/collective history and experience that shapes the individual and their expectations. Culture defines, extends and – if we let it – limits us as writers. In order to understand our writing and its range it is useful to

map our cultural experience, which, in itself, may contain the unresolved tensions of history and conflict. Placing your putative 'self' in the centre, make a radial 'molecular' diagram showing every 'atom' of your experience that may be considered cultural: language, ethnic origin, education, social class, geographical location/s, urban/rural origins, exposure to art, music, literature, civic space, and so on. Many of those 'atoms' will themselves fragment into more complex structures, showing that, rather than being a harmonious structure, our cultural selves are often fractured, discordant, unresolved and mutable.

2   Having explored your own cultural antecedents and experience, take an extended piece of your creative writing (novel, film or play script, short story or poetry collection) and reflect upon which elements were derived from formative or pre-existing personal experience and which elements were deliberately 'researched' from outside that direct experience. What further acts of invention/synthesis took place? What kinds of representations of culturally inflected experience does the reader need to engage with in order to realise the 'virtual dimension' that in turn transforms the text into their own 'experience'? How is the 'cultural' context and complexity of the text mediated for the reader? To what extent does the text depend upon tensions in identification and recognition to achieve realisation of its ideas and affect in the reader?

Notes

1   Homi K. Bhaba, *The Location of Culture*, Routledge, p. x, 2004.

2   Ansell Adams, *Yosemite and the Range of Light*, Little Brown & Co., p. 7, 1979.

3   See Raymond Williams, *Culture and Society: 1780–1950*, p. xvi, Chatto & Windus, 1958.

4   Roland Barthes, 'The Death of the Author', *Aspen*, No. 5–6. 1967. His essay argues against taking into account the intentions and biographical context of an author in an interpretation of text, maintaining that writing and its creator are unrelated.

5   http://www.transculturalwriting.com

6   An extensive events programme; a range of research projects in Africa; translation projects; a major research project with migrant writers in Manchester.

7   Wolfgang Iser, 'The Reading Process: A Phenomenological Approach', in *Modern Criticism and Theory*, ed. Lodge, David and Wood, Nigel, p. 194 Longman, 1988.
8   Donald Schön, *The Reflective Practitioner*, p. 68, London: Temple Smith, 1983.
9   Lancaster University PhD student.
10 Lancaster University PhD student.
11 Lancaster University PhD student.
12 Lancaster University PhD student.
13 Lancaster University PhD student.
14 Lancaster University PhD student.
15 Lancaster University PhD student.
16 Lancaster University PhD student.
17 Lancaster University PhD student.
18 F. Lorca, *Duende: Theory and Divertissement*, composed and delivered by Lorca during his stay in Havana *en route* from the United States in 1930; subsequently repeated in Buenos Aires for the *Socieded Amigos del Arte* in 1934.

Works Cited

Adams, Ansell, *Yosemite and the Range of Light*, Boston, Toronto, London: Little Brown & Co., 1979.

Barthes, Roland, 'The Death of the Author', *Aspen*, No. 5–6. 1967.

Bhaba, Homi K., *The Location of Culture*, London and New York: Routledge, 2004.

Centre for Transcultural Writing and Research (CTWR). Online. http://www.transculturalwriting.com

Iser, Wolfgang, 'The Reading Process: A Phenomenological Approach', *Modern Criticism and Theory*, ed. David Lodge and Nigel Wood, New York: Pearson Education, 1988.

Lorca, Federico Garcia, *In Search of Duende*, ed. Christopher Mauer, A New Directions Bibelot, New Directions Publishing Corporation, New York, 1998.

Schön, Donald, *The Reflective Practitioner*, London: Temple Smith, 1983.

Williams, Raymond, *Culture and Society: 1780–1950*, London: Chatto & Windus, 1958.

Further Ideas, Selected Reading

Jeri Kroll and Graeme Harper

1 Further ideas

Research Methods in Creative Writing offers a number of perspectives on creative writing research. As the contributors in this book make clear, their individual approaches to research draw directly from their lives as creative writing practitioners as well as teachers. Chapters reveal how each conceives of practice and, in particular, what techniques, methods and understandings were necessary for the projects they describe.

It would be counterproductive to produce a book like this without acknowledging the variety of voices here, or the choices the individual writers have made in pursuing their research; creative writing is certainly not an activity with a narrow range of methodologies, as will already be clear. Nor is it a field of endeavour where the number of methods used can be predetermined. That idea is inimical to what is being suggested. It is certainly not the suggestion in this book that we can categorise, tabulate and codify research in and through creative writing so that what we end up with is a decidedly singular blueprint for creative writing itself, fixed and uncreative. We trust that the readers of this book will use it as a starting point, not an end point.

Perhaps it is the notion that knowledge can only arrive via relatively codified means that is the real problem, rather than any specific suggestions relating to creative writing research. In the broader realm, there's little argument with the idea that research and methodologies associated with research benefit from being supported by the imagination and by being informed by creativity. Creative writing research exchanges, generates, explores and sometimes challenges knowledge, as the chapters here suggest, often revealing its interdisciplinary, connective and associative methods. Research in and through creative writing, thus, rarely benefits from being restrained by established parameters or disciplinary boundaries.

223

Perhaps this freedom suggests why, in the twenty-first century, creative writing as a university and college discipline is continuing to grow at a considerable pace. It is therefore an opportune time to share some of the exciting developments that have already taken place in creative writing research. As case studies, the models appearing in the chapters here are intended not so much as templates as ways of stimulating readers to discover what suits their individual interests. Thus, while the chapters in *Research Methods in Creative Writing* demonstrate the richness of theoretical and methodological pathways possible, the real success of this book will be if it generates new ideas, new explorations, and new projects that also seek to add to our store of knowledge.

Experienced creative writers frequently engage with their practices responsively. That is, they are aware of the creative actions they are undertaking and of the potential results of those actions. While something of our human fascination with creative writing comes from uncertainty, from not quite knowing how it might happen or what results might occur, undoubtedly experience generates knowledge, and that knowledge is applied to the work at hand. Creative writers are not often entirely isolated practitioners; rather, they are aware of the societies around them and of the streams of influence that flow between individuals and cultures. Likewise, experienced teachers and learners reflect upon the influences that cultures have upon them and on the potential influence that they have upon those cultures. They too are aware that learning and teaching are not always entirely fathomable enterprises but that open engagement with them, combined with a desire to know, will produce results.

In a more specific sense, creative writing researchers are always involved to some extent with articulating how they interact with their aesthetic environments. By aesthetic environments we mean those surroundings that relate directly to the pursuit of art and the ways in which art is informed by the world and also informs it in turn. In other words, writers are engaged with what is already in place as well as with what might be newly created.

With that in mind, what follows are suggestions for selected readings, providing a background for some of the work undertaken in this book. They might offer different perspectives on some of the arguments, or suggest new ways of connecting them, for example. They might be considered readings that contributors have personally found useful for one project or another – and, indeed, a number of them are exactly that. But they might also be considered exploratory suggestions, pointing this book's readers towards other avenues of investigation, helping them to personalise their research pursuits. Research is about finding out, about confirming the validity of what we know, about challenging that or about adding new perspectives. Thus, frequently the best way to approach research is to consider what others say about their undertakings and to ask if any more productive discoveries can be made, if any more advantageous methods be employed.

The chapters in *Research Methods in Creative Writing* as well as these selected readings, thus, illustrate how diverse conceptions of the field are; they encompass conventional as well as experimental research routes and continue to find inspiration in a wide range of disciplines, including other creative and performing arts and design. The goal, of course, in drawing from these diverse sources by responding to or adapting their methodologies is to generate innovative creative work as well as new knowledge. Creative writing research, which by its nature focuses on actions as well as outcomes and, therefore, engages creative, critical and practical faculties, often aims to bridge the artificial divisions that separate disciplines in academia and within the culture at large. This is a field that produces appreciable results. Perhaps, then, the best way to approach this suggested reading is to imagine the link between it and something that has not yet been written.

2   Selected reading

The following is not a definitive or exhaustive list of books. These texts are ones that we and our students have found useful. Obviously there are others that would be equally beneficial depending on the nature of a project. Ideally the list should give readers a sense of the range of material that can inform creative writing research. Readers can also find suggestions in the 'Works cited' lists in individual chapters.

Adorno, Theodor, *Minima Moralia*, London: Verso, 1994.

Allott, Miriam, *Novelists on the Novel*, London: Routledge, 1973.

Arana, Maria, ed., *The Writing Life: Writers on How they Think and Work*, New York: Public Affairs, 2003.

Atwood, Margaret, *Negotiating with the Dead: a Writer on Writing*, Cambridge: Cambridge University Press, 2002.

Auster, Paul, *The Art of Hunger*, London: Faber, 1998.

Bachelard, Gaston, *The Poetics of Space*, trans. Maria Jolas (French edn, 1958), Boston: Beacon Press, 1969.

Bakhtin, M. M., *The Dialogic Imagination: Four Essays*, M. Holquist, ed., trans. Caryl Emerson and Michael Holquist, Austin: University of Texas Press, 1981, 1998.

Balkema, Annette W. and Henk Slager, eds, *Artistic Research* (Lier en Boog Series of Philosophy of Art and Art Theory, Volume 18, Translations: Global Vernunft Amsterdam: Lier en Boog, 2004 (editions Rodopi B.V., Amsterdam/New York).

Baron, Dennis, *A Better Pencil: Readers, Writers, and the Digital Revolution*, Oxford: Oxford University Press, 2009.

Barth, John, *Further Fridays: Essays, Lectures and Other Nonfiction, 1984–1994*, Boston: Little, Brown, 1995.

Barthelme, Donald, *The Teachings of Donald B.*, Kim Herzinger, ed., New York: Vintage, 1998.

Berg, A. Scott, *Max Perkins: Editor of Genius*, New York: Riverhead, 1997.

Bergson, Henri, *Creative Evolution*, New York: Dover, 1998, first published in English in 1911.

Bhabha, Homi K., *The Location of Culture*, Routledge: London and New York, 1994: 1–18.

Blotner, Joseph, ed., *Selected Letters of William Faulkner*, New York: Random House, 1977.

Bohm David, *On Creativity*, Lee Nichol, ed., London: Routledge, 1998.

Bolt, Barbara, *Art Beyond Representation: The Performative Power of the Image*, London, New York: Tauris, 2004.

Borges, Jorge Luis, *Fictions*, trans. and ed. with an introduction by Anthony Kerrigan, London: Calder & Boyars, 1956.

Brewer, John, *The Pleasures of the Imagination: English Culture in the Eighteen Century*, London: Harper Collins, 1997.

Brophy, Kevin, *Patterns of Creativity: Investigations into the Sources and Methods of Creativity*, Amsterdam, New York: Rodopi, 2009.

Burke, Sean, ed., *Authorship from Plato to the Postmodern: A Reader*, Edinburgh: Edinburgh University Press, 1995.

Butler, Judith, *Bodies That Matter: On the Discursive Limits of 'Sex'*, New York: Routledge, 1993.

——, *Undoing Gender*, New York: Routledge, 2004.

Carey, John, *What Good Are the Arts?* London: Faber, 2005.

Cixous, Hélène, *Three Steps on the Ladder of Writing*, trans. Sarah Cornell and Susan Sellers, New York: Columbia University Press, 1993.

Claydon, Cherry, *Women and Writing in South Africa: A Critical Anthology*, Heinemann: Marshalltown, 1989.

Conroy, Frank, *The Eleventh Draft: Craft and Writing Life form the Iowa Writers Workshop*, New York: Harper Collins, 1999.

Darnton, John, *Writers on Writing: Collected Essays from The New York Times*, New York: Holt, 2001.

Day-Lewis, Cecil, *The Poet's Way of Knowledge*, Cambridge: Cambridge University Press, 1957.

Deleuze, Gilles and Félix Guattari, *A Thousand Plateaus: Capitalism and Schizophrenia*, trans. and foreword Brian Massumi, Minneapolis: University of Minnesota Press, 1987.

Derrida, Jacques, *Writing and Difference*, Chicago: University of Chicago, 1978.

Eco, Umberto, *Six Walks in Fictional Woods*, Cambridge: Harvard University Press, 1995.

Edel, Leon and Lyall H. Powers, eds, *The Complete Notebooks of Henry James*, New York: Oxford University Press, 1988.

Fitzgerald, Sally, ed., *The Habit of Being: the Letters of Flannery O'Connor*, New York: Vintage, 1979.

Foucault, Michel, *Madness and Civilisation: A History of Insanity in the Age of Reason*, trans. R. Howard, New York: Random House, 1965.

Fugard, Athol, *Notebooks of Athol Fugard: 1960–1977*, Mary Benson, ed., London: Faber, 1983.

Gardner, John, *The Art of Fiction: Notes on Craft for Young Writers*, New York: Vintage, 1991.

Gass, William, *Finding a Form*, Ithaca: Cornell, 1996.

Goodman, Nelson, *Ways of Worldmaking*, Indianapolis: Hackett, 1978.

Graham, Gordon, *Philosophy and the Arts: An Introduction to Aesthetics*, London: Routledge, 1997.

Grenville, Kate, *The Secret River*, Melbourne: Text Publishing, 2005.

—— *Searching for the Secret River*, Melbourne: Text Publishing, 2006.

Harper, Graeme and Jeri Kroll, eds, *Creative Writing Studies: Practice, Research and Pedagogy*, Clevedon: Multilingual Matters, 2008.

Harper, Graeme, *On Creative Writing*, Bristol: Multilingual Matters, 2010.

Halsall, Francis, *Systems of Art: Art, History and Systems Theory*, Oxford: Peter Lang, 2008.

Harwood, Gwen, *Steady Storm of Correspondence: Selected Letters of Gwen Harwood 1943–1995*, Gregory Kratzmann, ed., St Lucia: University of Queensland Press, 2001.

Heilbrun, Carolyn, *Writing a Woman's Life*, New York: Ballantine Books, 1988.

Hewett, Dorothy, *Memoirs: Wild Card*, Ringwood, Vic.: Penguin Books Australia, 2001.

Hodgins, Jack, *A Passion for Narrative: A Guide for Writing Fiction*, Toronto: McClelland & Stewart Inc., 1993.

Hunter, J. Paul, *Before Novels: The Cultural Contexts of Eighteenth Century Fiction*, NY: Norton, 1990.

Hughes, Ted, *Poetry in the Making: A Handbook for Writing and Teaching*, London: Faber, 2008, first published 1968.

Irigaray, Luce, *Conversations*, New York, London: Continuum, 2008.

Jaszi, Peter and Martha Woodmansee, eds, *The Construction of Authorship: Textual Appropriation in Law and Literature*, Durham NC: Duke University Press, 1994.

Johns, Adrian, *The Nature of the Book: Print and Knowledge in the Making*, Chicago: University of Chicago Press, 1998.

Kerr, Heather and Amanda Nettlebeck, *The Space Between: Australian Women Writing Fictocriticism*, Nedlands: University of Western Australia Press, 1998.

Knorr-Cetina, Karin, *The Manufacture of Knowledge: An Essay on the Constructivist and Contextual Nature of Science*, Oxford: Pergamon, 1981.

Krauth, Nigel and Tess Brady, eds, *Creative Writing: Theory Beyond Practice*, Teneriffe: Post Pressed, 2006.

Kristeva, Julia, *Revolution in Poetic Language*, trans. Margaret Waller, New York: Columbia University Press, 1984.

——, *Powers of Horror: An Essay on Abjection*, New York: Columbia University Press, 1982.

Le Guin, Ursula K., *Steering the Craft: Exercises and Discussions on Story Writing for the Lone Navigator or the Mutinous Crew*, Portland: The Eighth Mountain Press, 1998.

——, *The Wave in the Mind: Talks on the Writer, the Reader and the Imagination*. Boston: Shambala, 2004.

Manguel, Alberto, *A History of Reading*, London: Harper Collins, 1996.

Manhire, Bill, *Mutes and Earthquakes: Bill Manhire's Creative Writing Course at Victoria*, Wellington: Victoria University Press, 1997.

Marquez, Gabriel Garcia, *Living to Tell the Tale*, New York: Vintage, 2004.

Marr, David, *Patrick White Letters*, Chicago: University of Chicago, Chicago, 1996.

McHugh, Heather, *Broken English: Poetry and Partiality*, Hanover and London: Wesleyan University Press, 1993.

Mehring, Margaret, *The Screenplay: A Blend of Film Form and Content*, Boston: Focal, 1990.

Morrison, Toni, *What Moves at the Margin: Selected Nonfiction*, Carolyn C. Denard, ed., Jackson: University of Mississippi, 2008.

Motion, Andrew, *Philip Larkin: a Writer's Life*, London: Faber, 1994.

Murray, Les, *Killing the Black Dog* (revised and updated edition), Melbourne: Black Inc, 2009.

——, *A Working Forest: Selected Prose*, Sydney: Duffy & Snellgrove, 1997.

Myers, D. G., *The Elephants Teach: Creative Writing Since 1880*, New Jersey, Prentice Hall, 1996.

Nabokov, Vladimir, *Strong Opinions*, London: Weidenfeld and Nicolson, 1974.

Nicholson, Virginia, *Among the Bohemians: Experiments in Living, 1900–1939*, London: Penguin, 2003.

Oates, Joyce Carol, *Uncensored: Views and (Re)views*, New York: Harper, 2005.

Ostriker, Alicia, *Dancing at the Devil's Party: Essays on Poetry, Politics, and the Erotic*, Ann Arbor: University of Michigan Press, 2000.

——, *Writing Like a Woman*, Ann Arbor: University of Michigan Press, 1983.

Ozick, Cynthia, *Quarrel and Quandary*, New York: Knopf, 2000.

Perelman, Bob, *The Marginalization of Poetry: Language Writing and Literary History*, Princeton: Princeton University Press, 1996.

Phillips, Larry, ed., *Ernest Hemingway on Writing*, New York: Scribner, 2004.

Poe, Edgar Allan, 'The Philosophy of Composition', *Graham's Magazine*, XXVIII.4 (April 1846) 28: 163–7.

Pope, Rob, *Creativity: Theory, History, Practice*, London: Routledge, 2005.

Pound, Ezra, *ABC of Reading*, New York: New Directions, 1934, 1960.

Proust, Marcel, *Selected Letters: 1880–1903*, Chicago: University of Chicago Press, 1998.

Regge, Tullio, *Primo Levi: Conversations*, London: Tauris, 1989.

Rich, Adrienne, *Adrienne Rich's Poetry*, Barbara Charlesworth Gelpi and Albert Gelpi, eds, New York: Norton, 1975.

Sartre, Jean-Paul, *The Words*, New York: Brazillier, 1964.

Schwarz, Ronald B., ed., *For the Love of Books: 115 Celebrated Writers on the Books they Most Love*, New York: Berkeley, 2000.

Sennett, Richard, *The Craftsman*, New Haven and London: Yale University Press, 2008.

Snow, C. P., *The Two Cultures and the Scientific Revolution*, Cambridge: Cambridge University Press, 1959.

Solso, Robert L. *The Psychology of Art and the Evolution of the Conscious Brain*, Cambridge, MA; London, England: MIT Press, 2003.

Spender, Stephen, *Great Writings of Goethe*, New York: New American, 1958.

Sternberg, Robert J., *Wisdom, Intelligence, and Creativity Synthesized*, Cambridge and New York: Cambridge University Press, 2003.

Strand, Dennis, *Research in the Creative Arts*, Canberra: Department of Employment, Education, Training and Youth Affairs, 1998.

Thomas, Dylan, *Dylan Thomas: The Collected Letters*, Paul Ferris, ed., London: Paladin, 1987.

Thwaite, Anthony, *Selected Letters of Philip Larkin: 1940–1985*, London: Faber, 1992.

Vargas Llosa, Mario, *Making Waves: Essays*, New York: Farrar, Straus and Giroux, 1996.

Vargas Llosa, Mario, *A Writer's Reality*, London: Faber, 1991.

Vonnegut, Kurt, *A Man Without a Country*, New York: Random House, 2005.

Wandor, Michelene, *The Author is Not Dead, Merely Somewhere Else: Creative Writing Reconceived*, Houndmills, Basingstoke: Palgrave Macmillan, 2008.

White, Edmund, *Arts and Letters*, San Francisco: Cleis, 2004.

Wissler, Rod, Brad Haseman, Sue-Anne Wallace and Michael Keane, *Innovation in Australian Arts, Media and Design: Fresh Challenges for the Tertiary Section*, Flaxton: Post Pressed, 2004.

Woolf, Virginia, *Between the Acts*, London: Grafton, 1978, first published 1941

—— *The Diary of Virginia Woolf: Vol 2 1920–1924*, Anne Olivier Bell, ed., London: Penguin, 1981.

Wright, Judith, *With Love and Fury: Selected Letters of Judith Wright*, Patricia Clarke and Meredith McKinney, eds, Canberra: National Library of Australia, 2006.

Index